Other books in the New Explorer Series:

Red Salmon, Brown Bear by Theodore J. Walker

The Armies of the Ant by Charles L. Hogue

THE BLUE REEF

THE
BLUE REEF

A Report from Beneath the Sea

The adventures and observations
of WALTER STARCK, marine biologist and
authority on sharks, at Enewetak Atoll,
a coral reef in the Pacific Ocean

Told by ALAN ANDERSON, JR.

Alfred A. Knopf　New York　1979

Library of Congress Cataloging in Publication Data

Starck, Walter A. (Date)   The blue reef.

Includes index.
1. Coral reef ecology—Marshall Islands—Enewetak
Atoll.   2. Nuclear explosions—Environmental aspects—
Marshall Islands—Enewetak Atoll.   3. *Carcharhinus
menisorrah.*   4. Marine biology—Marshall Islands—
Enewetak Atoll.   5. Enewetak Atoll, Marshall Islands.
I. Anderson, Alan, jt. author.   II. Title.
QH198.E53S73   574.996'83   78–54892
ISBN 0–394–40035–6

*The drawing of display behavior in the gray reef shark on page 81
is reproduced from the article "Agonistic Display in the Gray Reef
Shark,* Carcharhinus menisorrah, *and Its Relationship to Attacks
on Man," by Richard H. Johnson and Donald R. Nelson, Copeia,
No. 1, March 5, 1973, pp. 76–84. The artist was Loraine Peterson,
and it is reprinted here by permission of the American Society of
Ichthyologists and Herpetologists.*

Created by Alan Landsburg Productions, Inc.

Manufactured in the United States of America

FIRST EDITION

CONTENTS

Introduction   vii

1   Arrival   3

2   Getting Our Bearings   7

3   The Creation of Enewetak   23

4   Secrets of Seawater   29

5   Color and Design on the Reef   35

6   A Short History of Enewetak Atoll   53

7   Some Notions on Scientific Research   66

8   First Encounter with the Gray Reef Shark   79

9   A Lesson in Reef Ecology   94

10   The Reef at Night   101

11   The People of Enewetak   121

12   Questions of Shark Behavior   130

13   Why I Do Science   136

14   Collecting Fish   143

15   The Ghosts of Explosions   149

16   The Channel Between Japtan and Medren   166

17 At the Concrete Barge 177

18 Pursuing Sharks 192

19 A Case of the Bends 205

20 Attracting Sharks 212

21 Learning Marine Biology 222

22 Winding Down 232

23 Shark Attack 239

24 Healing 246

Index 255

*Eight pages of illustrations will
be found following page 84*

INTRODUCTION

T HIS is the third volume in "The New Explorer" series—an ambitious project designed to allow biologists total immersion in the ecosetting of their specialty and to bring their observations to the public. For the first of these books, an entomologist studied a rain forest in Costa Rica, and for the second, an ichthyologist investigated a lake in Alaska. For this third volume, the term "total immersion" is more than a figure of speech: marine biologist Walter Starck spent much of his time underwater, exploring the blue waters surrounding Enewetak Atoll and its coral reefs some 2,400 miles southwest of Honolulu. The task of each of these scientists was to study—to live in, really—their biological environment and to report on the experience both in words (via tape recorder) and in pictures (via still and movie cameras). This series of books is a product of those words and pictures.

The key to Walter Starck's total immersion was a small submarine called the Perry Sharkhunter, which enabled him to mingle with the creatures of the coral reef almost as though he were one of them. He could cover distances and maintain speeds impossible with only an aqualung, and the little sub offered a mobile base from which to pursue tiny shrimps into their holes or giant groupers into their dens. He also had the benefit of his own small ship, the El Territo, on which he and his family and assistants lived, and the cooperation of the Mid-Pacific Marine Laboratory, run by the University of Hawaii.

Starck's own special interest was the behavior of the gray reef shark, *Carcharhinus menisorrah*. This aggressive fish is thought to be the only shark that gives behavioral signals when it is about to attack. Indeed, Starck, his wife, Jo, and his assistants, Jerry Condit and Dick Gushman, were attacked a number of times by the object of their study; only the slight protection afforded by the submarine and by their own wits saved their lives. The observations on the gray reef shark presented here are unique, and although Starck has not yet published them in formal scientific fashion, they will provide original and often surprising material for students of animal behavior.

O F all the atolls in the Pacific, Enewetak is in many ways a special case, particularly interesting for an environmental study. From 1948 until 1958 the Atomic Energy Commission and the U.S. military detonated forty-three nuclear "devices" there, obliterating, temporarily at least, much of the land life on several of the atoll's forty islands; two small islands disappeared altogether. This testing program raised questions about the compatibility of radioactivity and life as we know it, and many people predicted then that a nuclear war anywhere on earth would be fatal even to people living far from bomb targets. Since the halt of atmospheric testing in 1963, the Mid-Pacific Marine Laboratory and other groups have been studying just this question.

Starck's visit, a quarter century after the first explosion on Enewetak, has produced a detailed account of how life has fared since the equivalent of a nuclear war was waged on this atoll. Remarkably, he finds little apparent damage beyond the immediate vicinity of the blast points. Even there, he reports, the flora and fauna are not visibly different from life forms elsewhere in the atoll.

J UXTAPOSED with this use (or abuse) of the atoll is an "experiment" of another sort: the resettlement of the original human inhabitants, the Enewetakese people. These people were removed from their home in 1947, just before nuclear testing began, to a smaller, less desirable atoll named Ujelang. Only now—a full decade after severe food shortages forced them to protest loudly—are they being allowed to return to Enewetak. And even this concession may be mixed with danger: at least some portion of the atoll is still too radioactively hot for human safety.

About fifty-five people returned to the atoll on March 18, 1977, to take up life where they had left off—to fish, to raise pandanus and coconuts, to live with nature as they remembered it. At the same time U.S. Army troops, under the Defense Nuclear Agency, will continue "cleaning up" the atoll, a project expected to take three years and some $20 million.

Yet it seems likely that human life, at least, will never be the same as it was before the testing, not so much because of the bombs as because of other changes. The population, 136 when the people left, has swelled to 450 and is projected to grow to from 600 to 900 by 1983—probably more people than the traditional food sources can sustain. It will be hard to preserve a traditional hunting-gathering culture in the face of modern life; the people are already used to rice, flour, soft drinks, and soap. Some of the men have acquired a taste for beer and cigarettes.

A WORD about the creation of this book. Walter Starck is its progenitor—its eyes and ears, if you will. His observations provide the framework for the narrative and the bulk of the book's scientific content. As I worked at the task of editing Starck's daily tapes into narrative form, however, Enewetak began to grow for me until it was more than just an atoll. The environment itself was familiar enough; I worked for a year with the Smithsonian Institution studying seabird migration in the Central Pacific. But more than that, Enewetak began to take on importance not only as a place but also as a stage—an arena where humans are acting out, through both accident and design, turbulent scenes of a drama whose conclusion is not yet known. The primitive people who lived there are "discovered" by European traders; money is introduced, and their economic system changed forever. The islands themselves are assaulted by high technology; bombs are planted in the place of palms. The gray reef shark, one of the most primitive of fishes, is confronted at depth by a space-age submarine. The shelling stops and the natives return, their environment—and their entire way of life—changed. The submarine leaves, its propeller bent and its plexiglass canopy etched by the teeth of an enraged shark.

Does anyone "win"? Politically, Enewetak could become a symbol for all Micronesia, whose people are both lured and threatened by independence. They yearn to be free of the control of the superpowers, and yet they depend on the government jobs and handouts of these same powers. The people have been easily won by the flour and beer and what they perceive as modern life. When the first group of Enewetakese returned to their atoll last March, the item of most interest to teenagers was a kung fu movie playing that night on the pier.

Nature, by contrast, falls to no such temptations; it either dies or continues as before. The coconut crab still prefers its home-grown coconuts; the shrimp still keeps company with the goby; the shark has no yearning for a submarine. Life around the blue reef goes on.

Alan Anderson, Jr.

THE BLUE REEF

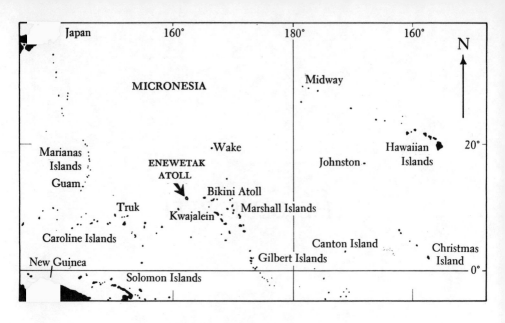

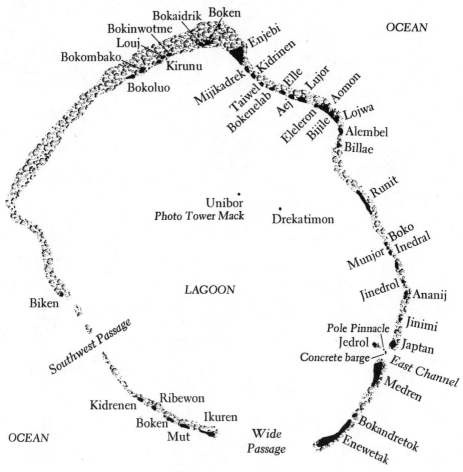

ENEWETAK ATOLL

1

ARRIVAL

TODAY, at 1:14 P.M. local time, I took a noon sight of the sun with the sextant. The sea surface was oily smooth, unrippled but undulating with the ocean swell. We had used up about 4,000 gallons of diesel fuel and about 1,500 gallons of water on the run down from Hawaii. We are lighter now, with less fuel and water, and in the calm sea that has prevailed for the past two days we have made better time than usual. At the noon sight I found that we were at latitude 19 degrees 20 minutes north, the latitude of Enewetak Atoll. I changed course from southwest to due west and reset the automatic compass.

When I looked up from the compass, I saw on the crest of a swell a dark line of trees: the islands of Enewetak, the first land we have seen since leaving Hawaii. We are 550 nautical miles southwest of Wake Island, 189 miles west of Bikini Atoll, and 2,380 miles southwest of Honolulu. It is July 29, but it could be many other days of the tropical Pacific year. It is Enewetak Atoll, but it could be many other tropical atolls in the Pacific. The low profile is typical, familiar, lonely in the vast sea. Beneath the surface of the water, life teems in a richness equaled in few environments on earth. But above the surface, the prospect is bleak, not inviting.

Like most atolls, Enewetak rises abruptly from the deep sea. Only a short distance offshore the depth of the water plunges to nearly 3 miles (15,000 feet). The land itself is insubstantial, consisting of a necklace of small islands arranged along the outer rim of the atoll. Seen from above, the islands form a roughly circular pattern or, more precisely, the flat-topped, sharp-bottomed profile of an acorn. Each is composed of sand

and other coral rubble that is constantly being remodeled by wave action. The rubble has also been shaped by human action, first in the form of devastating gunfire during World War II, when the atoll was the scene of a bloody battle between American and Japanese forces, and then after the war, when the Atomic Energy Commission exploded both atomic and hydrogen bombs on and above the atoll. There are a few coconut trees on some of the islands, but the rest of the vegetation has yet to recover from its rough history.

One of the islands that still has coconut trees is Enewetak Island itself, and the reason is that human beings lived there during the testing. Also on Enewetak are numerous corrugated iron buildings, telephone poles, and a forest of antennas that still service the radio and other electronic equipment. At one time, during the heyday of atomic testing, the human population of the island rose to several thousand men. Today only a skeleton crew of twenty-odd maintains the facility, mostly to support the loran (long range aid to navigation) equipment. Nonetheless, most of the abandoned barracks, bunkers, and other structures still clutter the land. In the last few years humans have begun a new, peaceful kind of research on the island through the Mid-Pacific Marine Laboratory, which is managed by the University of Hawaii. It was for MPML that we were heading.

Within an hour and a half of sighting the low-lying islands we were inside the lagoon and alongside the pier. After unloading a large outboard skiff, two drums of alcohol, and one drum of formaldehyde that we were delivering to the laboratory, we moved off, tied to a buoy, and went ashore for dinner. At the laboratory were several scientists that we knew and several more that we knew of.

After dinner every night in Enewetak there is a movie. That night *The Andromeda Strain* was showing. It's about a speck of life that invades the earth and finds human tissue so much to its liking that it threatens to erase the now-dominant species of the planet, us. The nature of this sinister seed proves so elusive that all the world's scientists are stumped—until it is almost too late. At the last second (our last second, that is) man manages to turn the thing against itself and stave off annihilation.

It's not that we expected to find anything so sinister at Enewetak. But there's an old saying among skin divers that what you don't know *can* hurt you, and this, in a sense, is true of our knowledge of the world. The behavior of the earth's organisms is far from understood, in terms of either origin, mechanism, or change. And coral reefs, in particular, are as rich with unanswered questions as they are with life: How can thousands of fish swim together in perfect formation without the aid of a computer? Why are some reef fishes so colorful? How do fishes communicate? Can answers to these questions help us in any way toward a better technology? A better food supply? A better understanding of ourselves?

As I shall discuss later, coral reefs are among the richest environments on earth in regard to the number of species of plants and animals vying for space to make a living. To a biologist this is more exciting than a laboratory because each species is put on its mettle, so to speak. Competition is intense, and each animal and plant must perform as well as possible to survive. On full display is nature's whole bag of tricks: camouflage, mimicry, predation, symbiosis, threat display, breeding display, growth, feeding, reproduction, and so on.

And Enewetak Atoll is—or has been—an unusually good place to explore this display. Not only are there abundant populations of fishes, plankton, corals, and bottom-dwelling organisms, but these populations are also more complete than usual. The reason is that the human population—at least the portion of it that preyed upon marine creatures for food—was removed in 1947, prior to the nuclear bomb tests, and is only now, in 1977, returning. Thus at the time of our visit in 1971 there had been almost no fishing by hook and line or by spear or by trap for two-and-a-half decades. The entire underwater reef ecology was in close approximation to the natural state. Above the waterline, of course, this was not the case; the nuclear detonations that rocked the atoll from 1948 to 1958 are the single great exception to the peaceful picture I have sketched. As we shall see, the long-range effect of the intense, though brief, exposures of radioactivity is still not clear. During our stay, however, we could detect nothing unusual in or around the reef.

Before I begin the narrative, I would like to make clear that one mystery above all others lured me to the shores of Enewetak: the behavior of the gray reef shark, *Carcharhinus menisorrah*. Despite continuous study during recent years, the habits of this fish are poorly understood. It's not that we don't know what it is made of (mostly water, like us, with predictable amounts of fat, cartilage, enzymes, protein, and so on), or what it eats (just about anything is possible, including humans), or how it swims. It's the mind of the gray shark we don't understand: its reasons for doing things; its rhythms; its furies. Perhaps the term "mind" is too generous. The brain of a human being weighs about 44 ounces; the brain of an adult gray shark weighs about one-tenth that much, and it has to command a body of equal or greater weight. What little brain it does possess is probably occupied full-time with housekeeping chores: directing fin motion; controlling heartbeat; recording what the eyes see and the scent organs smell; maintaining an upright attitude with respect to the center of the earth. It would be remarkable if there were brain left over for reflection, for dreams, for anger—for thought. And yet these sharks seem to have wildly differing "moods," if that word may be used. Why, in short, do sharks try to eat us at some times and not at others?

My concern is both academic and practical: I would like to understand the behavior of this shark for what it tells us about animal behavior in general, and I would like to reduce the danger to humans working or playing underwater. The answer probably won't be simple. In spite of many years of research, we still do not know why sharks occasionally attack swimmers. Statistically, they almost never do: for all the swimming, boating, fishing, and splashing activity that goes on along the full length of Florida's 1,200-mile coastline, for example, much of it obviously within the perception of any number of sharks, there are only about 3 attacks a year. Why should there be 3 instead of 3,000—or none? Could these be prevented? Could they at least be anticipated?

One reason I selected the gray reef shark out of the many shark species is that it is the only one that seems to give some warning before it attacks. It goes through an exaggerated arching of the back and a downward thrusting of the pectoral fins which seem to represent a warning to those able to "read" it. We hoped, by following the sharks around in the small Perry submarine we had brought with us, to provoke this warning display and, by observing when it was used and when it was not used, to begin to learn the body language of the shark. We would use ourselves as bait, in a sense, encouraging the sharks to attack us and hoping that we would be safe from injury in the submarine. As you will see, we had our successes—and our failures—on both counts.

2

GETTING OUR BEARINGS

WE had a lot of territory to cover, so we got started right away the next day. In the morning we went in the outboard around the southwest end of Enewetak Island to the outside of the atoll to make our first dive. The trade winds had picked up during the night, and the waves were choppy outside the reef. We stopped about a quarter of a mile across from the island at a depth of about 50 feet, and Jo and I put on masks and fins for a quick check over the side before we anchored the boat. I wanted to see what the anchor was going to get involved in on the bottom. As soon as the bubbles cleared away from my face, I looked down and saw two gray reef sharks. They didn't waste any effort greeting us, swimming away into the blue as though we didn't exist. The bottom held lush coral growth, and there were many fish, so we decided to dive there. We anchored, put on our scuba tanks, and Jo and I reentered the water along with Dick Gushman. I took the great Rebikoff camera with the wide-angle lens, and Jo took her Beaulieu setup for close-up work. We all carried bang sticks and a shark gun. A bang stick is basically a small section of pipe with an explosive charge in one end meant to drive off or even kill aggressive sharks.

Water visibility was fairly good—about 70 to 80 feet—but it wasn't crystal-clear ocean water. Even though we were on the outside of the reef, this was lagoon water coming out of the wide opening at the south end of the atoll and sweeping along the reef in this direction.

As soon as we got to the bottom, I noticed a gray reef shark at the limit of visibility. We began filming it, and after a couple of minutes I looked up to see another gray reef shark headed toward me from some distance off. I lifted the camera and started shooting, and it came straight in until it was about five or six feet from me. Then it began a slow circle, and I followed it with the camera. It made a complete 360-degree circle and then cruised off again into the blue. We saw four or five more over the next ten or fifteen minutes, and then they disappeared, and we didn't see any more until the end of the dive. It looks as if there will be adequate populations of this animal for some of the experimental work we want to do.

The gray reef shark is an interesting shark to study, as I mentioned earlier. It's not very big—usually from four to six feet in length—but it is a very fast-swimming shark and very aggressive. It has been involved in several unprovoked attacks on divers and is frequently present in large numbers. If any spearfishing is done and wounded fish are kept about, a great many sharks may gather. Their excitement starts to build as the numbers increase. As they swim about, their aggressiveness is self-reinforcing, and they may be triggered into a feeding frenzy in which they rush about and bite at almost anything. This aggressiveness makes sense when you consider the abundance of the fishes sharks feed on around a coral reef. There is also an abundance of other predators, so that to be really successful here a shark has to be very active.

Another reason I chose this species is its territorial uniqueness. Most of the other sharks we saw around the reefs live also in other nonreef habitats. They must be considered to some extent strays on the atoll. The gray shark, by contrast, is truly a reef shark, found only there and well adapted to feeding only on reef-dwelling fishes.

After coming up from the dive, we found that Jo had not seen any of the sharks; she had been busy observing and filming the smaller creatures of the reef. It is interesting that when your attention is fixed on the smaller animals, you often miss the larger ones. On the other hand, when you're carrying a wide-angle lens that is not really suitable for small creatures, you tend to notice only the big ones. Your perspective underwater seems to be related to the optical equipment you're carrying.

We have the *El Territo* tied at a mooring in the lagoon just off the shore of Enewetak Island. On the way back to the boat we stopped at some patch reefs in the lagoon and tried to spear a fish for Jo's pet otter, Mikka. The barb of the spear was missing, though, and after losing several small fishes, we gave up and came on in for lunch. We went ashore to eat, and while there I talked with Dr. Ernie Reese (now director of the Mid-

Pacific Marine Laboratory), a biologist from Hawaii working on the behavior of butterflyfishes. He mentioned that he had found seventeen different butterflyfishes around Enewetak Atoll; farther west, around Yap, he found twenty-one different species in one dive on one shallow reef. In the Caribbean we have only five reef species of butterflyfish. The pattern of distribution and evolution of reef organisms is interesting. It seems to start in the East Indies, and as one moves eastward from there across the Pacific, the number of reef species declines steadily. The Caribbean reef fauna was derived from the same source because at one time the Atlantic and Pacific were connected when the Isthmus of Panama was submerged. But the Caribbean is so far from the East Indies that the number of species there is low.

Out here the fauna is immensely rich. It is also poorly known, and just naming all the species is going to keep taxonomists busy for a long time to come. The presence of all these unnamed species makes broad-scale ecological work very difficult; often we're not even sure what we're dealing with. It will be a lifetime project to sort all this out. It seems strange that we've already explored the moon and are well into the process of exploring other planets, while here on earth we can go out almost any day and find an animal that has never been collected before and probably has never even been seen by a human being.

S INCE we were out to familiarize ourselves with as much of our new environment as we could that first day, we wanted to experience diving in our submarine. It was brand-new, built by Perry Submarine Builders in Florida, and we were eager to take our first test run. We returned to the *El Territo* and swung the sub over the side. It is a free-flooding craft, which means that there are no walls to keep the water out; you travel "wet" all the time. Two divers can ride at once, propelled at speeds of up to three knots by an electric motor that turns a propeller. We planned to use the sub for surveying long stretches of reef, for carrying heavy equipment around, and for studying shark attacks.

We were very pleased at the craft's performance on our first run; it really showed that it could do the job it was supposed to do. I'd been worrying about the problems I'd run into with other free-flooding submarines, which carry a tremendous amount of weight in the form of trapped water. Usually these subs have such a small electric motor, of only one-half or one horsepower, that they're incapable of controlling all that weight. If a coral head suddenly looms up in the murk, and you pull back on the stick to "fly" over it, you might as well be flapping your arms. You simply tilt the nose upward, changing attitude, and continue in the same direction, only to crash into the coral. At least that was my experience with one of the first subs I tried out, and subsequent ones showed little improvement.

This one, however, has two wings like a small airplane. These wings give it enough lift so that when you pull back on the stick, the sub not only changes attitude but actually starts climbing. Also, it seems to be adequately powered with a five-horsepower motor and a large propeller geared down from the motor. There is good torque, and you can stop it quickly.

W E found throughout our stay that it was always a little hard to snap out of our underwater world of fish, coral, and bubbles and adjust to the world of human beings above the waterline. There was, in addition, the enormous incongruity between nature's richness underwater and the barrenness above. It was as though the forces of nature had been concentrated on marine creatures here, lavishing all attention on the sharks and the shrimps and the sea cucumbers. When it came time to create the air-breathing birds and lizards and mammals and the dry-land plants, there just wasn't much energy left. Nor were there resources for them. There was almost no soil—only a small amount of fresh water hidden hundreds of feet below the surface, and precious little dry land.

By the time human beings reached the place there was so little to work with that their lives were more closely bound to the sea than to the land, although even that bond was a slender one. By catching fish and occasional turtles, humans could survive, but existence never came easy. The people had to live by nature's rules and these were strict rules. When it came time for a storm, for example, the rule was not to get caught on the water when it was blowing, or if it was a really big storm, not to get caught even near the water. The average altitude of the land here is 10 feet—not much protection against a storm wave.

As human beings become more "civilized," they become more specialized. That is, they learn to do fewer things better. A real specialist is one who knows how to do only one thing extremely well. The human beings who first came to Enewetak were generalists: they could fish, and weave mats, and open coconuts, and make clothing, and even grow a few basic food plants, like breadfruit and arrowroot. They fashioned crude huts from copra and drew their energy from the sun. The human beings who replaced these pioneers were specialists. Some were cooks; some were weather forecasters; some were nuclear physicists; some were policemen. They brought their food with them in special tins, their energy in the form of petroleum products, and their shelter in the form of cement. They came not as colonists, but as warriors, fighting noisy battles and later trying out noisy new weapons. It did not matter that the dry land was sparse and barely fertile; they brought what they needed.

There was another difference: men alone came as specialists. Only a handful of women have visited Enewetak since World War II, and most of them have been scientists. After that first day on the atoll we paid a visit to the small store at the base and noticed a consequence of the absence of women. The most prominent feature of the store was a large magazine rack, one side of which was devoted entirely to girlie magazines.

On the way back to the dock we stopped to look at the sign that commemorates the battle of August 1944, when United States infantry and marines captured Enewetak from Japanese forces. Thirty-four Americans and 700 Japanese were killed.

T HE next morning we headed up the reef to the East Channel, between Japtan and Medren islands. As we went I studied the local nomenclature in some confusion. Although the atoll has only forty islands, during our visit it had at least 120 names (not counting the old Japanese and German versions).

For most of the atoll's history, the Enewetakese people happily employed their own names for the forty islands, not bothering to write them (or anything else) down. Then, in 1944, the United States took the atoll from the Japanese and, finding the native names confusing, assigned English designations to the islands that sometimes approximated the original and sometimes did not. Japtan, for example, was called Muti; Medren was called Parry; Billae was called Piirai; and the island of Enewetak was called Eniwetok. These new forms were officially sanctioned in 1944 by the Board of Geographical Names, and appeared for nearly three decades on the charts of the U.S. Hydrographic Office. At the same time, however, elements in the military were impatient with such tongue twisters as Bogombogo, Bogallua, and Mujinkarikku, and an entirely different set of names was concocted on the time-honored basis of *A, B, C, D,* etc. The ludicrous list commenced with Alice, Belle, Clara, and Daisy and ran through Ursula, Vera, Wilma, and Yvonne, sparing us only names that began with Q, X, and Z. Thus Japtan was given the cognomen of David, Medren became Elmer, Billae Wilma, and Enewetak Fred. During the series of nuclear tests on the atoll these homey names were easy for American planners to deal with, as were other code names for the "events" themselves and their consequent craters. Thus we read in an account by the Department of Defense that "[Irene] was used as a ground zero island during Redwing, and contained instrumentation during other operations. Helen cannot be considered a true island, as all that remains is a sand spit bordering the Seminole crater where the island used to be."

The final set of names—those we shall be using in this account—was drawn up at the request of the Enewetakese people in 1972. It was in that year that American authorities agreed to let the people return to their atoll from the banishment that had begun in 1947. Although these "native" names are now the officially recognized versions, it will be some years before the confusion clears away.

T HE East Channel between Japtan and Medren, more than 100 feet deep, connects the lagoon to the ocean. Lagoonward the pass divides into two channels. Between the two is a shoal about 20 feet deep which is the resting place of a large concrete barge. We dived to the barge to see what we could find.

It was shaped like a small tanker, about 250 to 300 feet long. Half the vessel stood above water, so that it looked something like a ship at anchor. It apparently had been there for some time since all the heavy ironwork on it was badly rusted, but the concrete was still in surprisingly good shape. The ocean swell rolling in through the East Channel caused the water level inside the wreck to rise and fall, compressing the trapped air so that various hatches and access ports whistled and moaned as the air was forced through them.

The wreck was grounded between the two channels so that the stern projected over the blue water of the pass itself. A strong current of a knot and a half or two knots was coming in the pass, bringing clear ocean water with it. We made our first dive on the deep side of the wreck and found a steep slope from the edge of the shoal into the pass. The slope was about 75 degrees at first, then seemed to begin to level off at about 100 feet. It was completely covered with lush coral, mostly of the branching type of finger coral. Clouds of small plankton-feeding fish were hovering about the coral, picking their food from the ocean water that flowed in through the pass. It was difficult to swim in the flowing water, and we had to pull ourselves first down the anchor rope to get to the bottom and then hand over hand from one piece of coral to another.

We spent ten or fifteen minutes there, mostly observing the various kinds of fish, and then picked up the anchor and drifted along with the current for 100 feet or so. Then we hooked in again. If we watched closely, we could see the countless drifting specks of plankton that ultimately provide the food supply for every creature of every coral reef in the world.

Broadly defined, plankton include any of the small plants and animals that drift and float in the slow-moving currents of the oceans. Most basic are the phytoplankton, or plant plankton, that are the primary source of food for all life in the sea. The largest groups of phytoplankton are diatoms, dinoflagellates, and naked flagellates; there are about 200 species of these creatures drifting among the coral heads of Enewetak, and most of them are found throughout the vast reaches of the Pacific. Phytoplankton are considered primary because they, unlike animals, are able to capture the energy of sunlight and then to use this energy to manufacture starch out of carbon dioxide and water. This photosynthesized starch serves as energy to power the predators which eat the phytoplankton. The most important predators of phytoplankton are the omnipresent zooplankton, which drift and float everywhere in the company of their prey, leisurely gobbling them up whenever one is handy. These zooplankton, notably foraminifera and small crustaceans, are unable to produce their own energy, and hence unable to survive without the phytoplankton. So the living is easy when there are plenty of tiny plants to eat, but it is tough when the plants, through some subtle but inescapable change in sea temperature or salinity or current, decrease in number. Such is the life of the predator—comfortable and carefree when prey is abundant, desperate when it is not.

Most zooplankton, like the phytoplankton, are invisible or nearly so, but there is a host of less common drifters that stand out as visible specks when a beam of sunlight catches them: the eggs, embryos, and various larval stages of larger creatures such as fish and crabs. Larger still are larval stages of the jellyfish, Portuguese man-of-war, and other bulky members of the zooplankton. Some of these creatures are eaten by larger plankton or filtering animals like coral, and some of those in turn are eaten by small fishes. The small fishes are eaten by larger fishes, and so on up the food chain to the sharks and man, which usually are the last links. A notable exception here is that some sharks are eaten by some humans—and vice versa.

A s we held on against the current of the East Channel, the passage of plankton seemed as near to infinite as anything on this finite earth can be. Speck after speck swirled slowly past, swirl after swirl. By the time the current reached the far side of the atoll most of the specks would be missing, eaten by one of hundreds of kinds of predators operating day and night, filtering, biting, stabbing, trapping. Coral reefs with all their different plankton feeders from bottom to surface act as giant plankton nets. These nets are so effective at filtering the tiny bits of life from the water that the water coming off a reef has a markedly different composition of creatures than the water coming on. It still contains plankton, but on the down-current side the plankton is composed mostly of larvae and juvenile forms of the reef creatures themselves and specialized lagoon plankton members that have been swept out to sea. Because the ocean currents flow steadily around reefs, usually at the substantial velocity of a knot or even more, the reef as a whole is able to process and remove from astronomical amounts of ocean water enough nutrients to support itself.

In light of a persistent public notion about the fertility of tropical waters, it may seem strange that coral reefs have to go to so much trouble to gather their harvest of nutrients. In fact, the vast equatorial reaches of the Pacific bear a strong resemblance to terrestrial deserts. This analogy may seem stretched, and indeed, if you are thinking just of the watery aspect, it is. But deserts are located where they are largely because of quirks of atmospheric and oceanic circulation—and relatively barren spots occur in the ocean for the same reasons. The vast deserts of Africa, for example, do not lie along the equator, where one might suppose the heat would be greatest. They are found about 30 degrees north of the equator. This is because of global circulation patterns. The great heat at the equator, where the sun strikes the earth most directly, causes warm, wet air to rise rapidly and move away from the equator. As the air rises, it cools and drops its water; cool air can hold less moisture than warm air. Then, cool and dry, it descends again toward the surface as a heavy mass of dense, dry air. By laws of motion and thermodynamics, the place of descent tends to be at about 30 degrees north of the equator (the Sahara, for example) and 30 degrees south (the Kalahari in Africa and the Australian desert).

Similar rules govern oceanic circulation. I haven't mentioned the westward rotation of the earth, which tends to push both the atmosphere and the oceans eastward; this tendency is known as the Coriolis force, discovered by the French mathematician G. G. de Coriolis. In highly simplified terms, Coriolis's discovery was that the westward spin of the earth affects anything moving north or south across its surface—a cloud, an airplane, an artillery shell, even an automobile. The effect is greatest at the equator, where the velocity of rotation is highest. Thus a strong force is exerted on equatorial ocean water. This force is complicated by the presence of the continents, and the result is that in both the Northern and Southern Hemispheres of both the Atlantic and the Pacific, there are vast systems of slowly rotating current, or gyres. In the Northern Hemisphere the gyres rotate clockwise, and in the Southern Hemisphere counterclockwise.

The most famous ocean currents are the north-south sections of the gyres, which are adjacent to heavily populated areas. The north-flowing Gulf Stream is the strong western part of the North Atlantic gyre. The south-flowing California current is the weak eastern limb of the North Pacific gyre. The east-west limbs of the gyres move relatively slowly—about 2 to 4 miles per day—so that they adjust their temperature to the air temperature. The Gulf Stream, by contrast, moves more than ten times that fast—25 to 75 miles per day—so that it does not have time to adjust to its surroundings. Thus it remains warm during its long journey from Florida to northern Europe, transferring huge amounts of heat from one part of the globe to another. Without this heat, much of northern Europe would be almost uninhabitably cold.

Biologically, the most important kinds of water movement are upwellings. A typical pattern of upwelling results from prevailing offshore winds, which tend to blow surface waters out to sea. The waters are replaced by deeper, colder water that moves inshore. Deeper water tends to be richer in phosphates, nitrates, and other dissolved materials, because at depths of hundreds of feet there are few living creatures to use them up. Thus upwellings provide nutrient-rich environments that are continuously replenished by the circulation loop. Plankton flourish in huge quantities, as do the fish that feed on them and the birds that feed on the fish.

One of the most important and best-known upwelling areas is the band of ocean parallel to the coast of Peru where vast schools of anchovies have for many decades attracted flotillas of fishermen and have for many millennia sustained colonies of guano-producing cormorants, boobies, and pelicans. Several years ago the fishermen became so efficient at netting anchovies that the population plunged to record low levels. The Peruvians and others were forced to restrain themselves for a year or two, and the upwelling continued to nourish the plankton, which gradually nourished the anchovies back to something like their former abundance. Similar abundances of nutrients sustain huge plankton populations in polar seas, such as the extreme South Atlantic and Pacific reaches, where huge whales can make a living by swimming blindly ahead with their great mouths open, straining small crustaceans known as krill from the thick biotic soup.

Such a relaxed mode of earning a living is impossible around a coral reef. The biotic soup here is so thin and watery that a whale couldn't pick up enough food to fuel even one mighty fin. We didn't see any whales during our entire stay at Enewetak, and we didn't expect to.

There are no upwellings at most coral reefs. Almost all of them are within 25 degrees of the equator, and most are bathed by one of the slow-moving Pacific equatorial currents or the equatorial limb of one of the Pacific gyres. These equatorial currents (including the North Equatorial Current flowing west, the Equatorial Countercurrent flowing east, and the South Equatorial Current flowing west) are far from upwellings, so that the nutrients in them are constantly being depleted by their small plankton populations. In addition, the water temperature is fairly high (typically 70 to 80 degrees F). This is pleasant for skin diving, but not for plankton. Gases dissolve more readily in cold water than in warm; phytoplankton need carbon dioxide for photosynthesis, and zooplankton need oxygen for respiration. This makes life still harder for plankton, so most coral reefs must be extremely efficient filtering machines to survive.

Enewetak is no exception. It is located on the southern edge of the North Equatorial Current, and reef dwellers must work hard to extract a living from the clear, nearly empty water. On the other hand, their food supply, though meager, is nearly constant, so that the populations do not soar and plunge through the shocking peaks and valleys of the Peruvian anchovies.

There is a great abundance of species here, as we could see easily on the first day of diving, and few individuals of each species. This is not to say that some schools of fish, like the herrings or small jacks, won't number in the hundreds or thousands, but there is nothing like the seemingly infinite banks of anchovies off South America, or the schools of herring in the North Atlantic, or even the tremendous carpets of lemmings that regularly develop in the Arctic. The great number of species here makes for the kind of ecological stability one might find in a tropical rain forest; no one species predominates, and population explosions rarely occur. Predation is so heavy that any species that does begin to expand is quickly thinned out. Imbalances are soon righted by rigorous natural rules.

T HE East Channel began to give us a feel for the atoll quickly enough. We recognized some old friends from the West Indies and spotted close relatives of old friends. Most obvious during the daytime were the various species of plankton feeders. The larger of these tended to move well above the bottom, catching their small prey in the uppermost layers of the water. The smaller the species, the closer to the bottom—and the shelter it offered—they tended to remain. The presence of predators here is constant. The plankton can't do much about this presence, but the plankton-feeding fish can. Their predators are usually larger fish, so that the successful plankton feeder is alert for attack at all times. Bigger plankton feeders have fewer predators to worry about, and they can swim faster when they have to, so they dare to venture far from cover for food. The smaller plankton feeders, more vulnerable and slower-moving, do not usually get so far from the shelter of rocks or coral. On murky days all the plankton feeders hug the bottom, because they can't see their predators until they are close. The only small plankton feeders that move around freely, well above the bottom at times, are some of the species of small herrings that find safety in numbers and in their habit of forming dense schools. Such a school presents a confusing target for a predator, wheeling, sagging, and glinting erratically when threatened.

On the bottom itself there are innumerable other types of plankton-feeding animals. Around Enewetak we found quite a number of feather starfish (crinoids) perched on top of pieces of coral and rock, holding their arms outstretched into the current like beggars, waiting patiently for planktonic creatures to be brought to them. In addition, there are countless sponges that pump water through their porous bodies, filtering out the tiniest plankton; the night-feeding basket starfish; the coral polyps themselves, which snare the plankton with tentacles; and various types of bivalve mollusks, small crabs, and other creatures. Some of these, such as the bryozoans, are too small to see. There is even a component of the coral reef community known as nonplanktonic plankton: small creatures such as copepods, amphipods, tiny miscid shrimps, and others whose relatives are normally open-ocean plankton. These nonplanktonic plankton, by contrast, have adapted to life on a coral reef, often hovering among the coral during the daytime and emerging at night to feed on their true planktonic relatives as they drift in from the ocean. Like reef fishes, they are frequently brightly colored; their open-ocean (pelagic) relatives tend to be transparent or bluish. These small creatures manage to fight the currents and the surge of the surf that sweep other plankton helplessly along—as often as not into the maw of a plankton feeder.

It is interesting that almost all reef fishes that feed on plankton are particulate plankton feeders. That is, they do not cruise blindly through the water like whales, but instead select individual prey from among the plankton and snap them up one at a time. By necessity, reef plankton feeders tend to be relatively small fishes; otherwise, they could not, even by the greatest diligence, procure enough energy to survive.

The survival of all creatures, like that of the particulate feeders, is determined by strict laws of energy conservation; each must take in or manufacture by feeding or photosynthesis as much energy as it expends by movement, cell replacement, digestion, and all the other operations involved in maintaining life. Any shortfall is exposed relentlessly by weakness and often death. By even such harsh laws, a coral reef must be judged one of the most successful assemblages of life (some have compared it with an organism) on earth. A single reef, representing an exceedingly concentrated community of living things, must draw its energy and nutrition from a relatively impoverished environment, an equatorial current. The sources of nutrition in this environment are so tiny and so widely separated that a coral reef, to survive, must perform an operation of filtering and concentration that is startling in its efficiency. A single coral atoll community, such as the one at Enewetak, draws upon the nutrients of hundreds of thousands of square miles of ocean, acting as a vast energy sink with such success that it can support several thousand different forms of life. The existence of these reefs is surely a miracle of natural ingenuity, the extent of which we are only beginning to comprehend. Coral reef communities offer not only scenes of dazzling beauty that are perhaps unequaled in any other environment, but also biorelationships whose delicacy and complexity are rivaled only by those of the tropical rain forest.

Marine biologists are only beginning to explore these relationships here. The Eniwetok (old spelling) Marine Biological Laboratory was established on Medren Island in 1954, and small studies have been under way since then, many of them related to the effects of nuclear testing on the atoll. The laboratory has been operated since its inception through the University of Hawaii; on July 1, 1974, the old EMBL was reorganized, upgraded to a year-round operation, and renamed the Mid-Pacific Marine Laboratory (MPML). Operating out of the lab, visiting scientists have studied such topics as the movement of nutrients on the windward reef flat, the growth bands of corals, and the chemistry of the lagoon water.

But we have only begun to investigate the workings of the most interesting part of the reef: the outside. The bulk of reef plankton feeders work in and beyond the line of breaking waves; they are abundant inside the reef only in places like the passes where ocean water flows into the lagoon. Very little biological work has been done beyond the breakers, mostly because it is so difficult to work there. Ecologists have made many models of reefs and pronouncements about their energy flow and balance, but these models are really based on the more impoverished parts of the reef—behind the reef top where it is calm and easy to work. To date, the published literature on reefs leaves a good deal to be desired.

THERE is no question that the outer part of the reef is a difficult work environment. The crashing waves, some days so violent as to be unsafe for small boats, are not the only problem. There is also the persistent North Equatorial Current, sweeping along day after day from east to west, carrying away everything not tied down, including marine biologists. On the deep side of the wreck, where we were, it was difficult to work. So we moved to the shallow side; the wreck creates to some extent a large eddy so that on the shoal side it isn't necessary to fight the current. There is also a lot of coral growth, including a patch at the top of the middle ground of the pass itself, similar to the patch reefs in the lagoon. Innumerable small coral fish swam among them, and Jo photographed a number of these, mostly damselfish. Then we worked our way back along the side of the wreck to the deep end, to the stern, which overhung the deep water. Beneath the stern we spotted several large black jacks, a medium-sized fish of 10 to 15 pounds and very dark all over—almost black. They're a worldwide species, and we're familiar with them from the Caribbean. They were, in fact, described originally by a Cuban naturalist back in the mid-1800s from specimens around Cuba.

The scene beneath the stern was interesting because we were looking off into the deep water of the pass. The silhouettes of the black jacks were backed up by the intense luminous blue background, and the bottom of the stern of the vessel framed the sky above. It was a beautiful sight.

There were also a number of large surgeonfish of the unicorn type, the genus *Naso*, out beyond the stern. Several of these, we noticed at a distance, were pairing off and swimming vertically upward in the water. This is unusual behavior for any sort of fish. The only times that you normally see such activity is in spawning, when an upward rush apparently allows gas from the swim bladder to expand, thereby helping push the eggs and sperm from the body. Whether or not this is actually the reason for upward rushes we're not sure, but it is one possibility which has been suggested in the literature.

As we moved closer to these fish, I noticed that one, which was presumably the male, suddenly got white markings on the face—very pale, milky-white vertical markings and a white mark down the top of the head—while all the other fish remained dark. The one with the white markings would lead its partner about, and then they both would get quite excited and make the upward rush. We had seen similar behavior in the blue surgeonfish in the Caribbean when they were spawning. In that case, the whole face and head of the male got very white while it courted the female and remained white during the upward spawning rush. Many fishes change color when they are courting, and it is usually the male that does so.

From the wreck we proceeded back across the deep pass to Medren Island, which has a large abandoned military base on it. We tied up to a pier there and had lunch, and then Jo took the children for a swim off a beautiful powdered sand beach at the base of the pier. The sun was pretty brutal in the skiff, and the children were pretty hot by then, so they were glad to get in the cool water.

From Medren we headed back along the reef to Enewetak Island, stopping to make a dive at some patch reefs I had seen on the sand shelf inside the main reef, in about 15 feet of water. These small patch reefs are just mounds of coral about 12 feet high and 50 feet in diameter. They are like apartment houses for fish. Squirrelfish, small groupers, pomacentrids (damselfish), and various other types were tucked in the nooks and crannies all along the sides. We were able to stand on the sandy bottom and film and observe them. Most of the fish there, the ones back in the coral, were just resting. They are nocturnal species, and daytime for them is down time. The surgeonfish, which are daytime (or diurnal) species, were out grazing on algae, and the diurnal damselfish were out feeding on plankton.

The surrounding sand and rubble bottom was interesting. There were many beautiful cone shells and other shells, and there was also a considerable colony of snapping shrimps, living in burrows that are shared by a small goby. This relationship is fascinating. The snapping shrimp makes a burrow in the sand bottom by propelling itself backward and digging. It's a very ambitious, hard-working little creature, constantly repairing its burrow. It comes out like a little animated bucket loader, with the two big arms in front loaded with sand. All its little legs are churning as fast as they can, and as soon as it's clear of the burrow, it dumps its load. Then it backs up to the mouth of the tunnel, pops inside, and returns in short order with another big load of sand.

Meanwhile, the goby just lies in front of the burrow enjoying life. If a predator comes along, the goby dives for the burrow to seek shelter with the shrimp. The shrimp tolerates this arrangement—apparently because the goby serves as an early-warning system for predators. The shrimp can go about its excavating with peace of mind unless the goby dives for its burrow, in which case it follows right behind. Both of them stay inside until the goby comes out to check that the danger has passed. Then the shrimp reemerges and gets back to work.

What the goby, or even the shrimp, feeds on, I don't know. I presume that the shrimp consumes detritus and microorganisms from the sand bottom, while the goby feeds on some of the tiny crustaceans that live among the sand and perhaps on the small plankton that drift near the bottom.

Interestingly enough, the goby and the shrimp have the same sort of mottled color pattern. I remember seeing, in the Indian Ocean, similar shrimp-goby relationships. The pairs were different from the ones here, but again the pattern of the shrimp was like that of the goby. One of the gobies was strikingly banded, with alternating reddish and orange and white colors; its shrimp was marked the same way. Another shrimp I found was coal-black with a white stripe down the center of its head; this shrimp also had a goby of the same pattern living with it. Apparently, then, the shrimp-goby relationship is a highly specialized one that has evolved over a long period of time.

While easy to observe with the naked eye, the shrimp-goby system is difficult to photograph. Just as you are about to get close enough to get them in focus, the goby turns and dives for the burrow, followed by its shrimp partner. If you switch on a floodlight to take a movie, the same thing happens. But with patience I think we can get them, and it should be an interesting show on film.

From the patch reef we headed back to the boat and started cleaning up our gear and doing some work on the cameras. One of them has a 72-degree shutter which is not nearly wide enough for the wide-angle lenses, so I had to replace it. A couple of fellows from the Coast Guard loran station here offered to look at our loran, which has been malfunctioning. I think they found the problem was in some of the adjustments in the back of the set; it seems to be all right now. In talking with them, I was surprised to learn that of the fourteen men who run this station not a single one skin-dives, although they do a bit of snorkeling. I don't think they're impressed with the place, and since they don't dive, it's easy to see why. There are probably thousands of skin divers who would join the Coast Guard if they knew that they could be sent to Enewetak.

3

THE CREATION
OF ENEWETAK

B EFORE I go on with the account of what we saw at Enewetak and the pattern of life there, it might be helpful to tell what we know about the origin of coral atolls—a dark mystery until the end of the nineteenth century. By and large, the ocean floor is flat and featureless, covered, as a worldwide average, by about 12,000 feet of water. Why, naturalists asked themselves, should this monotonous floor break suddenly into a cone-shaped mountain, soaring to the surface to form a tiny coral pinnacle, and often no more? Much of our understanding of this process—as indeed of so many others—derives from the work of Charles Darwin, who sailed from 1831 to 1836 aboard HMS *Beagle* on its famous global surveying expedition. In addition to observing and collecting the great variety of organisms that led to the theory of organic evolution, Darwin was able to study coral reefs. In doing so, he was one of the first scientists ever to explore in detail the relation of organisms to their geologic environment. Many of his ideas on coral reefs are still accepted, partly on the basis of extensive tests conducted on two Pacific atolls: Bikini and Enewetak.

More than 100 years after the *Beagle* sailed, the coral reefs of the South Pacific became battlegrounds of World War II, and military and engineering problems sparked new observations. The most intensive studies were carried out after the war, however, on the coral reefs selected for testing the atomic bomb. To geologists, these reefs became famous because of the massive mapping and drilling program that was carried out to determine the origin and dynamics of reefs. In wanting to understand the effects of bomb testing, the U.S. military at the same time accomplished a lot of good basic research that no one else was willing to fund.

By definition, an atoll is a continuous or broken circle of coral reef and low coral islands surrounding a central lagoon. Most atolls have several features in common: (1) an outer wave-resistant reef front that slopes steeply seaward; (2) a flat reef platform in back of the reef that extends toward the center of the atoll; (3) a shallow lagoon in back of the reef platform that is protected from the waves by the reef; and (4) a central island. Some atolls, like Enewetak, have no central island, and this absence was to prove a cornerstone of Darwin's theory.

The main part of the reef is made up of actively growing coral. Coral is an animal in the family Anthozoa, closely related to the family Scyphozoa, which contains the jellyfishes. Corals grow in colonies of great numbers of individuals attached to each other in the form of branches, balls, stalks, and so on. The solid part of "a coral" is really the skeleton of a colony of coral animals. The skeleton is composed of calcium carbonate, or limestone, secreted by each individual coral as it grows. The animal itself is tiny, about the size of a pencil point, and it has invisible but effective tentacles with which it captures plankton.

But coral is not that simple. Each one can live only in partnership with small green algae (zooxanthellae) that dwell within the translucent tissues of the coral itself. By a symbiotic relationship, the coral provides protection for the algae and a place to live, while the algae provide oxygen for the coral through photosynthesis. Because of this dependence, reef-building corals need light to live. Their habitat is limited by this requirement to shallow waters, less than about 65 feet from the surface.

Another essential reef-dwelling organism is coralline algae, which, like the corals themselves, secrete carbonate mineral and thus help cement the whole reef into a massive rock terrace.

As the inhabitants of the reef and of the lagoon feed upon each other, or die of other causes, or are broken up by storms, their shells, skeletons, and other hard parts are constantly being fractured into smaller pieces, from sand- to silt-sized. These fragments provide the carbonate sand that makes up both the beaches of the atoll and some of the fine mud found on the bottom of the lagoon. Such information has enabled geologists to determine the whereabouts of ancient coral reefs. For example, during the Silurian period, some 400 million years ago, a vast series of reefs lay in a belt across what is now Indiana, Illinois, and Wisconsin; during the Permian period, about 250 million years ago, great reefs grew where west Texas is now. These were not, of course, atoll reefs, but huge barrier reefs adjoining a large landmass. A similar reef today is the Great Barrier Reef which parallels the east coast of Australia.

THE mystery of coral reefs, for Darwin as for later naturalists, hinged on the zooxanthellae, those minute green algae that exist symbiotically with corals. The algae must be close to the surface so that they can receive enough sunlight, and this means coral reefs can exist only in shallow water, ruling out the possibility that corals built their atolls all the way from the sea floor to the surface. How, then, did they get there? It is unreasonable to propose that the level of the sea was ever so near the bottom, and there is no evidence that the bottom somehow rose to the surface.

Darwin proposed that the best clue to the answer is the fringing reefs, or atoll-like reefs that grow concentrically around some volcanic islands where the water is of appropriate depth. After pondering the problem on and off for several years, he wrote in 1842 that the birth of an atoll begins with a volcano. The volcano, spewing out lava that piles up upon itself to greater and greater thickness, gradually builds a cone-shaped marine mountain that may, over hundreds or thousands of years, reach the surface. It may even go far beyond. Mauna Loa, on the island of Hawaii, today rises 2.5 miles above sea level, 6 miles above the sea floor, and covers an area 60 miles in diameter at its base.

After reaching the surface, suggested Darwin, a volcano may sag back downward as it cools. If this sinking is slow enough, upward growth of coral may be able to keep up with it, forming fringing reefs that maintain sea level. As the mountain continues to sink, the mountain peak itself may disappear beneath the waves, leaving only a lagoon surrounded by a ring of coral reefs.

Tests at Enewetak and Bikini atolls did more to confirm Darwin's general idea than any other research. At Enewetak, prior to and during the nuclear detonations, fifty holes were drilled through the islands themselves and through the outer reef. By geologic procedure that is now routine, slim cylindrical samples of earth material called cores were retrieved from various depths down to thousands of feet. And the vertical picture, or profile, that emerged was much as Darwin had predicted. We might imagine the atoll to have, in rough terms, the shape of an upside-down flower pot. The bottom three-fourths of the flower pot would be dark gray, to symbolize the dense, volcanic basalt which was built up by successive eruptions of molten rock from deep within the earth. The top quarter, however, would be light tan or cream-colored, to symbolize the limestone cap built by coral and coralline algae as the mountain itself slumped back into the earth's crust.

At Enewetak the whole structure towers about 16,000 feet above the surrounding abyssal floor; about 3,500 feet of this is limestone, hardened and compacted from the skeletons and shells of countless billions of individual animals and plants. Within about 150 feet of the surface of the island, this calcareous rock forms loose, unconsolidated rubble, much like coarse beach sediment. Below that depth, the rubble gradually becomes cemented, through a process known as lithification, into consolidated rock. Thus the foundation of the frail-looking wisps of land that we know from maps as Enewetak Atoll is solid, and as long as coral growth and lithification can keep up with the rate at which the mountain is subsiding, the coral reef will maintain itself—and its rich collection of flora and fauna, just beneath the waves, will continue to provide joy and puzzlement for marine biologists.

A MONTH or so after we got to Enewetak I happened to be on Medren Island when a geologist from the Scripps Institution of Oceanography in La Jolla, California, arrived. He said that he was looking for a "well" that had been drilled years before deep into the atoll, but that he was having trouble finding it. He said it was marked by a large block of concrete with a pipe sticking out of it. Since I thought I remembered seeing such a thing, I offered to help in the search. It turned out that trees had grown up pretty thickly around the general location where the bore hole was supposed to be. Worse, the company that had done the boring had informed the geologist that the hole would be between the airstrip and the CMR, but nobody knew what the CMR was. Since there was a building that looked to me as if it had been used as part of a marine railway, I guessed that the "MR" might be "marine railway," God alone knowing what the "C" stood for. We looked around the area and found nothing. But as we were going back along the road between the "marine railway" building and the airstrip, we saw a concrete slab just off to the lagoon side. There was a bunch of wires around, and supposedly the pole had had a thermistor (thermometer) chain going down in it with a cable attached, so we thought maybe these wires were part of that setup. The wires didn't look much like thermistor wires, and I continued walking around a large clump of brush to the north and saw that the concrete slab went on up under the trees. There was a small wooden building there, but it was empty and seemed to be falling down. Then I noticed still farther back in the trees, to the north and completely covered by the trees and heavy brush, a small wooden building about six or eight feet square. I could see one of the ubiquitous "off limits" signs that are on all the buildings around here, but this building didn't appear to have any bottom, and I started to dismiss it as just junk. Then I decided oh, what the hell, I'd go have a look. So I broke off some branches and cleared a little path to get into it, and there was a screen door on the place that was locked. The door was in such bad shape that I ripped the screen out to see inside the darkness. I saw a dirt floor with something sticking up in the middle. It looked like a pump, so I called to the others and then went ahead and crawled in through the hole in the screen and found that it was a standpipe and the casing of the bore hole. We knocked the door down and found the thermistor chain and cable leading into the bore hole. The Scripps people sounded it and found out that the chain went down for more than 100 feet without striking bottom.

The hole was actually more than 4,000 feet deep. That hole and one other are the only two that go all the way through the coral strata of the atoll to the basaltic base beneath—to the original volcano that formed the atoll.

It was exciting to see one of the original borings that had helped substantiate Darwin's theory. This reef is one of the most ancient that has yet been studied, going back 60 to 80 million years. As you go around the Pacific, you can find reefs in all stages of development. A relatively young island like Tahiti has just a fringing reef around it a short distance offshore; this means the volcano itself has been subsiding for only a brief time, geologically speaking. Then Bora Bora is a little better developed, with fringing reefs a little farther from the volcanic island—the beginning of a fair-sized lagoon. The island of Truk is older still, almost an atoll. Truk has only a few volcanic peaks sticking up in the center of a lagoon. Finally, Enewetak is a mature atoll, where the peak of the volcano itself has long since sunk beneath the surface, leaving only a large lagoon and a ring of islands that used to be fringing reefs. The lagoon is now about 20 miles long and 15 miles wide, with a maximum depth of about 200 feet. The lagoon floor sinks gradually with the rest of the atoll, and as it does, it is blanketed with the bodies and skeletons of dead organisms. And, as I've said, there is no longer any trace of the volcano—that is now several thousand feet beneath its limestone tombstone.

In any case, it was surprising that this bore hole had not been marked more carefully, since it was so important for geological research. It wasn't even capped off—just the open pipe standing up with a small wooden shed set over it. Any sort of storm could have blown the shed away, and a typhoon would have quite likely washed sand or debris into the hole. But at least it has been rediscovered, and the Scripps people have been using it to make more measurements. Around Enewetak, the thermocline in the ocean—the depth at which the water temperature drops abruptly—begins at about 330 feet, well below the depth where coral grows, and the Scripps people found that the temperature in the bore hole was almost exactly that of the same depths in the open ocean. This meant that the seawater was coming and going more or less freely through the porous rubble and limestone of the atoll cap.

This was good news as regarded the prospects of a program Scripps was now considering. Deep, cold water in the ocean (as I mentioned earlier) tends to be richer in nutrients than surface water; below the level of penetration by sunlight there are no plants, no photosynthesis, and hence no consumption of nutrients. The Scripps scientists were interested in pumping this nutrient-rich water to the surface to see if it would help grow plankton, and something that would feed on plankton—perhaps shrimp or fish. As possible sites for this experiment they had chosen, ironically enough, the now-peaceful craters that had been excavated by some of the nuclear "events" on the atoll several decades ago. It would be a nice touch of recycling if someone were able to convert these gaping holes into teeming reservoirs of marine food. It would also go far to counteract the idea that a nuclear war would mean the end of life.

4

SECRETS OF SEAWATER

THE next morning we woke up to a dead, oily calm. We set out to make a run down the outside of the atoll with the submarine. Conditions were perfect for this; we can't tow it when there is any wind at all.

We hadn't even gotten started when there was mechanical trouble. This will become a familiar theme, and I shall try not to belabor a sad fact about working in the sea: time spent productively underwater can be considered only time off from fixing broken, corroded, jammed, worn, ill-fitting, or poorly made equipment or looking for it when it's lost. There are many reasons for this, most of them having to do with the nature of seawater.

Water is a complex and in many ways surprising substance. Perhaps its most surprising quality is its chemical activity. It may not seem corrosive or dangerous to humans; after all, we drink it, bathe in it, and, to the extent of about two-thirds, are composed of it. Water seems as helpful and benign as the air we breathe. Yet, depending on time and temperature, it is capable of attacking and dissolving almost any substance—from the hardest metal or rock even to glass. The metal huts and equipment left behind on Enewetak by military forces and by the Atomic Energy Commission bear evidence to the corrosive power of rainwater; and beneath the sea, around the reef of the atoll, the rusted hulks of large and small vessels show even more dramatically the power of water to disassemble the stoutest works of man.

Water and petroleum are the only two naturally occurring liquids on earth; water is the only common liquid on our planet. Because it is so common, we tend to overlook its remarkable properties. As an example, it has the rare quality of being lighter as a solid than as a liquid; if it were not, lakes would freeze from the bottom up. Even the elements of which water is composed—oxygen and hydrogen—are chemically exceptional. Both are unusually reactive. Oxygen is our chief source of energy, the essential reagent in the respiration of living organisms and the combustion of fuels. Hydrogen is unique in having only a single electron, and it can attach itself to other atoms not only by sharing this electron but also by the attraction of its electronless, positively charged side. This positively charged side can weakly "hold" an electron from another atom in a link called a hydrogen bond. The hydrogen atoms of water molecules form hydrogen bonds with each other, joining the water molecules in a loose association that might be considered a single endless molecule. For this association to bend—as it must when water "flows"—many hydrogen bonds must be broken and re-formed. Thus there is in water a reluctance to flow that is much greater than there is in an "unassociated" liquid, like benzene. When benzene flows, its molecules simply slide around one another. In water, the motion is rolling, rather than sliding, as bonds are broken and remade. In this way it is possible for water to form waves when a force such as moving air is applied; an ocean of benzene would not have waves.

Perhaps the most important characteristic of the water molecule is its "rabbit-eared" shape. That is, the two hydrogens (positive charge) are joined to the single oxygen (negative charge) so that they make an angle of about 105 degrees—slightly more than a right angle. The consequence of this is that the "side" of the water molecule bearing the hydrogen rabbit ears is positively charged, while the side away from them is negatively charged. One side of this dipolar molecule responds differently to electrical charges than the other, lending a complexity to its behavior that has been discovered only in the present century.

This dipolar nature of the water molecule makes it extremely effective at combining with other molecules and even at pulling them apart. When certain compounds, such as sodium chloride (table salt), are dropped into water, they tend to dissolve almost immediately. Sodium (positive) is surrounded by the negative sides of water molecules, while chloride (negative) is surrounded by the positive sides of water molecules. The bond between sodium and chloride is weakened and broken. The sodium and chloride are then kept apart by swarms of water molecules that act as "cages." Water is so effective at breaking and keeping other molecules apart that it has been called the universal solvent.

It is not surprising, then, that the sea is a rich solution of dissolved material, or ions, such as sodium ions and chloride ions. Since the oceans first began to fill and atmospheric conditions produced rain on the earliest protocontinents, flowing water has leached minerals out of rocks and carried them, ion by ion, to the sea. There they have accumulated steadily, sometimes precipitating as limestone or other solids. Today, as a result of this accumulation, the ocean is a rich, complex, ionic soup. With some variation in different areas of the world, there are about 35 parts of dissolved solids for every 1,000 parts of water in what we call seawater. Most of this dissolved material is chloride and sodium ions, but virtually every element found on earth is thought to exist in oceanic solution. In a cubic mile of seawater, which weighs 4.7 billion tons, there are about 165 million tons of solids, including 89.5 million tons of chlorine, 49.5 million tons of sodium, 6.4 million tons of magnesium, 4.2 million tons of sulfur, 1.9 million tons of calcium, 1.8 million tons of potassium, 306,000 pounds of bromine, 132,000 pounds of carbon, 38,000 pounds of strontium, and so on down to 1 pound of silver, .2 pound of chromium, and .02 pound of gold. Of all these, sodium chloride, magnesium, and bromine are now being extracted directly from seawater in significant amounts worth several hundred million dollars a year.

THIS discussion of water may have seemed elaborate, but it is appropriate that it be so. Water is essential to all life on earth, and without its special qualities coral reefs and other ocean life could not exist. By being a powerful and persistent solvent, water is able to carry the nutrients needed to nourish phytoplankton, zooplankton, corals, and fish. If water molecules did not have a rabbit-eared structure, with one end negative and one end positive, they would not attract each other as they do. This would mean they would fly apart readily, or evaporate, instead of clinging together as liquid oceans. By the same token, the chemical character of seawater is so strong that only the foolhardy go against it. While living organisms need and make use of the dissolved material in seawater, inorganic substances fare less well. And this is where we were running into trouble. Almost everything we use as tools is made of inorganic material, notably aluminum, steel, and iron. And all these inorganic things, when exposed to seawater, come into contact with a multitude of dissolved ions that are eager to make chemical mischief with other ions. The most common form of such mischief is rust, and we could see it all around us coating abandoned ironworks and sunken ships. But it and other kinds of corrosion also formed on our submarine, cameras, spears, wrenches, flipper fastenings, outboard motors, bolts, nuts, and screws. Both the pure water of seawater and its ionic cargo were adept at seeking out chemical partners in tools that we considered solid and durable. The action is fastest below the waterline, but even aboard the *El Territo* or, for that matter, on any of the islands, the windswept particles of ion-laden water find their way into all of man's goods and possessions.

That morning's case study was a ballast control valve on the submarine. The valve was stuck, and the control arm was slipping, so I drilled it and put in a set screw. After doing this, we found that we had the arm locked rigidly, but when we tried to move it, we broke off the valve stem. This meant we had to take the valve out of the submarine, make a new valve stem on the lathe, and put it all back together again.

By that time it was about eleven o'clock. We towed the sub around to the ocean side of the island—a distance of a mile and a half or two miles—and prepared to make our first dive. We had to tow it slowly, so we trolled a fish lure on the way out and caught a snapper for Mikka, our pet otter. While we stopped for Jo to reel the snapper in, I noticed that the sub was listing. I got into the water and went back to it and found that I had left the ballast valve on one of the wing tanks open, and the sub was slowly sinking on that side. I closed the valve and blew the water back out and got it trim.

Meanwhile, Jo had dropped her lure down to the bottom and hooked a large type of fish known in Australia as sweetlips. I don't know of any American common name for it. When she finally got it to the surface, we heaved it into the boat. It must have weighed 12 or 15 pounds, and while we were getting the lure out, I noticed that inside its mouth was a fish it had swallowed. So I gave it a shake and out popped a large goby about six inches long—a beautiful pale fish with a yellow face and luminescent markings on the side of the head. It may well be a new species.

We put on our diving gear and picked up the cameras and got into the sub. Jo and I were going to run along the reef near the outer edge of the atoll where it drops into the abyss. We were planning to hold to the inside of that edge, in about 50 or 100 feet of water, toward the northeast along the line from Enewetak Island to Ananij Island. We blew the ballast in the sub, and it began to sink. Then we turned the power on and went into a shallow dive, leveling off at about 50 feet. We angled slightly away from the shore and down until we were over the steep drop-off at a depth of 75 feet. Large mounds of coral 25 or 30 feet high rose beneath us at intervals. They angled out from the reef like buttresses, so we'd have to come up over them, then proceed across the top and down into the next little valley, and so on. The buttresses were 50 to 100 feet wide, so we were swooping gently up and down like an aquatic roller coaster.

Flying along in a submarine like that creates a sensation totally unlike that of scuba diving. With scuba, your mobility is limited so that you see only the fishes of a small area. In a day, you might run across none or one of a species that has a dispersed population, and this is especially true of large fishes. In a submarine, you cover a lot of area and may see two or three of these large, widespread species. It's a little like fast-motion photography: events seem to be speeded up, many of them packed into a smaller time frame.

One of the first examples of this that we ran across was a giant wrasse, *Cheilinus undulatus,* the largest member of the wrasse family. It reaches a weight of at least 300 pounds, and there are unconfirmed reports of specimens 10 to 14 feet long that would probably weigh well over 1,000 pounds. It is a deep-bodied fish; a *Cheilinus* 4 feet long would measure 2½ feet from top to bottom, so that it looks much like a miniature barn door swimming along. It is bright green, with some pretty markings along the side of the face. It swims in a curious fashion, using its pectoral fins instead of its tail. This is typical of all the wrasses, and at first the sight of these heavyset beasts sailing along under "armpower" was ludicrous. The wrasses reserve the use of their large tails for emergencies; if pressed really hard, they will shake their tail for a short burst of speed to get cover. Normal cruising, however, is all done with the tiny, but remarkably efficient, pectorals.

The *Cheilinus* we ran across was a fairly large one—3½ or 4 feet long, about 100 pounds. We turned toward it with the submarine. I'd seen these before, when diving in the Indian Ocean and around Tahiti, and had tried in scuba gear to approach them. But, although they look ungainly swimming with their pectoral fins, they can still move at 2½ or 3 knots, which is faster than a diver can swim. So in the past I have been able to get only a short look at one before it easily flapped out of sight. With the sub, however, we found that we were able to keep up, and we flew along in formation side by side. I held the sub steady, and Jo stuck the movie camera out the window. We continued in that way for several hundred feet.

At that point I looked up and noticed a large white shark. It was a reef whitetip, not an oceanic whitetip, but this one was large for its species—about seven feet long. I turned the sub away from the wrasse and started toward the shark. By this time we were out over the blue edge, and the bottom was sloping very steeply into the deep-sea abyss. I followed the shark a short way, and then it dodged us as we came over the top of one of the buttresses of coral. It went down on the other side, and as I came over the top, it doubled back under me, and I lost it. So we turned and again proceeded up the reef. We noticed a number of large groupers and various species of surgeonfish. There was a lot of fish life of all kinds, and we seemed to move through clouds of them. Some of them dived for cover, and others just seemed to look us over. We felt like large, cumbersome fish-creatures ourselves, moving along at fish cruising speed over lush coral growth with many beautiful and delicate plate corals. We would gladly have cruised there for hours, watching the three-dimensional scenery reel past us like a total-experience movie. But we were bound to our air-breathing identity and had to head back before the hour's worth of oxygen was exhausted.

5

COLOR AND DESIGN
ON THE REEF

A N equally good name for coral reefs would be "color reefs."
There is no natural environment on land to equal them, with
the possible brief exception of bursts of wildflowers or flocks of bright-
plumaged birds, like flamingos. But even these exceptions are not compa-
rable. In the case of the wildflowers, they do not last very long and are limited in space to a carpet within a few inches of the ground. In the case of
the flamingos, they are brilliant but monstrous; that much pink can over-
tax the senses. In the case of a coral reef, the brilliant colors are part of
heterogeneous natural sculptures that are present year round and soothing
to the eye.

The next day was a bright one, the kind of day when reef colors are
really pulsing with life. There was only a light breeze and so, while Jo
caught up with some work back on the boat, Dick Gushman and Jerry
Condit and I made a dive at the concrete wreck. We caught it just at slack
tide so that we didn't have to fight the current. Without the clear incoming ocean water, the visibility wasn't as good as it is during the rising tide,
but it was still about 60 or 70 feet. We anchored near the stern of the
wreck, and I swam down from there into the East Channel. The overhang
of the concrete vessel extends into the deep water of the pass and shelters
a number of large fish in its shadow. There was a large school of *Caesio*,
some black jacks, blue-tailed jacks, and a large black snapper. The overhanging portion of the boat was covered with delicate colonies of pink
and orange corals. Large sea whips grew from the hull, extending downward like bent metal rods for six or eight feet. Immediately beneath the

stern of the wreck I came across a pair of Moorish idols grazing on the algae of the coral. They were near the edge of the overhanging portion of the hull, so that the sunlight struck them full on their sides. They were quite tame, so I could move in close with the camera. Their color patterns were remarkable: the body was barred with coal-black bands interspersed with snow white, tinged with yellow around the fins, and the face was painted with orange.

Biologists have spent a good deal of effort trying to guess the significance of some of the elaborate and beautiful color patterns of coral reef fishes. In most terrestrial environments, we are accustomed to muted colors and patterns designed to camouflage animals from potential predators. Since the time of Darwin, scientists have been baffled by the apparent violation of this tradition on coral reefs. For a long period, many biologists assumed that there were so many hiding places on coral reefs that color made no difference. In such an abundance of coral shapes and colors, they thought, it seemed possible that even fish with the most outlandish designs could persist without being eliminated. More recently, Konrad Lorenz and other behaviorists have argued that brilliant and distinctive color patterns allow species to recognize other individuals of their own kind and, conversely, to defend their territory against members of other species with different patterns.

From an extensive amount of work we did in the West Indies it has become apparent that several factors are involved in selecting the color patterns of reef fishes. Color is uniquely important to these creatures. Unlike birds, they cannot call to each other to identify themselves or their intentions (although many species of fish are capable of some vocalizing). Unlike mammals or reptiles, they cannot perceive the presence and, in some cases, the emotional state of another individual by a sense of smell. For purposes of communication and social interaction, fish are limited largely to vision. And because of the tremendous competition for space and food on a coral reef, the range of visual signals is accordingly great.

The matter of designing a color pattern is made difficult by the fact that the pattern must accomplish several tasks simultaneously. To complicate the challenge further, these tasks may be conflicting. At times, animals need to be concealed to avoid predators or to approach their own prey. At other times, they need to be conspicuous and recognizable in order to attract a mate or to announce to competitors the boundaries of their territory and their intention to defend it. And in still other instances, where no amount of camouflage would be successful, a pattern should be able to confuse a predator that has moved within striking range.

To give one example, a number of reef fishes have narrow, horizontal stripes of contrasting colors. Schooling fishes, in particular, commonly share striped patterns, and these can serve several functions at once. Take a design of alternating blue and yellow stripes. When a predator approaches a school of blue-and-yellow fish from a distance, it may not notice the school at all. This is because the primary colors of blue and yellow together tend to mix and diffuse into an overall greenish cast, blending in with the greenish background of the water. If the predator moves closer to the school, it may face yet another problem. If the yellow striping is dominant, as it is in the case of the French grunt, for example, the dominant yellow begins to blend with yellows in the coral (these fish are often found around coral which also has yellow as its dominant color). In addition, in shallow water sunlight is broken into flashing yellowish patterns, forming another kind of backdrop into which the grunts blend. If the predator gets still closer, to a distance where no amount of camouflage would aid schooling animals that are hovering in midwater, the fish huddle together and mill about so that their patterns blend into a seething maze of stripes. It becomes almost impossible for the predator to distinguish an individual, and without being able to mark the outlines of a prey organism, the predator has difficulty compensating for its evasive tactics. If the predator just rushes openmouthed into this maze, it has little chance of success. The schooling fishes simply move an inch or two out of its path to escape. This lack of success is parallel to that of the inexperienced quail hunter who, when a covey is flushed, fires blindly into the middle of the flock, killing nothing or perhaps wounding a bird. To make a successful kill, he must learn to pick out one individual and lead it as though it were flying alone. The explosion of the covey makes it difficult to do this at first. A spearfisherman faces the same visual challenge in a school of fish. It is very difficult to single out and lead an individual, and the temptation to fire into the "school as a whole" is a strong one. The predator fish and the quail hunter and the spearfisherman all must learn to pick out a single face in the crowd or return home hungry.

Some nonschooling fishes, too, like the Moorish idol, have strongly contrasting elements of color that would seem to make the animal shockingly conspicuous. But in fact, the strong spots or lines or other elements serve to break up the outline of the animal into a series of blotches. The overall effect is that the predator no longer sees the typical fish-shaped silhouette but a series of seemingly disjointed segments of color and shape. This may be a "deliberate" attempt at confusion—the ultimate goal of any successful "prey" fish.

The purpose of color is very different when it comes to fish of the same species, which have little or no interest in eating each other. At the close distances within which conspecific animals deal with one another, distinctive patterns of stripes, circles, or curves offer essential visual cues. These cues allow each fish instant recognition by its fellows and speed the orderly transaction of such behavioral business as mating displays or territorial defense. By the same logic, the cues must change when the behavior of the individual changes. Thus it would make no sense for a juvenile fish to draw the attention of an adult interested in mating. If such an adult had to chase and attempt to mate with every member of its own species, juvenile as well as adult, a great deal of time and energy would be wasted. Thus the juveniles of many reef fishes have a different color pattern than the adults. Other aspects of the life of a juvenile differ as well; the juvenile may not be able to forage for food over the same long distances as adults, or it may eat different kinds of food. Since its predation or hiding habits are different, it needs a different color scheme to go with these habits.

Almost every fish on the reef has its own particular color pattern for a good reason; by this I mean the reason seems "good" to us humans. To our way of thinking, any fish that didn't have a good reason for its color would not be successful in the struggle for survival.

One kind of coloration that seems logical to us is the camouflage adopted by many bottom dwellers. A fish that must lurk motionlessly on the bottom, waiting for prey to come within reach, has perhaps the strongest stake in invisibility of any kind of creature. An unsuccessful coloration here would be spotted by prey fish and avoided. Flounder, sole, anglerfish, and toadfish are good examples of drably colored, well-camouflaged bottom predators. There are many on the coral reef also, including turkeyfish and lionfish. Often these are not drab at all, as it turns out, but brightly decked out in reds, whites, and oranges. On a coral reef this coloration serves much the same purpose as does brown or gray on a sandy or muddy bottom; the surrounding area is also rich in reds, whites, and oranges.

Fishes that cruise through midwater watching for prey face still another challenge in devising the right color scheme. Sharks, snappers, jacks, and other large, roaming predators are seen by observers from many different angles, against many different backgrounds. This presents an unusual quandary: there is no way to blend with them all simultaneously from all viewpoints. One observer may be watching them against a dark patch of sea grass, while another watches them against a light sandy bottom. Because it is impossible to have a camouflage suitable to all possible backgrounds, these animals tend to exhibit a compromise pattern of generalized gray. Because the sky above is usually brighter than the bottom below, this gray is two-tone: darker above and lighter beneath. Thus, if an observer sees a shark from below, the light belly blends well with the sky. To an observer above, the dark back blends with the bottom.

One of the most important considerations in the disguise of a fish is the eye. The eye is often the most conspicuous moving part, especially the black center spot, which stands out against the surrounding white. A common means of camouflaging the black spot is to duplicate it on the body or on the upper or lower tips of the tail, so that instead of one black spot there are two or three or four. If a series of black spots swims by, it is more difficult for a predator to know which end to attack or for a prey fish to know which end to evade. Another common way to mask the eye spot is by running a dark bar through it. Many fishes use a dark vertical bar to hide the eye. In fishes that roam about in the open, however, such a permanent dark line would attract too much attention by itself—perhaps even more than an unbarred eye. So some of these wide-ranging species have a dark stripe that can be turned "on and off." The stripe shows only when they become excited in a feeding situation or when they are actually attacking their prey. Certain species of jacks and snappers have this feature.

There seem to be certain exceptions to the laws of coloration in fishes such as the butterfly- and angelfishes and Moorish idols whose lifestyle involves moving about near the shelter of coral as medium-sized, rather awkwardly shaped fishes. They have very deep bodies and a somewhat rigid skeletal structure with stiff dorsal spines and heavy neural and hemal spines on the vertebrae. These spines make them effectively much larger than they actually are, and predators have great difficulty getting such a spiny mouthful down. Consequently, they learn to leave them alone. As a result of the habit of sticking close to an abundance of shelter and the successful evolution of a particularly unpalatable style of body, most of these species have largely freed themselves from the need of camouflage to avoid predation. Nor do they need camouflage to mask their own movements; they are grazers and browsers and eaters of small sessile organisms such as corals and sponges. Thus their dominant concerns, in the realm of styling, are those of easy species recognition. Freed of any need for subtlety or deceit, this group of species has produced some of the most distinctive and brilliant coloration of all the reef fishes.

AN interesting variation on the principle of camouflage is mimicry. Like a human being who is successful as, say, a comedian or rock singer or athlete, the evolutionarily successful fish often inspires imitators. The business of mimicry is one of the more intriguing adaptational quirks that a biologist can study. In many cases the job of mimicry is done so effectively that in the field it is impossible to tell the impostor from the model. Only after capturing the mimic and dissecting it in the laboratory can you really pin down its identity; it is often unrelated taxonomically to the animal it mimics.

I would guess that more such mimicry goes on around coral reefs than in any other kind of environment. But the requirements are strict. For real mimicry to develop, the animals involved must have a great deal of time in a highly stable ecosystem. If the "real" animal is changing, or the surroundings are somehow altered, the mimic's advantage may be lost, and the entire effort may go for naught. Coral reefs, being stable, offer a wide range of bizarre imitators that we are only gradually getting to know.

One of the cleverest mimics on coral reefs is a little blenny that mimics the cleaning wrasse, *Labroides dimidiatus*. The cleaning wrasse is not only tolerated by almost all the fishes on the reef, but welcomed. Even large predators entertain this busy creature without violating a kind of two-way trust that has built up over the millennia. The cleaning wrasse, as its name implies, removes annoying parasites from larger fish, earning a good living for itself in the process. It even swims into the mouths of large barracudas and moray eels, which open wide and hold still while the little *Labroides* darts about amid the teeth and gums.

The clever imitator, which is not a wrasse at all but a true blenny called *Aspidontus taeniatus*, is virtually indistinguishable from *Labroides*. It even mimics the swimming of the wrasse by using its pectoral fins, instead of the normal snakelike motion of other blennies. In addition, although it has the telltale underslung jaw of most blennies, it has developed a false nose extending in front of the mouth, coming to a pointed snout much like that of *Labroides*.

However, the most important difference from *Labroides* lies hidden: four large fanglike canine teeth inside the underslung mouth, two in the upper jaw and two in the lower. The blenny behaves just like the wrasse, puttering up to a large fish which stops to be cleaned, fluttering its fins in trusting anticipation. Instead of removing parasites, however, the little blenny picks out a soft, fleshy spot, such as the gills or the flesh around the eye, and charges into it, removing a chunk of meat. The startled victim immediately takes off, and in an area where one of these mimics is operating, it isn't long before the legitimate cleaner, *Labroides,* can no longer make a living. The large fishes become so shy of *Aspidontus* that they flee at the approach of *Labroides.*

Nor does the arrogant blenny confine its attacks to fish: the unsuspecting diver seems to be just as appealing as the unsuspecting fish. I've been swimming along when all of a sudden, out of nowhere, one of these little fishes comes slamming into the middle of my back and takes out a mouthful. Fortunately they are only a couple of inches long and do very little damage.

F ISHES mimic each other in ways that at first may seem strange or meaningless. One day Jerry Condit and I were diving around a sunken barge off Pole Pinnacle, which we named thus because it is a pinnacle reef marked by a pole; it is about a mile from Jedrol Island. I had the telephoto lens on the movie camera, and I was trying to film some of the smaller fishes around the barge, particularly a very interesting blenny, *Meiacanthus atrodorsalus.* Most blennies are small fishes that live on the bottom right among the rocks, and many of them inhabit the intertidal or surf zone. But a few, in addition to the devious imitator of the cleaning wrasse, have specialized in other ways. This particular species has become a plankton feeder. Like other plankton feeders, it spends its life free-swimming far above the bottom, and unlike other blennies, it has become a schooling fish rather than a solitary feeder. It has a blue head and a bright yellow tail, and like a number of schooling fishes that hover away from the coral and bottom, it has developed long streamers along the tail. The uppermost and lowermost rays of the caudal (tail) fins have, through evolution, become long filaments several times as long as the fin itself. When the animal swims, these filaments wave in an S-like pattern back and forth. The function of these graceful filaments is not known with certainty, but it appears to me just in looking at them that their brightness and length cannot fail to draw attention away from the rest of the fish. In a group of these blennies swimming together, you see not a collection of individual fish but a sea of waving filaments. This seems to be an effective means of confusing a predator by preventing it from focusing on an individual within the shimmering crowd.

Some years ago, when I was diving in the Amirante Islands, near the

Seychelles in the Indian Ocean, I was watching a group of *Anthias* feeding on plankton. *Anthias* are members of the sea bass family, spread throughout the Indo-Pacific area, that also have long filaments on the tail; many of the species are a bright golden color. I was watching them at a depth of about 90 feet when I noticed among them a very slender-bodied fish. It was very hard to distinguish amid all the waving filaments, but it was definitely slightly smaller and more slender than the *Anthias*, even though its color was also golden yellow. As I got within five or six feet of this school of *Anthias*, this strange animal dived quickly into the coral; not until I got closer did the *Anthias* do the same.

I was intrigued enough to want to identify the "false *Anthias*," so I went back to the surface and got some rotenone, which is a poison derived from the derris plant that we use to collect fishes. I put out a large dose of rotenone, and among the fish affected were quite a few *Anthias* and several individuals of this stranger, which turned out to be a previously unknown species of blenny. It was distinct enough from other blennies to warrant at least subgeneric ranking, so I called it *Anthiablennius*, meaning an *Anthias*-like blenny, and gave it the specific name *midas*, in allusion to the golden color.

In any event, this blenny too was a plankton feeder, and apparently it was taking advantage of the presence of the common and abundant *Anthias*. It had left the near-bottom environment of most blennies, grown imitative fin filaments, and moved up into the water column to feed on plankton as though it were a bona-fide schooling fish.

THE next day was heavily overcast and raining, with strong squalls and winds from 30 to 40 miles an hour. Despite the fact that we were only 11 degrees north of the equator, the weather felt raw. When you are used to bright, beating sun and then one of these windy, drenching days comes along, it seems as if there is no warmth left in the world, even though the temperature may be in the 60s.

After breakfast we discovered a leak in the water pump of both the starboard main engine and the generator. We had to replace the seal assemblies and some other parts inside the pump, and the whole operation took until noon.

After lunch, since it was too rough to go out, I made a dive beneath the *El Territo*. The water visibility was only about 30 feet—not very good—and the depth about 60 feet. The bottom in the area under the boat was silty sand with small patch reefs 10 or 12 feet in diameter scattered about. I spent about thirty minutes down there with the close-up lens and artificial light, filming some of the smaller reefs and colorful reef fissures. After dinner I again worked on equipment, repairing a battery-operated underwater movie light that fluttered out last year. I rebuilt it completely and put in new batteries and a new switch and fixed up some electronic flash units for underwater use, and then I straightened out a synchronization problem on an underwater still camera.

Looking back on it, I'd say that those mechanical problems are more wearing than a long day diving on the reef.

THE next morning the weather had settled down, so we went out for our first day's diving in the lagoon. As I've said, the lagoon is shaped roughly like an acorn, having a total area of about 370 square miles and a maximum depth of somewhat over 200 feet. The ocean waves are blocked by the islands, so that the lagoon, as per the traditional South Pacific romantic literature, is a smooth and placid body of water. This calmness implies a number of things about the kind of environment in the lagoon and about the kinds of creatures living there. The bottom is protected from the main force of the oceanic currents, for one thing, allowing silt and other fine sediment to accumulate. Without much wave action, the upper layers of water are not nearly as rich in oxygen as is the water on the outer part of the reef. The water is by no means stagnant, and there are more than 2,000 coral pinnacles scattered throughout the lagoon. But circulation is relatively sluggish, and the composition of the plankton community is noticeably different from that on the reef. With the larger amount of sands and muds on the bottom, the bottom-dwelling fauna is richer, featuring an abundance of snails, clams, crabs, sipunculid worms, and sea urchins. The numerous sea cucumbers churn through the bottom material like giant earthworms, ceaselessly ingesting mud and sand, gleaning the bacteria and algae from it, and egesting the waste.

We boated out to two of the pinnacle reefs in the lagoon where there is a sunken concrete ship. The first pinnacle rose to within 12 feet of the surface, plunging from there to a depth of about 50 feet. From there the sides sloped more gently to the lagoon floor, which at that point is about 145 feet down. The top of the pinnacle was forked, with a narrow pass between the two tines, which joined at about 40 feet. One of the peaks had a hole through it. Quite elaborate and beautiful.

There were three species of schooling fishes of the genus *Caesio*. One was a brilliant blue with a bright yellow tail, another was a gun-metal blue with two golden stripes and black tips on the tail, and the third was blue with a large yellowish mark on the side. All are plankton feeders, and all are about six to eight inches long. They seemed extremely friendly, swarming around us in clouds. On one side of this pinnacle I found a single specimen of a large alcinarian, or sea whip. In the Caribbean, the sea whips and sea fans are dominant members of reef communities, some growing to a fairly large size, their constant swaying in the surge of the current adding grace and beauty to the life of the reef. In most of the Pacific, however, these alcinarians are far less common, so that at first glance, at least, the reefs don't seem as lively as West Indian reefs. But the big difference lies in the stony corals, the true reef-building corals. Here they are far more luxuriant and diverse than on Caribbean reefs. As an illustration, there are 2 species of a genus *Azuaflora* I am familiar with in the West Indian region; in the western Pacific there are more than 100 species. In the West Indies, there is a total of 50-odd species of reef-building corals, whereas here there are that many genera alone, and hundreds of species.

The second pinnacle we went to was the more interesting of the two. It was much smaller, with a diameter of about 50 or 60 feet across the top, and very steep-sided, plunging almost vertically to a depth of more than 100 feet. There a sloping base continued to the lagoon floor at 135 feet or so. The water was much clearer here, and the current much stronger. The clean ocean water coming through the deep pass in the reef sweeps this far into the lagoon, accounting for both the clear water and the current.

On the up-current side of this pinnacle was a variety of large fish. There was a large school of the unicorn surgeonfish, which has a large, peculiar spike sticking straight out in front like that of the mythical unicorn. There were schools of *Caesio* as well, hovering in the current and feeding on the plankton that came in with the ocean current. There was also a large dog-toothed tuna. The dog-toothed tuna is unusual in that it looks like a strange, heavy-bodied mackerel armed with prominent teeth; most other species of tuna have very tiny teeth which are normally hidden. The specimen we saw was about three-and-a-half or four feet long. That's about average for the species, although it has been recorded as large as 160 pounds. Its very husky body makes it appear quite formidable. The dog-tooth differs from other tuna species in one other important respect: it hangs around in reef passes in the lagoon, whereas other tunas are open-ocean animals.

The pinnacle seemed to be a favorite hangout for other large carnivores as well. We ran into a school of about twenty Pacific barracudas. They were about three or four feet long and looked and behaved in general like the great barracuda of the West Indies, which also lives in the western Pacific. But instead of having the black spots along the lower posterior portion of the body, they have a series of indistinct vertical bars down the side. We also saw two gray sharks and a whitetip shark. The smaller of the gray sharks was waiting for me as I swam ahead of the others to the up-current side of the pinnacle. It was about 4 feet long, and immediately, at a distance of about 30 feet, it went into its aggressive display, or preattack display. I stopped and filmed some of it. I tried to move in a little closer, trying not to make it more agitated, but the display seemed to intensify, so I backed off. It continued to display even when I went all the way to the surface, so it seems that even a complete retreat doesn't satisfy it. I returned to the boat and got a bang stick to try to get a little closer to the shark, but before I could get back, I ran out of air.

T HAT afternoon was taken up by some more of those minor challenges that technology throws up, one of which grew into a major challenge to Dick and Jerry.

Every time we go out on an expedition it seems as if it takes a couple of weeks to get all the equipment functioning. This time it was some of the scuba regulators. The hoses had cracked and were leaking, and the check valves had gotten gummy, so it was necessary to replace the check valves and the exhaust flutter valves and the hoses.

Those were the minor challenges. The major one involved the submarine. It is only a little sub—some might consider it a toy—and you can't go very far or very deep in it, but any time you do anything on or beneath the sea, nature and technology can team up to scare you. Jo took a practice run in the sub, doing well and handling it effectively. Then Dick and Jerry had a go at it and didn't have so much luck. They went off without realizing that one of the ballast weights had slipped forward. This put them out of trim so that they were nose-heavy. At the surface, with the nose down, the propeller was raised uselessly out of the water, where it simply fanned air. This meant that they could not descend with the prop but only by blowing some air out of the ballast tanks. Then, when they got down, they found that they couldn't get back up again. They got almost to the surface, and the nose just wouldn't rise any more, so they ran along about 10 feet below the surface, unable to come up the rest of the way. Finally, they blew the water out of the ballast tanks to rise the last 10 feet, but when they did that, the propeller came out of the water first and they were still helpless. Finally, they blew the ballast tanks completely and floated all the way up. They still didn't know what was wrong, so Jerry got out, and Dick went down again by himself to give it a final try. But they had inadvertently left on the air in the ballast system and used almost all of it. When Dick got down to about 80 feet, he ran out. This meant that he was also out of breathing air since he had been using the same supply. So he had no air to blow out the ballast tanks and no air to breathe. Fortunately there was another tank in the back seat that Jerry had been using. Dick breathed off it for a while and then managed to transfer the last little bit into the ballast tanks. This last bit turned out to be just enough to get the sub to the surface. We spotted him and went over in a skiff and threw him a rope. He had been swimming around, mostly holding the sub afloat by himself. We got it squared away and stuck a new tank in and went back down, and that was when I discovered that the ballast weight had slipped forward. I threw it in the back, and the sub reassumed proper trim, and there was no further problem.

I T wouldn't be fair to give the impression that the submarine was a lemon or a sullen sea creature of evil spirit. On the contrary, she served us well most of the time, affording a mobility and underwater freedom unmatched by any other craft I have used. On good days, when the wind was low and the water clear, we were able to glide and soar in the midst of spectacular beauty with an exuberance that is known perhaps only to birds. Flying the machine is very like piloting a silent helicopter, and it puts us on an almost equal footing with the creatures we are studying.

The next day we towed the submarine out around the southwest corner of Enewetak Island. It was a clear, calm day with a broiling sun. Jo and I submerged in the submarine on the outer edge of the reef. Our objective on this mission was to count the shark populations along a stretch of reef and to test their reactions toward various approaches and "postures" of the sub. The water was extremely clear, and we could see the bottom plainly from the surface down to depths of more than 100 feet. We descended in rather a steep dive, and on the way down I noticed some blurry patches on the windshield. They turned out to be muddy footprints that had dried; I had made them when I was on the surface, standing on the sub and pushing it away from the *El Territo* after I had lowered it into the water by the crane. We stopped on the bottom at about 80 feet, just inside the steep outer slope of the reef, and I hopped out and wiped off the windshield.

I got back in, and as we started up, I pulled back sharply on the stick so that we could maneuver cleanly out of the little sand pocket where we had settled. The sub responded beautifully, lifting rapidly and reminding me again of a helicopter. We glided on down the slope of the reef, spotted a large silvertip shark, and turned to follow it. It turned and started back in the direction from which we were coming, so we then had to double back and chase it the other way. In the process we came across two more silvertips, one of which was going the way we wanted to go. We turned and followed it. We could get quite close to this shark—within about 20 feet—but it did not respond at all like the gray reef shark. There was no threat behavior at all, no erratic swimming. If we tried to "threaten" it by pulling in close, it would simply swim away a little faster. The only deviation from normal swimming routine that we thought we detected was a slight swinging of the head from side to side, but this may have been only an attempt to keep us in view, to see how close this strange, huge "fish" was approaching.

In the process of chasing after one silvertip, we had gone out beyond the edge of the coral grove onto a steep sandy slope that began at about 80 or 90 feet and continued downward rather steeply to unknown depths. As we doubled back after the third shark, we noticed a large leopard ray below us on the bottom, so we broke off and headed down to have a look at him. The rays belong to a large order of fishes which, like sharks, have skeletons not of bone but of cartilage that has been hardened by lime. The body is flattened, and the pectoral fins are highly developed as broad lateral lobes, or "wings." The tail is slender and whiplike. Rays move by flapping their large wings in slow, graceful motions. Well-publicized species include the huge, often playful manta, or devil ray, which may attain a wingspread of 20 feet or more and is sometimes seen cavorting and leaping at the surface; the barndoor skate, which lives at depths greater than 100 feet along the Atlantic coast; and the torpedo, or electric ray, which generates enough bioelectricity to produce a severe shock. Rays, generally camouflaged against the bottom, prey on crustaceans and other bottom dwellers.

The leopard ray is an extraordinarily beautiful fish, coal-black on top and snow-white beneath, patterned with a series of spots on the back which gradually become white circles as the animal grows older and larger. The silvertip sharks are apparently no respecters of this beauty, or of their close family relationship, since they often make a meal of leopard rays. But the silvertips we had been following seemed to pay this ray no notice, even though they were certainly big enough to have eaten it.

The ray has a long whiplike tail with a set of several barbs at its base. It also has a "tongue" made of a heavy plate (its teeth are inconsequentially small), which it uses, in concert with a smaller, corresponding plate in the roof of the mouth, to crush the mollusks on which it feeds. In the ray we were watching, this "tongue" would have been about three inches wide and five inches long.

As we approached the ray, it was flapping up the slope toward us; we met—ancient, primitive beast and twentieth-century submarine—at a depth of about 150 feet. Since it showed no inclination to change course, we turned to follow it up the slope. When we got back up to about 125 feet, it banked to our right. Just before the ray turned off, a blue-tailed jack rushed in, and started following it like a shadow. The ray flapped its wings and then turned both wings up and went into a peculiar glide with the wing tips arched upward. The jack maneuvered into a position between the wing tips and maintained that position so that they went sailing off together in tight formation.

I know it stretches the imagination to lay before you such an improbable partnership, but queerer ones exist. We already know of the shrimp/goby and the cleaning-wrasse/predator symbioses and several others, and there are surely many more on the coral reef. Jacks follow not only rays in this way but also various species of sharks. At times when they are following a shark, they seem to be scratching themselves on the shark's rough hide; at other times they probably feed upon the small fish that are frightened out of grass beds as the shark swims through them. When they follow a ray, they are often presented with a smorgasbord of small bottom fish, crabs, shrimps, and other creatures that are startled from cover as the ray grubs about.

Since we didn't seem to be able to provoke any attack behavior in the silvertips, we cruised on down the reef, slowly climbing until we leveled off at about 75 feet along the outer break where the bottom was more nearly level. We came upon a number of sizable groupers of various sorts. Groupers, along with similarly shaped sea basses and jewfishes, comprise a large group of big fishes that have the general appearance of ordinary small- or largemouth basses. The kelp bass is a small species of grouper that lives among the kelp beds off California, where it is frequently taken by anglers; the sand bass is another. Jewfishes are much larger, including the black jewfish of the region around Florida, the spotted jewfish living south of Florida, and the Pacific jewfish.

Among the groupers we spotted was a large Pacific jewfish of about 50 pounds. At maximum size, this species approaches 1,000 pounds and reputedly has swallowed native pearl divers in the Great Barrier Reef waters off Australia. The Caribbean species reaches a similar size. I once took one of these with a bang stick for teaching the osteology of the fish skull at the University of Miami. To boil the meat from the skull, we needed a large kettle of sorts, and we seized upon a 55-gallon drum. The head weighed more than 100 pounds, and was so big that it would just barely fit inside the drum. My father once caught one that weighed 756 pounds, and I have heard stories of jewfishes caught commercially that weighed more than 1,000 pounds. I remember reading an article in the local paper of Key West, Florida, that described the adventure of a Navy underwater demolition team diver. On his day off he decided to have a busman's holiday of sorts, going spearfishing off Key West. He spotted a large jewfish, which he began to stalk; but the fish was too quick for him, and it suddenly grabbed him in its huge mouth, seizing his head and one shoulder and arm. The teeth of these animals are too small to amputate an arm, but they are sharp enough to create a horrible pattern of skin lacerations. As they were accomplishing just that, the UDT man managed to get out his knife with his free hand. He stabbed the fish as best he could, to discourage any further swallowing efforts, and the fish finally spat him out. He was badly raked, and spent time in a hospital.

So far we haven't seen any large ones here, but we expect to before long. We flew on down the reef and came across a large pufferfish that was hovering in midwater like a little animated dirigible, sculling with its pectoral fins and holding motionless. We circled around and headed toward it. It was so preoccupied, or thought itself so invisible, that we actually bumped it with the sub before it moved out of the way. It was quite large—about 2½ feet long and weighing somewhere around 15 or 20 pounds. There are several extraordinary things about these fishes. One is that they are able to puff themselves up to several times their normal size if they are frightened; hence the name puffer, or blowfish. Another is that their teeth have become fused together into a parrotlike beak. The beak is sheltered inside thick, fleshy lips and is an extremely powerful shearing tool. Once when I was diving in Fiji, one of our party had speared a puffer and put it in the boat. I offered it the hard plastic tip of a snorkel to bite, and the fish obliged by severing the snorkel cleanly with one bite, just like a pair of mighty scissors. A puffer the size of the one we saw today would have a fearsome cutting power. Fortunately, they also have docile dispositions.

After about half a mile of cruising we angled upward and broke the surface. Jo was getting chilled, and she had also used all the film in the camera on the sharks. So she got out, we unloaded the cameras, and I got back into the sub alone to take it back around the southwest point of the island into the lagoon. I flew along at depths of only 25 feet, in 30- to 50-foot water. I didn't want to go deeper because of the decompression obligation that I would have taken on. There are precise tables telling you how long you can free-swim at certain depths before you have to go into a decompression tank after you reach the surface. We have one on the *El Territo* for emergencies, and it is a very good thing to have.

The principle behind "the bends," or compressed air disease, is simple. Gas has a greater tendency to go into solution under high pressure than under low pressure, and when one is diving, the pressure gets higher with depth. The deeper you dive, the greater the pressure, and the more gas goes into solution. In this case the relevant gas is nitrogen, which composes more than two-thirds of the atmosphere. Nitrogen gas is inert, so the body doesn't use it up; it continues to dissolve in greater amounts as long as you stay down at depths of, say, 100 feet or more. Then, when you return to the surface, lowering the pressure on your blood, the dissolved nitrogen comes out of solution, returning to the gaseous state. This may mean large bubbles if you come up too fast, and the deeper you dive, the longer you stay down, and the faster you come up, the bigger the bubbles. It doesn't take much of a bubble to block a blood vessel to nerves, muscles, or brain tissue. If enough blockages occur, a diver is suddenly afflicted by localized pains in the abdomen or limbs, vertigo, lack of coordination, and even a collapse into unconsciousness. The only known treatment is to return the diver to deep water or a pressure chamber, where compressed air performs the same function as deep water, forcing nitrogen bubbles back into solution. Decompression is then managed slowly over a period of an hour or more so that the nitrogen can be eliminated gradually without forming bubbles. I had been down at 150 feet, and if I'd gone deep again with the sub, I would have had to go into the chamber after coming up.

On the way back I saw four blacktip sharks and tried to chase each one of them. They are shy animals, however, and none would let me get very close. They are usually small; these were about four to five feet long, the normal size for adults. They are similar to the gray reef shark, with less streamlining, but they have a striking black tip on the dorsal fin which is conspicuous in shallow water. Often the tip protrudes from the water when they are near shore, and it is easy to track the shark's movements even while standing on the beach.

At several locations in this shallow water I passed very large schools of surgeonfish. A hundred individuals or more, each 10 to 12 inches long, were slowly moving across the reef like a herd of sheep or cattle. This is a good simile for them because these are herbivorous fish that literally graze on the marine algae, serving very much the same ecological function as the herbivorous animals on land, that of converting vegetable matter to protein.

As I reached the southwest end of Enewetak Island—or rather came abreast of it underwater—I turned north to head into the lagoon through the broad pass which runs to the west of Enewetak Island. The water was only about 30 feet deep, and as I cruised over the sandy bottom, I could see that it was rippled by wave action into corrugations about a foot or two apart. Here and there the pattern was broken by coral outcroppings. It was a perfect environment for garden eels, and at several points I came across large groups of them. This is an unusual little eel that lives in colonies and burrows in the sandy bottom. Each one is like a snaky jack-in-the-box, living with its tail anchored in the burrow and its head outside. It feeds on plankton that it grabs from the drifting current. The tail end of its body, which never leaves the burrow, is very pale—almost colorless. The head is usually chocolate brown above and paler beneath, with some markings around the head. On the head is a set of exceptionally large eyes that give good binocular vision—essential to accurate sight fixing on the tiny planktonic prey. This gives it quite a different appearance, bug-eyed and short-snouted, from the more predatory types of eels. It is remarkable how job-specific these creatures are: they are entirely useless for swimming, or crawling, or gnawing, or doing much of anything other than grabbing tiny organisms that float within reach of their burrow. They pop abruptly back into their "box" whenever this simple routine is broken. As a human swimmer approaches a colony of these eels, they rapidly draw back into the sand and disappear as though they had never existed. They are extremely difficult to approach when one wears scuba gear, because every time a diver exhales, a cloud of bubbles bursts loose from the regulator and startles them. You can get within 20 or 30 feet, with care, but the only way to get closer is to use a blind, like the moving trees in *Macbeth*, and closed-circuit breathing gear. Our Electro-lung gear, for instance, puts out no bubbles, and when we wear this, it is possible to lie down on the bottom and inch along toward a colony of garden eels to within four or five feet, as we have done with the West Indian species. This approach ability has come only in recent years; before that, little was known about these shy bottom dwellers, which, unlike many others, are not caught in trawling nets because they duck into their holes whenever any such device approaches. Only since the advent of scuba have most of the different species of garden eels been discovered.

Finally, after about an hour of cruising by myself, I surfaced. I was well inside the lagoon by that time, and we took the sub in tow and brought it back to the boat.

6

A SHORT HISTORY OF ENEWETAK ATOLL

URING days of bad weather, when the winds came at a steady 25 or even 30 knots, roiling the water and spoiling visibility, I read up on Enewetak Atoll's place in human history. In contrast with the marine richness in which I was immersed as often as possible, the subaerial barrenness raises the question of why humans would bother about such a place, let alone struggle violently for it. The geological upheavals that raised the atoll above the waves achieved a miracle in accomplishing that task, but the resulting dry land must be called inadequate for the needs of most terrestrial organisms, let alone humans. Yet humans have indeed struggled over this poor real estate, and they have struggled violently. Victims of the violence have included both the strugglers—members of the world's mightiest nations—and the native peoples who originally settled this and other atolls of the western Pacific.

The natives of Enewetak are Micronesians (literally, "people of the small islands"), descendants of ancient oceanic sailors, who today wrest a living from the sparse and mutually remote pinpoints of land between Hawaii and the Philippines, generally north of the equator. Micronesia is one of the three divisions of Pacific islands. (The other two are Melanesia, which includes the Solomon, New Hebrides, New Caledonia, and Fiji islands to the south; and Polynesia, which includes the Hawaiian Islands to the east and Samoa, Tonga, and others to the southeast.) The 2,141 islands of Micronesia are spread over 3 million square miles of ocean—an area almost as large as the United States—and fewer than 100 of them are inhabited. On these 100 islands, which total 700 square miles in area, about 115,000 Micronesians live as wards of the United States in what is known as the Trust Territory of the Pacific Islands.

Little is known about the earliest Micronesians. Their islands are physically unstable places, periodically scoured by storm waves, and the people themselves left no monuments or writings. Separated by vast expanses of ocean, they are related only distantly in unremembered history, and they have never had strong cultural ties. In their isolation from each other, they have developed at least nine distinct languages, with further dialectal variations. Experts disagree on the extent of historical contact between the islands. Some believe that the only thing they have in common has been the need to develop specific strategies of subsistence on meager land resources. Others, in the words of a State Department report to the United Nations, believe that "Much trading, visiting and, very likely, war raiding took place." There is little doubt that settlement patterns were complicated and that each island periodically received new immigrants.

The first known contact between Micronesia and Western civilization took place in 1521, when Ferdinand Magellan sighted Guam during his round-the-world voyage. Magellan found that foreigners were not always received courteously; his ship was stripped of most of its portable goods by enthusiastic Micronesian treasure hunters. His visit had little immediate effect, but the subsequent activities of Europeans in Micronesia were usually destructive. Within recorded history, the depredations of soldiers, administrators, missionaries, whalers, "blackbirders" (slave-gathering pirates), and invading armies have taken an immense toll of lives and cultural patterns.

Guam soon became a vital watering stop for Spanish galleons sailing between Mexico and Manila. In 1668 the first permanent Spanish residents—six Jesuit priests—arrived with troops to establish a mission in the Marianas Islands. The native Chamorro peoples of the Marianas were all but obliterated by the end of the eighteenth century through warfare, disease introduced by the Spanish, and intermarriage with Spanish, Mexican, and Filipino soldiers and colonists.

Although Spain claimed sovereignty over the Marshall and Caroline islands as well as the Marianas, it did little to extend its influence in them. Carl Heine, a Marshallese by birth, writes in *Micronesia at the Crossroads*, a first-rate account of the political status and history of the area: "Outside of the Philippines and Guam little remains to suggest that the Spaniards were ever here. The history of Spain in Micronesia, excluding

Guam, is largely the story of a few galleons, a handful of military governors, and a small number of priests."

By 1900 Spain had declined as an imperialist power and control over its Pacific possessions had shrunk. At the same time the whaling and copra industries had attracted the attention of other great powers, which had begun to move into the Pacific. Rivalries sprang up among, in particular, Germany, Japan, and the United States. In 1885 Germany seized control of the Marshall Islands, and in 1899 it "bought" the northern Marianas and the Carolines from Spain for $4.5 million. The Marshallese, including the Enewetakese, accepted coconut seedlings from German traders and sold the harvested copra back to the Germans for trade goods and food. The new rulers did not keep a resident agent on the island, so the Enewetakese were more or less on their own; foreign visitors were kept to a minimum. The Germans were autocratic, but at the same time they were efficient and concerned with the details of living; they built roads, improved health and sanitation, and, to a certain degree, protected the natives from unscrupulous traders. They also, according to Carl Heine, attempted to "ease the movement of the natives into the Western world."

German control over Enewetak was relatively brief. It came to an abrupt end when Japanese military forces swarmed across Micronesia in 1914, at the outbreak of World War I, as part of a well-planned attempt to expand the Japanese Empire and relieve the overpopulation of their own islands. After the war Japanese occupation of the former German territories was sanctioned by a League of Nations mandate, and Japanese colonists moved into the islands, bringing the trappings of a more sophisticated world. Coconuts, sugar, and rice became important agricultural crops, and deep-sea fishing and phosphate mining became important enterprises. By 1935 so many Japanese had emigrated to the islands that the population ratio stood even at 50,000 Micronesians and 50,000 Japanese.

Enewetak Atoll itself was not strongly affected. The Japanese Navy visited it in 1920, and traders stopped at the atoll frequently, but no attempts were made to establish a full-time administration. Both Enewetak and Ujelang, an atoll to the southeast, were administered from Ponape in the Carolines, and the only Japanese residents on Enewetak were a trader and two assistants. Aside from a modest weather station, established in the 1930s, Japanese contact with the atoll languished for two decades.

Beginning in 1939, however, thousands of Japanese military personnel were moved in to construct an elaborate military base from which to

strengthen their grip on the Pacific as a whole. A large airbase was built on
Enjebi Island, across the lagoon from Enewetak Island, and strong fortifi-
cations were planted nearly everywhere.

These works violated the League of Nations mandate, by which Micronesia was designated a Class C area; this included the stipulation that
the islands were to be unfortified and open to visitation. Japan had sought
outright annexation, but the United States, which had acquired Guam in
1898 as a result of the Spanish-American War and which had interests in
the Philippines, opposed this plan. The United States pushed instead for
the "mandate system," embodying the principle of international account-
ability; the well-being and development of the dependent people consti-
tuted a "sacred trust of civilization." In the case of Enewetak and the rest
of Micronesia, the Class C designation meant that the people were
thought incapable of self-government for the foreseeable future.

The fortification of Enewetak lasted through most of World War II
until the United States began its ambitious sweep across the Pacific in
1944, and American troops attacked Japanese strongholds in Micronesia.
They moved first against Kwajalein and Enewetak and then neutralized
the great naval base at the lagoon of Truk Atoll. Moving to Taipan,
American forces won one of the bloodiest and most decisive victories of
the Pacific campaign (resulting in the resignation of Prime Minister Tojo
and his entire cabinet) and then proceeded to capture Guam and Tinian.
Most of these islands and their people were devastated during the campaign (all the Enewetakese people were moved to another island on their ·
atoll called Aomon), and thousands of tons of metal and unexploded ammunition were left lying about. For many years after the fighting had
ceased, the principal export from Micronesia was scrap metal. Some 70,-
000 Japanese military personnel and civilians were removed by American
forces from the scattered islands of Micronesia and returned to their
home country. This often meant the breakup of Japanese-Micronesian
families. When it was all over, a war-weary and desolated population of
50,000 Micronesians were left to resume their lives.

With the defeat of both Germany and Japan, the decision as to what
to do with Micronesia was left largely to the United States. There was
some conflict between America's promise not to seek territorial aggran-
dizement as a result of the war and its future strategic interest in the Pacific. This conflict was resolved, at the San Francisco Conference that
created the United Nations, by the establishment of a "strategic" trusteeship. The final agreement, approved on April 2, 1947, gave the United

States almost unlimited power over Micronesia—as long as its activities furthered international peace and promoted the political, economic, social, and educational advancement of the inhabitants. The formal name for Micronesia under this arrangement is the Trust Territory of the Pacific Islands, including the Marianas Islands, the Marshall Islands, Palau, Ponape, Truk, and Yap, with their total population (as of 1973) of 115,-000 people.

In the case of Enewetak, the furtherance of peace and the advancement of the inhabitants were pursued in a peculiar fashion—namely, a combination of noisy and violent operations that might have seemed to the natives, had they been there to see it, like a continuance of warfare. After Enewetak was made part of the vast Pacific trusteeship of the United States, the 136 inhabitants were removed from their atoll and taken to Ujelang Atoll, 124 miles to the southwest. For the following decade, beginning in 1948, the U.S. Atomic Energy Commission and the Department of Defense proceeded to rock the atoll with a violence never before seen on earth, setting off forty-three nuclear explosions consisting of both atomic and hydrogen bombs. Some of the enormous craters can still be seen on and around the islands, and traces of the radioactivity loosed during the tests are detectable in leftover debris, soil, animals, plants, and lagoon bottom material.

Enewetak Atoll was not the first choice of the nuclear weapons testers. In 1945 and 1946 explosions were set off first in New Mexico (Operation Trinity) but also at Bikini Atoll (Operation Crossroads). Although Bikini was satisfactorily remote from other land areas for nuclear testing, its land area was small, and what land there was lay in an awkward orientation with respect to the prevailing winds. This precluded construction of an airstrip large enough to accommodate the huge transport planes that would have to haul the bulky matériel needed for a lengthy nuclear development program.

So the Navy and the AEC began scanning their newly conquered collection of atolls and came up with Enewetak, with its extensive ring of islands, and Kwajalein, nearly 400 miles to the southeast. Enewetak was especially appealing, both for its extensive land area and with regard to fallout: several hundred miles of landless sea stretched in the prevailing downwind direction. On December 2, 1947, President Truman approved the atoll as a nuclear weapons test site.

Construction began almost immediately. Enewetak Island itself, which at a length of two miles was the largest island, became the main support base for a planned population in excess of 4,400. A form of intra-service segregation was arranged, so that Enewetak housed only military personnel, and Medren, just a few miles away, became home for AEC and scientific personnel. Enewetak acquired an abrupt patina of civilization as it was hurriedly endowed with an electricity generating plant, a water distillation plant, an infirmary, a mess hall complex, an airport, metal warehouse buildings, a cargo pier, tennis courts, golf courses, a swimming pool, and so on. Medren was likewise modernized to house, to feed, and generally to support up to 3,000 people.

Most of the other islands were accorded lesser roles, in relation to their land area and their general appeal to humans: Kirunu got a concrete bunker with radiation- and electronically-shielded instrumentation; Kidrinen got several buildings to house biomedical sampling equipment; Taiwel got a submarine cable terminal building; Alembel got a scientific station to house research animals; and so on. The most fortunate islands got nothing; the least fortunate were chosen as "ground zeros"—explosion sites. Eluklab (Flora) and Dridrilbwij (Gene), for example, were used as ground zeros in 1952 and 1958 respectively. In their places today are large, overlapping underwater craters.

In short order, the entire atoll was wired and ready. Airplanes had brought in complete facilities for housing, messing, laundry, recreation, freight handling and storage, and maintenance and repair. A complete air transport complex, with a paved runway and airplane parking areas, was built on Enewetak; smaller airports were maintained on Medren, Bokoluo, Enjebi, Bijile, and Runit islands, and several smaller islands got helicopter landing pads. Fresh water was distilled from seawater and piped throughout the atoll to faucets and hoses. Electronics experts laid an interisland network of power-telephone-signal submarine cables along the lagoon floor.

Then the nuclear experiments began. They were given such names as Greenhouse, Ivy, Hardtack, Redwing, and Castle. The first explosion came in April 1948, and they continued at an average of four a year until July 1958. The international moratorium on nuclear testing went into effect the following Halloween, October 31, 1958, and the program came to an end. During that eventful decade Runit was shaken by eighteen nuclear tests; Enjebi by ten; Eluklab by four, Aomon by three; Eleleron by two; and Bokoluo, Dridrilbwij, Bokaidrik, Lujor, Mut, and Boken by one each.

The moratorium was short-lived. On September 1, 1961, the Soviet

Union announced its intention to resume testing, which it did within a matter of days. The United States then did some further testing itself in the Pacific, but near Johnston Island and Christmas Island. Both are far to the east of Enewetak, and the detonations there are thought to have had no effect on the atoll. These tests were completed at the end of 1962, and the Limited Test Ban Treaty was signed in September 1963, prohibiting all nuclear tests except those done underground. Since then the United States has exploded nuclear devices on the U.S. mainland and in Alaska, but none at Enewetak.

This is not to say, however, that Enewetak was to enjoy peaceful times under the test-ban treaty. The U.S. Air Force now took over, and from 1963 to 1968 its missile scientists used the atoll as an "impact and scoring area" for intercontinental ballistic missiles launched from the United States. Then, in 1968 and 1970, the atoll was used for the testing of rocket motors. A misfire in 1968 was reported to have resulted in a "local" deposition of the toxic metal beryllium. Finally, the U.S. Air Force Weapons Laboratory carried out a series of small, nonnuclear, high-explosive detonations in 1972.

W HILE the atoll of Enewetak was receiving so much vigorous attention from its guardian nation, the rest of Micronesia—and indeed the people of Enewetak as well, unhappily resettled on the much smaller atoll of Ujelang—was being virtually ignored. In 1951 President Truman transferred the administration of the trusteeship from the Department of Defense to the Department of the Interior, and for the next decade the United States followed a policy of benign neglect, which has also been described as "frugality and non-disturbance" and the "squirrel philosophy." In the words of Edward C. O'Connor, writing in the *National War College Forum* (Spring, 1970): "The islands became a treasured 'nut' to be buried in the South Seas and not to be disturbed until 'winter'—when the hardships of political climate would stimulate growing hunger for a reliable western Pacific defense line." The United States, having conquered and disrupted much of the eastern Pacific, now saw fit to leave the natives to return to their original society, to take up the raising and tending of coconut trees and the weaving of copra huts and the catching of fish as though nothing had ever happened. The Micronesians were "free," like reservation Indians in North America, to do what they wished, recognized but ignored as the dominant faunal specimen in a vast, watery game preserve.

THE next day was a calm one, good for skimming around the lagoon in the outboard. There was only a light breeze, which picked up in the afternoon to perhaps 10 miles per hour, and the sun was extremely bright and hot. We decided to take a ride up the reef to look at some of the islands and visit one of the sites where nuclear bombs had been tested.

We ran up the eastern side of the atoll for a distance of about 12 miles to Runit, or, as the military called it, Yvonne. On the way, leaving from Enewetak, we passed Bokandretok (Walt), Medren (Elmer), Jedrol (Rex), Japtan (David), Jinimi (Clyde), Ananij (Bruce), Jinedrol (Alvin), and three more little ones before coming to Runit. The difference in the phonetic, elaborate Enewetakese names and the American nicknames of convenience seemed ludicrous at first, but we all got used to it.

On the way we stopped for a short while at Japtan, the island just across the deep eastern pass from Medren. Japtan has good growth on it and a lot of coconut trees and generally looks lusher than most of the other islands. The reason for the lush growth on Japtan, I've heard, is that it is the only one with any topsoil. When the Germans administered the islands before World War I, they did what they could to improve the copra trade with the Micronesians. When the ships came over from Germany, they would carry topsoil as ballast. When they arrived, they would throw the soil onto the island and replace it with coconuts. So Japtan has a good—and very unusual—layer of topsoil from some faraway place like Hamburg or Bremen.

The remaining islands between Japtan and Runit are rather small and bear only scrubby growth. They are really just sandspits with a few trees and bushes. As we ran up the inside edge of the reef, we were surprised to see quite a large swell on the lagoon side, even though there wasn't much wind. Many of the coral heads were out of the water. It was spring low tide, and as the swell came in, there would be nothing but an expanse of water ahead, and then, as it passed, several small patch reefs would be left sticking a foot or so above the surface. So we had to look sharp and constantly weave back and forth among the reefs.

After about a thirty-minute run we arrived at Runit. It was almost noon. There was a strong surge breaking on the lagoon side of the island where we tried to land. Because the reef in that area is continuous for miles in both directions, there was no way to get around to the ocean. We searched in vain for a place to get onto the island. Failing to find one, we went around to the south end and managed to find a spot on the reef top with just enough water to get the skiff in for 100 yards or so. There was very little wave action that far in, so we had our lunch there.

It was broiling hot, and Jerry Condit and I walked up toward the middle of the island, where there was an aluminum tower with a small aluminum house on top. That was the only structure on the island other than a half dozen or so large concrete blockhouses and a half dozen landing craft abandoned and beached on the western side. The tower was on top of the largest blockhouse and apparently had been used for determining the impact point of missiles during the "impact and scoring" program subsequent to the nuclear tests. The blockhouses are substantial structures covered with earth. The doors are huge, heavy steel numbers, and it is surprising that in only fifteen years or so they have been almost completely rusted away by the near-constant mist of seawater. Likewise, almost all the landing craft have been eaten away to their skeletons.

As we walked up the island, it was unbearably hot. The scattered trees stopped whatever saving breeze there might have been, and the sun was dazzling. We got to the tower, and I went up with the movie camera to get a panoramic view of the islands and the reefs. The top of the tower was about 75 feet above the island, and it was a beautiful view: the deep indigo of the open ocean and then the white line of breakers and then the various turquoises and greens of the shallower water in the lagoon. There was more: the darker blue of the deep parts of the lagoon and the snow-white sand of the island and the other islands nearby. And each time a cloud went over, it all changed.

Directly offshore from the tower, off the outer edge of the reef, was a wrecked ship, a Japanese fishing vessel that had gone on the reef a little more than a year before. After we came down from the tower, we walked out to the wreck, about a quarter of a mile from the shore of the island. About half this expanse was submerged; the rest was rocky limestone shelf that would be under water at high tide. The last half or third of the trip was through water up to four feet deep, where there were a great number of fish grazing about. There were schools of different species of surgeonfish and quite a few blacktip sharks. The blacktip reef shark normally feeds around on top of the shallows of a reef. We saw half a dozen or more as we waded slowly out to the ship. If we stood still, some of them would come up close before they saw us and turned to dart off at high speed. Like any fish in the shallows, they are vulnerable and ready to run if anything threatens—even us.

T HE fishing vessel was a type known as a long-liner. The Japanese have an open-ocean fishery for tuna that goes back several hundred years or more. The vessels themselves are like this one, about 125 to 150 feet long with a large refrigerated hold. In general, they have the appearance of small freighters, and they can be seen at sea and in ports great and small from Rio de Janeiro to Samoa. Apparently this one had come straight onto the reef just between two buttresses of coral extending out from the reef and up a deeper trough known as the surge channel. The bow came right out of the water and was high and dry, although the stern showed signs of beginning to slide back down into the surge channel.

We managed to stumble our way over the coral, getting knocked down several times by waves breaking on the edge of the reef and then foaming on in toward us, but we finally reached the boat with the movie camera intact and climbed aboard. Some adventurers—probably from the base on Enewetak—had stripped the compass and other valuables from the vessel, although the fishing tackle and the longline puller and various other gear were still lying about. The ship was amazingly rusted and corroded for having been on the reef for only a little more than a year— another graphic demonstration of just how corrosive the marine environment can be. Other than that, it wasn't particularly interesting, as wrecks go, but it had a special appeal for me: for several years I had studied the statistics of this fishery while working out the worldwide distribution of billfishes, which include the marlin and the sailfish. The longline fishery records are very thorough. They keep records not only of the tuna, which is the principal prey, but also of billfishes, sharks, and all other, smaller kinds of fishes brought in on the longlines. These records were the best source of information available on the distribution of these large fishes, and as an undergraduate at the University of Miami I worked as an assistant on a project whose goal was to compile and analyze this information. Despite all that work, and despite what came to be an intimate knowledge of the workings of the whole fishery, I had never been aboard one of the longline vessels.

These ships use a long rope, as the name implies, which comes in sections about 1,000 feet long. At intervals of about 100 feet are suspended shorter drop lines about 30 feet long, and at the ends of these are huge baited hooks. At each 1,000-foot interval is a float line reaching up to the surface. When a series of these sections are attached to each other, as they normally are, you have floats about every 1,000 feet suspending the main line at some depth, off which hang the drop lines, or hook lines.

To most people, and especially to tourists who have visited the Pacific, the best-known component of this system is the floats, which are the familiar greenish glass balls enclosed in a heavy net of rope. They are found awash on beaches the world round, and they are sold in curio shops from Hawaii to Australia. Glass floats are used because despite their fragile and often beautiful appearance, they can withstand great pressures. Large tunas, when hooked, sometimes pull the floats beneath the surface to considerable depths at which metal floats, or even ordinary cork or plastic, would be crushed and useless.

Setting longlines is a frantic job, with no time to correct mistakes. It is done while the vessel is steaming ahead at 10 or 12 knots—nearly full speed. The line rushes out of great tubs or baskets and over the stern, and as it goes, the hooks are baited, and the hook lines attached to the main lines. As one section of main line ends, and a basket empties, the section is connected to the beginning of a new section in another basket. The fishermen lay as much as 60 miles of longline in this fashion at one set. They leave it floating for several hours and then begin the tedious process of taking it all back in again. The retrieval is accomplished over the forward quarter of the vessel by a mechanical puller. This operation is a little slower than the setting, with the ship steaming at about six knots, but that is still a substantial speed. As the line comes in, it is coiled automatically in the baskets by the puller. Then the drop lines are detached, and if a fish is on one, it is gaffed and swung aboard, or hooked by a gaff hook on the end of a line and swung aboard aft by other men. This fishery is extremely efficient at gathering tunas in areas where they are not concentrated enough for nets to be used, and it is the technique of choice in most parts of the Pacific Ocean between the latitudes of 30 or 40 north and south.

AFTER looking around the longline vessel for twenty or thirty minutes, we had seen everything, and we came on back to shore. The tide was coming in by then, so the water was a little deeper. The sun was also beginning to have its effect on us; we were pretty hot after the half-mile walk to the skiff. We met Jo and the children, who were swimming on the sandspit at the very southern end of Runit Island. The skiff was now in neck-deep water instead of knee-deep; the spring tide comes in fast. We all loaded aboard and headed back for the *El Territo*.

It was a long hot run, and we put up the top so that Jo and the children could lie down for a rest. As we ran along the calm lagoon, I tried to sort out how it felt to visit the experiment chamber of the first rough tools of the nuclear age. The northern end of Runit Island, only a few hundred yards from where we climbed up the tower, had been ground zero for a number of atomic tests. The blasts had devastated the island and largely erased signs of life. Yet, looking at it fifteen years later, I had to say that the long-term effects were inconspicuous to the eye. The area still bears radioactivity that can be detected by sensitive instruments, and some of the scrap metal lying about is probably dangerous to humans who come in more than occasional contact with it. But the flora and fauna do not seem noticeably different from the life forms elsewhere on the atoll, and I gathered from talking to some of the researchers who have studied the aftereffects in some detail that they are less than many people had feared.

By contrast, radical and widespread ecological damage was accomplished throughout the atoll by the thousands of humans who manned the base while the tests were going on. Nearly all the vegetation on Enewetak Island was erased, for example, in the interests of construction, although some of it may have disappeared during the battle with the Japanese during the war.

All in all, the atoll has had quite a going-over above the waterline. Even so, the forces of nature being what they are, the system seems to be righting itself. Judging from the rate at which metal corrodes here, I would estimate that in another twenty years or so virtually all the untended creations of man will have disappeared. It will probably take considerably longer than that for the original flora and fauna of the islands to return. But they seem to be well on the way. Ironically, islands like Runit, which were seared by a nuclear blast, seem to be coming back faster than islands like Enewetak, which were just lived on.

This condition of rejuvenation may bear a message for citizens of the United States who have been trying so hard over the last few years to decide whether nuclear power plants are safe. The answer seems to be that nuclear power is not as frightening as some of its opponents make it out to be. Whether it is economically feasible is, of course, another question, as is waste disposal. But when you've seen a place like Enewetak, which has been subjected to really devastating radiation and is recovering rapidly without major identifiable effects, it is difficult to believe that widespread use of nuclear power plants would be of great detriment to the environment. In the final analysis, the damage or danger of living next to a nuclear power plant would be considerably less than the damage Jerry Condit and I sustained today in the sun. Solar radiation in large doses is known to cause skin cancer; the solar dose we gathered on the lagoon was certainly far more debilitating than the normal radiation "leakage" from a nuclear power plant.

We got back at around four o'clock in the afternoon.

7

SOME NOTIONS
ON SCIENTIFIC RESEARCH

I MUST admit to having mixed feelings about the removal of the Enewetakese people from the atoll. From their point of view, it can be viewed only as a heartless infringement upon an entire "nation," small as it was. From mine, however, and from that of any scientist interested in studying the atoll itself, the absence of humans is beneficial. We have a word for populations of animals or plants that have been free of human manipulation: "undisturbed." The word is arrogant in its connotations, tacitly putting the interests of scientists above those of people who might like to use an area or its creatures for purposes other than study. Yet there is little point in studying a population of deer, for example, in a place from which man has exterminated all the wolves which prey on the deer. And if fishermen prey upon all the fishes that taste good to them around a coral reef, the ecology is artificially skewed. This is the case around most Pacific atolls, where spearfishing and hook-and-line fishing have reduced some populations to the benefit of others. I found that Enewetak, where little fishing by humans had been done since 1947, was an exception to this condition. At this point, what we have is essentially a balance of fish populations as it would be if humans had never existed. It is a combination of ironies that the application of all the destructive force humans could muster has produced what could be considered an underwater wilderness.

Despite the presumption involved in wanting to study "undisturbed" populations, there are good reasons for doing so—the most human of reasons. Take modern agriculture, for example. The use of increasing amounts of chemical fertilizers and herbicides and fungicides on midwestern cornfields has drastically changed what used to be the prairie ecosystem. Indeed, the simplification of the ecosystem in much of Indiana, Illinois, and Iowa to corn and soybean crops has perforce eliminated not only the hundreds of species of wildflowers and grasses that used to flourish on the prairie, but also the myriad insects, microorganisms, and other forms of life that were part of the original system. A poorly understood, but generally accepted, law of ecology is that diversity breeds stability. That is, the greater the number of species in an environment, the greater the biological stability of that environment. By this law, a vast cornfield, allowing just one kind of organism, is a simple and unstable ecosystem. It is deemed unstable because it invites insurrection; in the ceaseless competition of the bioworld, too much success is a bad thing—a challenge to be met by predators or competitors in one way or another. In the valueless world of nature, a cornfield is such a challenge, one that is met by hoards of rootworms, corn borers, molds, fungi, and other organisms known by us as pests. The fact that we call them pests betrays our bias; they are really nature's attempts to right an imbalance. We react against such pests with strong chemicals designed to kill them but not the corn. Unfortunately, these chemicals also kill the relatives of the pests, so that the soil in our vast corn belt has taken on an increasingly sanitized aspect, devoid of the earthworms, centipedes, bacteria, and other life which go to make up the soil ecosystem. When a pest does get by our chemical barriers, as a strain of southern leaf blight did in 1971, it finds no natural competition or predators. In trying to industrialize farming, as we have so rapidly done, we are working against natural laws. It may soon prove easier—though not by standards common today—to grow crops on vast sheets of plastic infused with nutrients, forgoing the troublesome complexities of soil altogether.

Until then we are faced with the problem of dealing with old-fashioned soil and the rules of biology. The more we defy them, the more effort and energy we require to enforce our system of farming. It would, of course, be much easier to work within the rules, using them to our own advantage in raising food. And this is where basic ecological research comes in. There is no way to work within the rules unless we understand the rules in the first place. And the only way to understand them is to witness their operation in an undisturbed environment, since the disturbance is the very thing we are trying to compensate for.

Let me give an example. A number of big-farming enthusiasts would like to "solve" the world's food problems by "farming the Amazon" and similar tropical rain-forest areas in other parts of the world. Already, in fact, the Brazilian government, eager at once to relieve the unemployment and starvation in the northeastern part of the country and to produce huge food supplies for its soaring population, has tried to open the Amazon Basin to agriculture. There has been some limited success, in cases where farmers are sensitive enough to the fragility of the tropical soil ecosystems. But there have been more failures, and in fact, the whole program has slowed drastically.

The reason for the failures is that the enormous productivity of the tropics is misleading. It is true that the constant conditions of warm air and high humidity are nearly perfect for growing plants; anyone who has been in a rain forest would agree to this. But it is not true that this productivity is limitless. The Achilles' heel of the Amazon, and of other rain-forest regions, is the soil. It is poor in organic material, which is replenished as long as the forest grows above it, dropping leaves, branches, and trunks. If the forest is removed—and it must be to initiate farming—the soil's protective cover disappears, as does the source of its organic material. The sun is allowed to bake it; the hard tropical rains pound it; its nutrients wash and leach away. Unless care is taken, the alternate drenching and heating can, in a matter of a few years, produce a kind of protorock known as laterite.

The point here is that conditions that seem perfect for the introduction of modern agriculture are really not so. They are substantially different from the conditions found in the North American corn belt, for example, where the soil is routinely left unprotected for months at a stretch. When Brazilian pioneers began to rush into the Amazon to clear their plots of land, little basic research had been done on the effects of such activity. And what little research had been done did not bode well for the experiment. One of the fundamental purposes of science is to gain predictability: we know that if certain weakened viruses are injected into our bloodstream, we can be immunized against yellow fever; we also know that if a certain amount of liquid oxygen is ignited, it will lift a Saturn V rocket off the ground. These are relatively simple predictions to make; ecosystems are much more difficult. We might ask, what would be the effect of removing all ants from the tropical rain forest? We could begin to guess: there would be no army ants to kill ground-dwelling insects, no carpenter ants to eat dead wood, no leaf-cutting ants to cut leaves, and so on. But these are not general effects. Would the rain forest change in a fundamental way? We don't know.

The replacement of forest by crops is a far more profound change, and its effect—in the short term, at least—more obvious. But we complicate the matter by asking if there is anything we can do to reduce this effect, without causing further trouble. Simply to march into the forest and begin clearing it with axes and machetes and fire implies a willingness to experiment through mistakes. There have been many cases in the history of science where "mistakes" have led to great results; the telephone and penicillin come to mind. But both these cases involved small, controllable situations. And the mistakes turned out to be good ones. In the case of a large area of rain forest, a major mistake might be both bad and irreversible, and few responsible scientists would advocate going into large tropical plantations without a good idea of whether they would succeed.

Now we are back to my original point. It is possible to predict the success of conventional agriculture in the tropics only through many tests on undisturbed areas. A lot of these tests must seek to define how the areas function if they are left alone: what plants harness the sun's energy; how animals tap this harnessed energy; how stored energy is recycled; and so on. Other tests must alter the ecosystem in some way and monitor the effects of the alteration—or disturbance, if you will. If there has already been a disturbance, it is not possible to relate cause and effect.

In the case of Enewetak, one disturbance has been replaced by another over the last few decades. When human predators were removed, the large carnivorous fishes were given a chance to move back into the area in "normal" numbers, establishing a balance with the amount of food available. Then the bombs were set off, between 1948 and 1958. The blasts themselves killed unknown numbers of organisms around the atoll through heat, shock, and intense radiation; the residual radiation killed more organisms during the years that followed. By now much of that residual radiation has dissipated, and the particles that emitted it have been washed away by rainfall and carried away by the sea. But some is left, in measurable quantity, bestowing on scientists a clear-cut, if distasteful, field of study.

The atomic scientists of the 1940s went ahead with the nuclear equivalent of farming the Amazon. Without knowing what the effects would be on the fishes or the plants or the people who might someday reinhabit this atoll, they put Enewetak through an extended version of a great nuclear war (what region on earth could be expected to take forty-three direct hits during even the fiercest nuclear attack?). The experiment is over, and to the great amazement of some scientists, life has persisted. The terns are nesting, the corals are filtering, the *Scaevola* bushes are fruiting; by external appearances, at least, life goes on. The final results are not yet in, of course, and radiation experts and biologists affiliated with the Mid-Pacific Laboratory here will continue to monitor the long-term effects of the irradiation. But we can perhaps take some solace from the fact that the atoll is not today a poisoned wasteland.

AFTER a couple of days of wind and rain, perfect diving weather returned. The wind was very light—only a couple of miles per hour—and the sky was almost cloudless. So we moved the *El Territo* into the pier to take on fresh water. Jo took the opportunity to give Mikka a swim in the old salt-water swimming pool that had been built for the military during the nuclear testing program. Mikka is a Malaysian otter that Jo bought from an animal dealer in Los Angeles just before we left. He was only a couple of months old when we got him, and very tame—so tame that he didn't even know how to swim. He must have been captured before his mother had had time to teach him. Since we've been under way from California, there hasn't been much chance for him to learn, except in an inflatable child's wading pool that Jo has for the children to use on deck. Jo did get him into that a couple of times, but it was only a couple of inches deep.

The old swimming pool on Enewetak had been classified as inoperable, so we didn't think anyone would object to its use as a training tank for the little otter. At first, Mikka didn't like the idea, and when Jo launched him anyway, he screamed and hollered shrilly and dog-paddled stiffly around on the surface. But he quickly began to realize that he and the water were made for each other, and caught on right away to the idea of diving. He would streak along the bottom at a depth of three or four feet until he couldn't hold his breath anymore, then would come to the surface to utter a loud shriek and take a gulp of air. Jo would hold out her hands, and he would come over and hang on and rest awhile, and then he'd dive some more. He seemed to be a little bit out of shape for that sort of thing, after having lived the easy life on the air-conditioned boat and being fed by hand. I would judge by the way he was swimming underwater that day it won't be too long before Jo will have him out on the reef diving.

Since the water tanks take several hours to fill, we left the boat at the dock. Dick stayed behind to do some touch-up painting on the crane and to watch after the children, Marissa and Varrina, as they paddled around in their wading pool on deck. Then Jo and Jerry and I headed out for Pole Pinnacle. Running up the inside edge of the reef was like flying an airplane. The water was glass-calm, and the surface unrippled and very clear. The shadow of the boat could be seen on the bottom as we passed over corals and groups of fish, and we had the sensation of being suspended in air instead of water. Jo sat up on the bow with her feet hanging over the gunwale, watching, until finally we moved away from the inside edge of the reef and the water depth increased in the lagoon beyond the range of visibility.

We reached Pole Pinnacle at slack tide, unfortunately. The two previous times we had dived there we had had great visibility but a strong current that had made maneuvering difficult. Today there was no current, but the water visibility was only about 60 feet. We went down and were immediately approached by the usual gray shark. We moved on around to the east side of the pinnacle, where most of the large fish seem to hang out, and were immediately greeted by several large groupers. This species of grouper was rather streamlined, weighed about 20 pounds, and was colored a dark chocolate brown with small, iridescent blue spots all over its body. It has another color phase, in which the fish is so pale as to be nearly white, with chocolate-brown saddle-shaped markings across the back and bright yellow fins—a striking combination.

We moved to the front side of the pinnacle and saw several more sharks, but they stayed off in the distance. A large school of surgeonfish hovered above us, seemingly intrigued by our exhaust bubbles. On the bottom at 135 feet there was a small group of sea whips growing up from a rocky patch in the sand bottom. On one of these I spotted a tiny goby that seemed to be living right on the sea whip. I had seen a similar relationship in the Indian Ocean once—a goby living full time on a sea whip—and a colleague of mine, Bill Davis, has collected a new species of goby living in similar company on the Solomon Islands. This was the first time I had found a goby/sea whip pair at Enewetak, and we immediately laid plans to collect the goby at least. Gobies are very easy to collect. You simply put your hand around the sea whip (which I did, just for practice) and run the hand along the stalk. The goby invariably proceeds along just ahead of your hand until it gets to the end of the stalk. The trick is to have a net or jar waiting at the end of the line, where the fish has nowhere else to go. That first time I simply ran the goby off the end of the stalk; it jumped off and came unsuspectingly over to my hand to hover for a while. When I withdrew my hand, it returned to the sea whip.

We didn't make a long dive at Pole Pinnacle because the water wasn't very good for observing. We went instead to a small island about half a mile away, just adjacent to the concrete ship on the middle ground of the east pass. This small, unnamed (as far as I know) island is about 100 to 150 yards long, with a beautiful sand beach on the western side. Despite its tiny size, the weapons testers seemed to have found some use for it, as evidenced by a large, abandoned bunker. The structure seemed to be made of a Quonset hut completely covered with rubble and rock. We anchored a short distance offshore and waded in to look around. Inside the bunker we found a large rat, a box of quarter-pound blocks of TNT, and a number of empty crates. Uninspired, we moved outside and over to some trees that covered the eastern end of the island. They turned out to be the nesting area for a small population of fairy terns, pure white robin-sized birds with coal-black eyes. There were also some noddy terns, slightly larger terns of uniform brownish-black plumage. From the island, looking through the breaks in the trees, we could see the beautiful turquoise and blue water around us and hear the breakers on the reef offshore. The bright snow white birds stood out sharply against the bright green colors of the trees.

Compared with most other Pacific seabirds, fairy terns are especially endearing to humans. For one thing, they are unfailingly sociable. If you walk along the beach near a population of fairy terns, the chances are very good that if you turn around suddenly, there will be five or six of them hovering soundlessly two or three feet above your head and peering down. No other bird of the region lavishes such attention upon humans, unless in the form of hostility. Other terns, especially the sooty terns, raucous, cosmopolitan creatures with striking black and white plumage, will actually attack humans who wander near their nesting area, calling shrilly, hovering, and finally diving from a height of six or eight feet to make a sharp stab at the top of your head with their pointed bills.

Fairy terns also win our admiration for the daring way in which they fashion their homes in this demanding environment. Unlike the shearwaters, which play it safe by digging burrows in the sand, or albatrosses, which simply plop themselves down on a mound of sand and pebbles, or tropic birds, which seek the refuge of dense bushes, the fairy terns lay their eggs in the small, swaying trees of the atoll. Having chosen this precarious perch, each deposits its single egg on the flimsiest of twiggy structures—or on no structure at all but the bare notch of a junction of branches. Some of these places are so small that it seems inconceivable that the females can lay their eggs and then alternate nest-sitting duties with their mates, without the eggs rolling onto the ground below. I saw that there were a number of nests in the trees, but when I crawled up to a level where I could see into them, there were no eggs. Finally, I did spot one and photographed it.

Also among the trees were many large hermit crabs. They were bright red, and some were a couple of inches in diameter. They lived at the base of the trees, and several crawled up into the bushes, where they were as much as several feet above the ground. I presume they were feeding on vegetation, but I can't be sure because as soon as they saw us, they would stop moving about and just cling.

From the fairy tern nesting island we returned to the boat and ran on up to Japtan Island—the second island of any size up the atoll from Enewetak. To the outside of Japtan are the remains of a vessel, probably a freighter, that ran aground on the reef just off the island. All that is left is the bow section, which is about 70 feet long and 70 feet high. This maritime corpse is so rusted and corroded that I found it difficult to see how it could still stand. Since it was as tall as it was long, it was hard to imagine anything less stable. On the very top—the former foredeck of the ship— was an old gun mount and what was probably a five-inch gun; this was a common armament for freighters trying to protect themselves against aircraft during World War II. Twenty-five years of wave action had taken away the rest of the ship; there was nothing to be seen of the hull. International treaties had taken away the war; there were no warplanes in the sky. Yet the five-incher remained, still vigilant, still pointing skyward, on guard not because there was anything to guard, but because history—and the sea—had determined this role for it. The bow section lay more or less parallel to the incoming ocean swell so that the waves broke with regularity against the side of what remained of the ship, and as they broke, the spray shot straight up toward the sky.

From Japtan we ran on back to Enewetak and arrived at about one o'clock. We found that the swell, which rolls in all the time without respect to the weather, had been mischievously at work on our ship while we were away. Even though the surface of the lagoon appears perfectly calm, the large ocean waves are always heaving in through the passes and swinging around in the lagoon so that the waterline surges up and down as much as 10 feet. This means that at the pier the boat constantly moves out and back, and as it moves, paint is ground off. Since one fresh-water tank was full and the other was almost full, we decided to move on out to anchor. We started the engine and went out to a buoy, and then we used gasoline and soap to clean off the creosote that had smeared on the sides from the end of the pier.

W HEN we got back and settled down, we learned from the Armed Forces Radio station on Kwajalein that the lunar astronauts had successfully explored an area around a stream-bed-like feature called Hadley Rill, and returned to orbit around the moon. This last was a crucial accomplishment (who wants to be stranded on the moon?) that was soon to be followed by the equally crucial maneuver of escaping the moon's gravitational field (who wants to be stranded in lunar orbit?). These maneuvers had all the elements of high adventure and drama, and all the disputes over the value of the space program did not and never will diminish those aspects of it.

We were following the lunar venture from a peculiar perspective, as were people at other isolated outposts on earth. There are some places— Antarctica, Greenland, the middle of the Sahara—that bear some resemblances to the moon, and Enewetak was one of them. We were at the mercy of an alien environment, dependent for our lives on tenuous technological arrangements. Any disruption of these arrangements could terminate the program, so to speak; later this almost happened to three astronauts, and in similar fashion, Jo and I came perilously close as well. But more of that later.

From the perspective of Enewetak, I experienced strong feelings about the space program. I made notes on some of them and still feel, years after the program's end, that they are worth sharing. We all remember the controversy over the huge sums of money that were spent on our half dozen or so visits to the moon—money which some people argued could have been better spent on social programs, health research, or any number of earthly activities. Whether or not this money would have ever been diverted to such "practical" activities is doubtful; the money spent sustaining the war in Vietnam seemed to disappear after the war ended.

But this dispute misses the point, as do discussions of "technological spin-offs" that can (and have been) applied to medicine, aviation, household goods, and so on. The really important point is that humans were for the first time able to leave this planet and to begin to gain some firsthand understanding of the immediate universe around us. The importance of such a philosophical interpretation may never seem as great as the pressing problems of the moment. But once we as a species become overwhelmed by the pressing problems of the moment, we lose much of what distinguishes us from fish, or coral, or plankton. All those dollars and cents have made us—all of us—acutely aware that we inhabit one small planet in a very cold and hostile universe and that as far as human life is concerned, we had better take care of our tiny but best-possible world.

For the first time in human history, we are sufficiently advanced technologically to be able to think globally. Satellites bind us in communication to every part of the world; no place is more than a day's journey by jet; economic systems are strands of the same web. The *ability* to think globally becomes a *duty* to think in this way; if we do not, the whole suffers. If one strand breaks, the web is weakened. And it seems to have taken half a dozen trips to the moon for us to realize this fully.

Many critics of the space program, and of science generally, fail to admit a basic historical truth: progress is almost always the province of an elite. The labor of the masses has always supported the activities of this elite, and always will. The few members of this elite make social and scientific and philosophical progress because they are free from the problems of just surviving. Conversely, the benefits of this progress sustain the masses in the form of better medicine and better technology and better food. Those who disparage modern technology should consider closely what is feeding them, sheltering them, clothing them, and healing them. On one level, it is fair to question the correctness of one man's tinkering with something that might one day be called a wheel, while all his fellows are out on the plains and in the forests gathering nuts and roots. On another level, such tinkering is essential. Today the effects of the wheel are obvious; once they were not. Much of human progress has been the result of someone's fiddling while others performed the routine tasks.

Ultimately, of course, in a democratic society, the citizens will determine how much money goes for basic research. And if, in the long run, the sciences fail to produce results that are commensurate with the amount of money being spent, then the amount should be cut back. This sort of cutback occurred toward the end of the moon program. A backlash set in among people who suddenly discovered tremendous waste and bureaucracy, both of which had burgeoned during the post-Sputnik boom days when science—especially the "hard" sciences—became a national cause. However, the cutbacks of recent years are probably not altogether a bad thing, simply a paring of some of the fat. It is to be hoped that the more competent scientists will now go back to science rather than running

back and forth to Washington, promoting bigger and bigger grants and
then spending the rest of their time administering these grants and attending to the inevitable bureaucracy that grows like algae in the presence
of so much money.

There's another implication of our global reach these days. We have
achieved, for the first time, the capability of despoiling our planet and
perhaps even of altering its climate or life systems in ways that could make
it uninhabitable for humans. For example, if we burned all the coal and
petroleum available to us and continued to produce as much electricity by
means of nuclear power plants as we could, we could theoretically raise
the "heat balance" of our atmosphere catastrophically. It would take
about a century, but beyond any doubt it can be done. The effects of putting out huge amounts of heat by such means are uncertain, but specula-
tions include the creation of a permanent cloud cover. This would block
incoming sunlight and lead to a series of related atmospheric/oceanic
changes that cannot be predicted yet. The processes to be concerned
about are those that trigger ice ages, for example—the wide swings of the
climatological pendulum that must run their full course before they return to "normal."

Because we have, or soon will have, the ability to wreak catastrophe
upon the earth, it is foolhardy not to try as hard as we can to understand
the details of its normal functioning. We have never been able to predict
the consequences of our actions—partly because our actions have so far
been puny in relation to the size of the earth and its systems, and partly
because we don't have enough information. The world's largest computer,
for example, is unable to do enough calculations fast enough to predict
the weather accurately for any place on the planet for even a few hours in
advance. We are at a point where it is genuinely crucial to develop a rational philosophy for dealing with human/environmental interactions.
And the only way such a philosophy can be developed is by our probing as
never before into every natural system we can find.

Such a rational philosophy must not be confused with dogma. Abso-
lutist dogmas of the past were possible only in the *absence* of real knowledge. Our modern philosophy must be flexible enough to discard obsolete
beliefs when they are proved wrong. There is already evidence that this
can happen. Only a decade ago we truly believed that DDT was an environmental miracle drug that did the impossible: killed pests while sparing the rest of us. Once we found that this was not true—that we cannot
kill some creatures without affecting others—we reversed our thinking

with a speed that many of us have regarded as nothing short of remarkable.

The development of such a rational system requires the "hard data" obtained by science—even the kind of data gathered by the space program. And yet it need not result in the inhuman, brutalized, computerized society that some of us have feared from the time *1984* was published. The kind of rational philosophy I am thinking of does not differ in goals and means from basic religious concepts. If you go to something as basic as the Ten Commandments, you find that these are fundamentally a carefully thought-out and ultimately rational set of rules for living. If we put ourselves in the mental shoes of biologists for a moment, we may see a remarkable parallel. On a very simplistic level, animals follow a set of rules for living that could be defined as survival of the fittest, as Darwin once wrote, and that could be interpreted further as the Ten Commandments of Evolution. "Fitness," in an evolutionary sense, has been a much-abused concept, giving rise to such excesses of enthusiasm as "social Darwinism," in which misuses of power are rationalized as "natural." Fitness has also been criticized as a tautology: what is a "fit" gene anyway? Nonetheless, the idea of fitness is a convenient basis for thinking about populations of animals—the important unit when it comes to survival. And populations must obey some rules in order to be fit, to survive. The individual members collaborate in many ways to allow smooth social interaction: they generally do not kill each other; they do not steal each other's mates once a pair bond has been consummated; they do not practice trickery or deceit in order to gain territory; and so on. The rules vary widely from species to species, but in general, animal populations have somehow developed sets of social rules that allow them to function. We perceive these rules as "rational" in the sense that without them there would be social chaos: breeding schedules would be interrupted, feeding would become chancy, the attention of predators would be attracted, and so on. In the same way, it is fair to say that the Ten Commandments are rational in specifying certain tried-and-true social rules for humans. Today we have codified them into laws specifying property rights, protection of the individual, the sanctity of social bonds, and so on. In the long run, these laws allow human society as a whole to function far better than it would if the strong were always killing off the weak.

Similarly, the gathering of scientific facts does not preclude the nourishment of human values. It allows this nourishment to continue. An individual who understands the consequences of actions is in a far stronger position than a person who simply obeys a set of rules out of fear of some supernatural power or of social censure. And if he understands the workings of systems, he knows why it is advantageous to follow certain rules. If, for example, we understand fully the effects of exploding atomic bombs on coral reefs and the effects of long-term disposal of radioactive wastes from nuclear power plants, we are better equipped to make decisions about using atomic energy.

Only in recent years have we begun to understand that ecology is not just a word in the vocabulary of dotty birdwatchers and academics. Through a number of apparently accidental discoveries, we have begun to appreciate that our activities can change the entire environment—air, land, sea. This is a revelation fundamental to our own survival—and that of even such far-flung bits of life as the coral reefs of the Pacific. Enewetak, in a small way, will help us make rational decisions about the use of atomic energy. By my cursory inspection, the effects of the nuclear testing program are today not obvious. But the Mid-Pacific Marine Laboratory intends to probe into the workings of the environment by far more subtle means during the coming years. In this way we hope to learn just how careful we must be with the atom.

8

FIRST ENCOUNTER WITH
THE GRAY REEF SHARK

THE next day was a good one for diving, and we took advantage of it with an outing in the submarine. It turned out to be a considerable adventure, featuring the first time we were attacked by the gray reef shark. And it was just the kind of behavioral situation I had been anticipating.

During the last decade a great deal of research has been directed at shark behavior in an effort to learn just why sharks attack human beings when they do. The premise for most of this research from the very beginning has been that sharks go after humans because they are hungry and would like to eat them. Then in 1969, in a journal called *Military Medicine*, D. H. Baldridge, Jr., and J. Williams published an article entitled "Shark Attack: Feeding or Fighting?" This was the first formal suggestion of a motivation for shark attack other than hunger. The motivation itself was not identified, but just the proposal that there could be one other than feeding was novel.

The best evidence that some sort of social activity (such as communication) was involved came from the gray reef shark. A report as early as 1961 described what seemed to be a highly ritualized display preceding at least five separate attacks on humans. A display of this sort implies some sort of communication, such as a warning to other sharks. When a dog growls, bares its fangs, and raises its hackles, any other dog is fairly warned to expect aggressive or defensive behavior. This display is so familiar to humans that they, too, have learned to beware of it. In the case of the gray reef shark, it seemed entirely possible that by going through its exaggerated swimming routine, it was trying to warn other swimmers—divers, in these cases—away. The purpose of most displays of this type in nature is to avoid violence, not to provoke it. But if the signal is ignored—say, by a human diver ignorant of its meaning—then the threatened violence is carried out.

About half a year before we arrived at Enewetak, two biologists, Richard H. Johnson and Donald R. Nelson, had visited the atoll to observe the behavior of the gray reef shark. Both men, from California State University, Long Beach, had studied the literature on this species and had decided that the best way to test the threat display hypothesis was to use themselves as human guinea pigs. Their task was to show that an aggressive approach by a diver would trigger the shark's display and that this display was "agonistic"—forewarning of an attack. Johnson and Nelson took a straightforward approach toward demonstrating these points. In ten separate trials (they have since written in a paper that "no further were attempted due to the danger involved"), they simply swam straight at an approaching shark when it had closed to within a distance of about 20 feet. In all ten cases, the sharks went into an elaborate posturing routine involving a laterally exaggerated swimming motion, using the whole body, and rolling movements. Accompanying the wagging and rolling were an upward pointing of the snout, arching of the back, and dropping of the pectoral fins.

The displays lasted from fifteen to sixty seconds, occurring when the diver-shark distance had shrunk to about 12 or 13 feet. The display was most intense (that is, the pectorals pointed most sharply downward, the snout lifted so high that the teeth were bared, the rolling motion exaggerated, and so on) when the shark was most nearly cornered by rock or coral formations. If the shark had a free escape route, the display was milder. Intensity of the display was also affected by the angle of approach: it was most violent when the divers charged head-on, rather than after a shark that was already retreating. By contrast, in six other encounters in which the diver did not charge, there was no display.

Although these sharks never actually attacked Johnson or Nelson, the display they observed closely paralleled agonistic behavior in other animals, particularly fishes. In the Siamese fighting fish, *Betta splendens*, for example, an attack is preceded by a display of finnage, lateral orientation, and slow, distinctive movements. Other common indications of threat in animals are extreme muscular tenseness and the exposing of teeth. Such characteristics, wrote Johnson and Nelson, "suggest a ritualized communicative function which we believe to represent threat. Since in the context of diver-shark encounters displays occurred in response to rapid diver approaches which are essentially aggressive, this behavior is considered defensive in nature. Although display during interactions with man appears relevant, its development certainly seems dependent upon broader usage under natural conditions. It would, therefore, seem likely that this behavior plays a significant role in the shark's normal social encounters— possibly in dominance, territoriality or courtship (if such exists)."

DISPLAY   NON-DISPLAY

Comparison of display and non-display postures in the gray reef shark.

So what we had when we got to Enewetak was good evidence that an aggressive charge by a human can trigger a ritualized display in the gray reef shark and a strong suspicion that this display itself is defensive-aggressive. As it turned out, we fell into the guinea-pig role ourselves, using our own behavior to evoke agonistic behavior in the shark. We did have one great advantage over Johnson and Nelson and other biologists who had studied sharks: we were protected by the submarine from the consequences of actual attacks.

Or so we thought. As it turned out, and as anyone with experience knows, there are no certainties around the ocean.

We had been running along the reef for about twenty minutes, seeing groupers and wrasses and other large fish, but no sharks. At last, after about half a mile, I finally did spot a gray reef shark. It was swimming in the same direction we were, and was on the outer slope of the reef at a depth of about 75 feet. We were slightly farther out, so that it was more or less between us and the reef. We approached the shark, and when we were about 50 feet away, it began the kind of posturing that has been variously termed preattack or threat or aggressive or agonistic behavior: It turned its head upward and backward, arched its back slightly, and extended its pectoral fins downward as if trying to touch the bottom. It also swam in an exaggerated fashion, with lots of side-to-side motion, and shook its head slowly and deliberately from side to side as if to say, "No, no, don't come any closer."

We continued nonetheless, so that in a matter of a few seconds we were within about 10 feet of the shark. At this point it became very agitated, made a sudden dart to the left of our path, and wove around the sub in an arc of about 20 feet, disappearing from our view. Before we knew where it was, it had come in behind us and attacked the propeller of the sub. It did this extremely fast; from the point when it was in front of us to the point when we felt it hit was a matter of perhaps one second. It was large for a gray reef shark, about six or seven feet long, so that when it hit, there was a heavy thump. After the first collision we felt more blows, but because the shark was behind us, we couldn't see what it was hitting. Each blow was strong enough to shake the whole sub.

I then found that we had lost headway, even though our electric motor was still running. By this time the shark had left off attacking us and circled around in front again. It became clear to me just how vulnerable we now were. At each side of the sub is a "window" about three feet long and a foot high which offered no protection at all. As I have said, this was a "wet" sub, with water freely circulating through the cockpit by way of these windows. The beast was still very agitated, and I was enormously concerned that it might charge at us from the side. Sharks can't swim backwards, and if this one did come inside the sub, it wouldn't be able to pull back out.

Jo had the bulky Beaulieu camera with the large aluminum housing, and by shoving this into the window space, she was able to afford us some protection on that side at least. The shark had several marks on its head from the aluminum propeller and the shroud around it, and seemed to be still in a very aggressive mood. It came in by the propeller again but this time didn't attack.

I then found that we had totally lost mobility; the shark had apparently knocked out the propulsion system. Even with the motor working, the propeller wasn't turning, so we blew air into the ballast tanks and started our ascent. Without power this is a somewhat tricky maneuver. The normal procedure with this particular sub is to fly it as you would a small plane: to reach the surface, you just pull back on the stick, rising in a climb. You blow the ballast tanks only if you want the sub to float high out of the water or if you are ready to terminate the dive alongside the ship. When you blow the tanks at depth, there are a couple of problems. The ballast tanks are low in the sub, so that when they fill with air, they reduce the stability of the submarine so much that they may overturn it. Also, even if you blow only a little air into the tanks, that amount of air expands as you ascend because the pressure decreases. As the air expands, it pushes more and more water out of the tanks so that you go up ever more rapidly. This poses two dangers. The first is that the sub wants to overturn. The second, much more serious, is the danger of the bends. Because our cockpit was open, we were essentially scuba diving and had to obey the rules of decompression I've described earlier. Coming up too fast in the sub poses the same threat as free-swimming too fast to the surface.

Trying to keep these things in mind while the shark patrolled outside, I blew in only a small amount of air. As the submarine began to accelerate, I blew some of the air back out of the ballast tanks, trying to keep the rate of ascent steady. I managed to juggle to the surface in this fashion, blowing air in and blowing it out as it expanded. We reached topside in about a minute. Then I closed off the ballast tanks and blew them completely full of air. We floated high and dry and were glad to be so, since we still didn't know what the mood of the shark was or even where it was.

Dick and Jerry, accompanied by Marissa and Varrina, had followed us on the surface in the boat. They threw us a line, took the sub in tow, and brought it to shore in a place where the drop-off was steep, so that there was about 50 feet of water under the sub. I went in to examine the prop, which seemed to be turning but didn't have any power. I couldn't figure it out. And since we couldn't use the sub anymore that day, and we no longer felt like antagonizing sharks (some more were circling in the water beneath us), we decided to tow the sub back to Enewetak to check it out.

The thought occurred to me that in the movies there would now be a fade-out and the tale would take up the following morning after the submarine had been repaired. No such luck. We towed it around to the lagoon side and stopped in about 15 feet of water over sand bottom, and I got in to see if it would operate. Nothing seemed to be bent out of shape, and the propeller was turning, but not fast enough. I couldn't even make the sub dive. So we brought it back to the boat and swung it aboard. There I discovered that the propeller has a shear pin like that of an outboard motor and that the shark had jammed the propeller so tightly that the pin had sheared off. When this happens, the propeller just drifts freely, independent of the shaft that is connected to the motor. The only reason it was turning at all was that there was some friction from the nut that holds it in place; mostly it was just slipping. I also found that the half-inch-thick plastic rudder was deeply gashed by teeth, but nothing was really damaged.

We made up a new shear pin out of stainless steel, an adequate replacement for the brass original. Then we set about doing something for those nonwindows that had us so worried. The answer was some sheets of plexiglass I found in the *El Territo*. We made some side windows that could be folded up when we were observing or photographing, or dropped into place in the event of shark problems. We also put a rear-view mirror inside the sub, so that I could keep an eye on what is happening behind my field of vision, which is very narrow when I have a diving mask on.

THE fact that this shark attacked the sub so readily offered us some really interesting possibilities for research. For many years, a great deal of work has gone into trying to understand what makes these animals attack humans and what might be done to prevent it. It appeared from our first attack experience that there may be two totally different kinds of shark attacks. One is a feeding attack, in which the animal simply desires something to eat, whether or not that "something" is a human being. Then there is the kind of attack we took part in today with the gray reef shark. That one seemed to involve not feeding, but some impulse of defense or some form of aggression other than hunger, corroborating the earlier research of Johnson and Nelson on threat display in this species. If

"We have the *El Territo* tied at a mooring in the lagoon just off the shore of Enewetak Island."

"It was always a little hard to snap out of our underwater world of fish, coral, and bubbles, and adjust to the world of human beings above the waterline."

"One mystery above all others lured me to the shores of Enewetak: the behavior of the gray reef shark, *Carcharhinus menisorrah*." (above) Whitetip reef shark, *Triaenodon obesus* (below).

"Bottoms can be deceptively rich." Feather starfish, contracted sea anemone (above); giant clam, underwater vegetation (below).

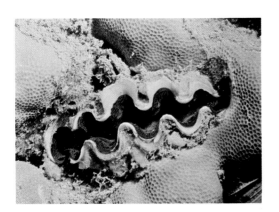

"The main part of the reef is made up of actively growing coral."

"Many lionfishes are highly venomous and are often so cleverly camouflaged against the background that it is quite easy to touch or step on one without ever seeing it."

"The diurnal clownfish habitually seeks protection at night within
the anemone. It was nestled among the anemone's tentacles,
motionless and asleep."

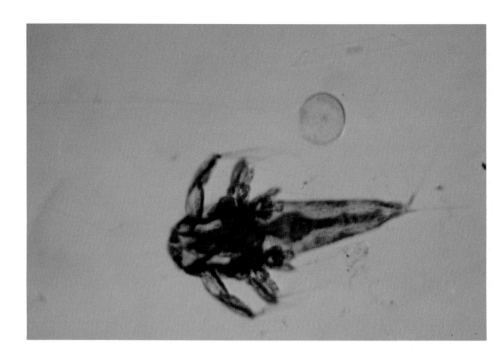

"As we held on against the current of the East Channel, the passage of plankton seemed as infinite as anything on this finite earth can be."
Planktonic crustaceae, magnified approximately 1500 times.

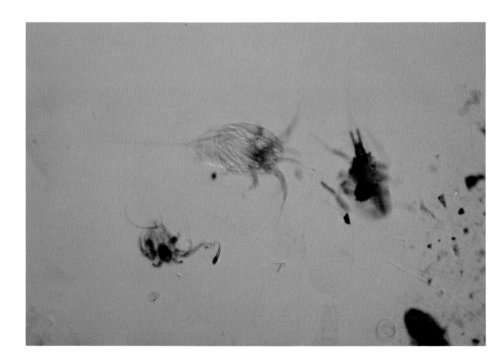

that is indeed the case, then the proper behavior of a diver in the presence of a shark might vary widely from species to species. Large hammerheads and tiger sharks, for example, apparently do not feel threatened at all by a diver and can sometimes be driven off by aggressive behavior on the part of the diver, such as his swimming rapidly toward it. Judging by our experience with this gray reef shark, I would say that for this species just the opposite is true: by acting aggressively toward it, you might just trigger the attack you are seeking to avoid. The gray reef shark has attacked divers on a number of occasions, and in virtually every case that we're aware of, the diver was not eaten, simply bitten. This indicates that it was not a feeding attack.

If we find we can elicit an attack from a shark at will, we have a number of interesting possibilities that involve using the submarine. First we can film and closely observe the behavior leading up to the attack; we may be able to learn just how far we can go before preattack behavior turns into the attack itself. Then we can try modifying the sub in various ways. For example, the shark attacked the propeller very vigorously; if we carried a propeller of some sort in front of the sub, we might be able to focus the attack there. We might paint a false eye on the front, since an eye spot forms a target for most predators. We might try breaking up the outline of the sub by painting a series of black bands across it. If we can learn to manipulate the attack or misdirect it in any way, perhaps a diver can be prepared to do the same.

The submarine is really the essential tool here, and although we were within its shelter, the shark attack was a fearsome thing. It was so fast that even a diver with a powerful bang stick would have been helpless. The shark could easily have run completely behind him before he could have turned around. There is no question, after seeing an attack like that, that once the shark goes into its move there would be no way for a human to defend against it; the only defense would be to avoid triggering the attack in the first place. In persisting in our course toward the shark after it had begun its display, we had violated the rules. The display function is essential in many animal species to avoid constant and draining fights between individuals. Presumably, if we in the submarine had properly "read" the display and obeyed its message, we would have been left alone. By getting to know the details of the display better and perhaps even by filming both display and attack from the sub and from the surface, we can learn what *not* to do, and teach it to skin divers as a rule of behavior around this species of shark.

THE next morning we moved the boat into the pier to take on fuel. Fuel had to be brought to us in 1,000-gallon lots in an antiquated truck, so it took us all morning to top off. By noon we had finished and moved the boat back out to the mooring.

We spent the afternoon doing some work on the submarine and the outboard. The outboard was cutting out whenever we suddenly advanced the throttle under load. It also stalled when we shifted from neutral into either forward or reverse, so it was necessary to rev it up before shifting. The problem turned out to be a vacuum switch that would stay closed only under conditions of little or no load. On sudden acceleration it would break contact, just like the vacuum-operated windshield wipers in an automobile that will momentarily stop functioning when you accelerate. We managed to repair it, and that was a good thing; for the past couple of days, our landings had been in the form of controlled or semicontrolled crashes. Because of the switch problem, we would come in toward the shore, trying to judge our distance carefully, then cut the engine and coast onto the beach or up to the pier from there.

For the submarine, I was a little worried about the plexiglass panels we had put in the day before. They were about a quarter of an inch thick, and I had decided they were not heavy enough to keep out a determined shark. We found an old plexiglass desk top ashore that was half an inch thick and made new windows from that. After we rigged them up, I put the sub in the water and gave it a trial run. I wanted to make sure the shutters wouldn't flap up and down from the motion of the sub moving through the water. It turned out that they worked beautifully—the sub even seemed to gain about half a knot of speed, since the plexiglass eliminated the turbulence around the side windows.

IT seemed as though we were in for a goodly number of shark encounters, and we resolved to test our defensive gear, such as it was, and also to try collecting several sharks in order to see what they were eating. So today we ran comparison tests on two different types of shark gun. Dick Gushman has a .223 Remington powerhead that is reputedly very potent. It uses the same cartridge as the M-16 military rifle. The cartridge sits behind a short, water-filled barrel only about an inch longer than the cartridge. Our own bang stick uses a .357 magnum pistol cartridge in a six-inch barrel that is sealed with a plastic cap, so that the bullet fires in an air-filled chamber instead of in water.

Dick fired both of them against a six-inch block of wood, and we found that the bang stick penetrates about the same distance as the .223 powerhead but does considerably more damage. The .223 is a more powerful cartridge than the .357 magnum, but having it fire in the water-filled barrel is inefficient. The barrel must of necessity be very short; otherwise, pressures would run dangerously high as the slug was forced against the water and the powerhead would blow apart. With such a short barrel, a rifle cartridge like the .223 blows most of its powder out unburned. Smokeless powder must be under pressure to burn explosively, and here the bullet no more than gets moving before it's out of the barrel. Then pressure drops abruptly, and the remaining powder does not burn. So in effect you are using only a small fraction of the power available. The magnum pistol cartridge, by contrast, is designed to burn all of the powder and generate all its velocity within the six-inch barrel we use; that is why it's a superior weapon.

After lunch, Jo and Dick and I went up to Pole Pinnacle. The wind was stiff and the lagoon water a little cloudy, but Pole Pinnacle is near the deep eastern pass, and clear ocean water comes in there. We got in and Jo and I went to the down-current side of the pinnacle where we were sheltered from the strong current. We were down to about 40 or 50 feet when a shark showed up, and then another and another. All three were gray reef sharks, but none was showing agonistic behavior even when we moved quite close to them. Several times one came within five or six feet of us but appeared to be simply curious. They soon seemed to satisfy this curiosity, so that when Dick came down with the powerhead, he was unable to get close enough for a shot.

Then the sharks began to follow us, moving down and up as we did along the face of the pinnacle. Gradually it dawned on me that there was something special about this place that drew such a contented group of not only sharks but other large fish. At the base of the up-current side, at a depth of 60 or 70 feet, the vertical wall of the pinnacle begins to slope outward, reducing its angle to about 45 degrees before plunging on down to a depth of about 135 feet, which seems to be the lagoon floor in that area. The 45-degree slope is irregularly broken with mounds of corals and boulders of coral rock that have probably fallen from the pinnacle above. This formation, facing into the current as it was, served to deflect the flow of water upward into a rising stream. It was along this stream that the majority of the larger fish gathered, hovering negligently together as they were buoyed by the incoming ocean water. The buoyant effect seemed the same as that of the bow wave of a ship, where porpoises can often be seen taking advantage of a virtually free ride. Here there was a large school of about twenty barracudas, great clouds of small plankton-feeding fish, *Caesio*, various *Anthias*, wrasses, and large unicorn surgeonfish, all arrayed out in front of the slope of the pinnacle at various levels.

And, of course, the sharks. The other fish didn't seem to pay them much attention, even though I counted six gray reef sharks and three whitetips. At one point I descended to the base of the pinnacle, at a depth of about 100 feet, where I was quickly surrounded by great clouds of *Caesio* and jacks, and through this cloud of fish I could see five gray sharks in line, one behind the other, slowly moving along the edge of sand at the base of the slope. It was a spectacular sight. The presence of so many large predators—particularly sharks—around this small pinnacle (which is only about 75 or 100 feet across the long axis, and 50 feet in width) was a surprise to all of us.

Shortly after we had got around to the front of the pinnacle, I had used up the last of the film in the camera, and Jo had used hers, so we went back to the boat to change cameras. This time I wanted to take some close-ups with the micro lens on the Beaulieu, and Jo was going to shoot some stills, so I went down on the back side of the pinnacle to work in the lee of the current, and Jo and Dick moved around to the front side to shoot some stills of the sharks and other big fish. I'd shot about 35 feet of the arms of a feather starfish and some small damselfish when the light suddenly went out, so I had to bring the rig up and put it back on the boat. I decided to take the bang stick down this time to see if I could collect one of the sharks. This was the only way to get an idea of why all those large predators were gathered there. Were they feeding there or just resting before their feeding activities in other areas, or perhaps at night? If we could see what was in a few stomachs, we would have some indication.

I got out to the front of the pinnacle, and just as I started down, I spotted Jo with a whitetip reef shark about six feet long coming around from the side of the pinnacle toward her. She was at a depth of about 90 feet, and the shark was just swimming lazily along while she was looking in the opposite direction. I yelled at her through my mouthpiece, but she didn't see or hear me, so I swam down toward the shark. When I was about five feet from her, she turned and noticed it and began to film. About that time I poked at it with the bang stick, but the shark was just slightly out of reach. It darted off and disappeared. I then moved on down the slope and soon got close enough to another shark to hit it, but just a glancing blow—not enough to detonate the bang stick. Then I found Dick and exchanged sticks with him; he had one of the seven-foot sticks with a better reach, while mine was only the four-foot type we use for defense. I tried to get close to several other sharks, but each time I approached they would move away just before I came within range.

Finally, I spotted a whitetip coming along and saw that it was going to pass on the far side of a large coral block about 20 feet long and 6 or 8 feet high, so I quickly ducked behind it and moved around to the opposite end in ambush. Sure enough, a few seconds later it popped out where I thought it would, and I hit it just behind the gills. The bang stick exploded, and a big cloud of blood came out. The shark started to thrash around in various directions, crashing into the coral; it seemed to be in its death throes. There were large snappers in the area, weighing about 15 to 20 pounds, and they immediately charged in and appeared to be biting at the wound. As the shark churned back and forth, they followed very closely, like a pack of dogs after a zebra, and then the other sharks in the area began to get excited. At that point my tank ran out of air, so I had no choice but to start toward the surface. Dick, running out also, followed close behind, and with all the other tanks empty as well we called it a day and headed back to the boat. I hated to kill the shark without carrying through with my purpose of collecting the stomach. On the other hand, things were getting a little wild down there, and even the option of bravery in the face of a blood-in-the-water feeding frenzy vanished along with the air supply.

ALTHOUGH there were many sharks in the area, it was not easy to find them when we wanted to collect them. That's how the sea is, in general: if you go out with firm plans for a specific mission, chances are you'll be disappointed. Another day you'll be wandering along with nothing special in mind, and suddenly there before you is that new subspecies or that unique symbiosis or that novel shark behavior. The only hope in doing the kind of basic research we were doing is to be prepared as best you can for anything that happens.

At any rate, we had been so impressed with the variety and number of large carnivores at Pole Pinnacle that we resolved to go back as soon as we could.

Some windy weather held us up, but a few days later, with the wind down to 12 to 15 knots, we left the boat at the pier to take on water and headed out to Pole Pinnacle in the skiff to take a dive. Dick stayed behind to keep an eye on the *El Territo* as she took on water, and since Jo's toe was too sore to swim for any length of time with swim fins, she elected to take the children to the beach. We dropped them off on the way at the beautiful white sand beach at Jedrol Island. Jerry Condit and I then headed for Pinnacle, which is only about a mile from Jedrol.

We arrived just before slack tide, so the water was still crystal-clear and we could see the bottom from the boat at about 135 feet. We put on our gear and descended, and in the clear water the view was thrilling. The steep-sided pinnacle, rising from the bottom almost to the surface, was brightly lit; the top, because of its living coral crown, was yellowish, and the deeper sides were bluish and darker. Great clouds of surgeonfish and *Caesio* hovered and trailed out from the eastern side of the pinnacle. On the southern side, where we entered the water, there was a large school of barracudas hanging motionlessly in the water 40 feet below the surface. I swam over to them and filmed a short sequence and then moved to the front of the pinnacle. I was gradually going deeper and looking back up, watching the plankton feeders silhouetted against the bright surface. From that angle the colors and silhouettes were beautiful, with the dark form of the pinnacle swooping up and the dazzling shapes of the fish swooping and darting against the sky above.

We had been on the bottom only a few minutes and I was watching the small goby that lives on sea whips when Jerry tapped me. He pointed to a large shark that was swimming away from us. I signaled to him to shoot it if he could, because I still wanted to look at the stomach contents of the sharks to get some idea of the frequency of feeding, the time of feeding, and the nature of the food. The shark was only a short distance off, but it was moving faster than we were. As we stopped to watch it disappear in the distance, another, smaller gray reef shark about five feet long came in from Jerry's left, and he didn't see it. As it moved in on him, I watched until it came into his view (with a diving mask on you have almost no peripheral vision, much like a horse with blinders; consequently, you can't see the fishes and other creatures that approach from the side until they suddenly pop out in front of you. Another diver a short distance away can, of course, see them, but not those around *him*, so we are always coming up from a dive and saying, did you see so-and-so, no, but did you see so-and-so?). As this shark suddenly popped into Jerry's view a few feet in front of his mask, he started momentarily, then cocked his bang stick. But by the time he was ready the shark had begun to move away. Jerry swam after it (I was filming meanwhile), and eventually he came up from beneath it and hit it on the underside of the head with the bang stick. There was a sharp explosion, and the shark was temporarily stunned. It began to swim in slow circles directly above me, and I continued to follow it with the camera. Then the shark regained its balance and started swimming away very erratically. We both followed it for a while, but finally lost it in the distance. The charge had not been powerful enough, and I decided to make up some special hand loads that I have used before for collecting sharks. They have enough powder to disable a shark no matter where you hit it, whereas a normal cartridge blows a neat hole through the fish without doing much damage, and it recovers pretty rapidly and swims off.

By this time it was slack tide and the water was getting turbid. Visibility had dropped from more than 100 feet to 60 or 70 feet. I went up the side of the pinnacle to a depth of about 30 feet, just below the top, and then perched on the coral to watch the various plankton feeders operate. I was particularly interested in the *Naso*, or unicorn surgeonfish. There were two species present—one a true unicorn type of surgeonfish with a long spine on its forehead sticking straight out in front. Whole phalanxes of these, with clear white tails and lances projecting forward, were parading by, wheeling and returning in the current. The sunlight coming down would catch their sides, especially as they turned, glinting brightly on their scales.

The other species of *Naso* was quite large, but the male had only a slight bump on his forehead rather than a long, projecting spire, and the female was slope-headed. Several of the males of this species were courting the females. Since they were only six or eight feet from me, I could see, in addition to the white markings that we had observed a few days ago, other markings that flashed in the light. Normally this fish is a dull brownish black and not very attractive from the standpoint of color. But when the male is courting, he undergoes some brief and rather startling changes. He gets not only a very pale head, but also a blue "mask" in the region of the eye and a bright yellow pattern on the upper and lower regions of the tail. He initiates the courtship dance by approaching the female, then stopping suddenly and erecting his dorsal and anal fins, expanding them in saillike fashion and flashing his brilliant blues and yellows. As he moves in close to her, either she responds positively (and who could resist!) or she doesn't. If she does, they swim off together, angling up toward the surface; if she turns him down, he veers away, defeated, striking his colors and reverting to his normal drab self.

After watching these displays for about half an hour, I began to run low on air, so we returned to the boat and went back to pick up Jo and the children. When I got to Jedrol Island, I saw Jo up on the beach, piling up a large heap of sand. We anchored the skiff off the beach, waded in, and found just Marissa's head protruding above the sand. Jo had completely buried her and molded a little body-shaped mound around her. Just as we arrived, Marissa decided to unbury herself and broke through the mound, emerging into daylight coated with sand. Varrina then had to have her turn, and afterward showed me the game that Jo had invented for them with an old section of aluminum ventilating duct that they had found on the island. It formed a large hoop about two feet in diameter which the girls would roll down the sloping beach, chasing it down to the waves, and then watching and shrieking as the waves hit it and brought it rolling back. They got into the water to wash the sand out of their bathing suits, and we piled into the skiff for the ride back to the *El Territo* and lunch.

After we had finished, before moving back out to the mooring, Jo decided to go into the water with the hand spear to hunt a fresh fish for Mikka the otter. She got in and looked all around under the pilings of the pier, but didn't see anything large enough to spear (sometimes even the richest marine environment on earth lets you down). There was a group of small fish near shore, in the shallows at the foot of the dock, so I made a couple of throws with the cast net, but they were extremely shy, and as soon as the net flew through the air, they would scatter before it hit the water. I had put the net back, and started the engines to warm them up, when Jo called and said there were a couple of squid in the neighborhood. A few minutes later she came back to the boat, and I could see that she had speared one. I was checking over the engines, reading the oil pressure and fresh-water flow and so forth, when she put the squid down on deck in front of Mikka. He immediately grabbed it, and the squid let out a spurt of ink. Mikka began to chew on it, and the squid writhed and twisted and squirted more ink, whereupon the otter decided that he pre-ferred to dine below in air-conditioned comfort. He grabbed the beast and took off through the open door of the wheelhouse, the squid pulsing ink at every step and Mikka leaving a set of black, precise footprints of squid ink all the way across the deck. As he raced up the steps, it occurred to us that we preferred to have him dine on deck rather than below, given the active role his dinner was playing, and Jo yelled while I headed him off at the door and turned him around. He was distinctly annoyed and tried to come in again, but we finally convinced him he should stay outside and got the movie camera to film this meal. By that time he was chewing on the body up next to the head, and the enormous eye was directly opposite his own small eyes. Soon it seemed as though only the eye were left, and although the tableau appeared gruesome to us, Mikka didn't seem to notice. I filmed for a minute and turned to the controls to back the ship away from the dock. Mikka took this cue to make another dash for the door with ink still dribbling from the carcass of the squid. Jo met him at the door this time and, thwarted, he went up to the forward deck (which we had just scrubbed down with fresh water), where the ink sac apparently burst. Mikka, again on cue, proceeded to march about the foredeck, producing beautiful black otter footprints throughout, and then returned to devour the rest of the squid.

9

A LESSON
IN REEF ECOLOGY

THE next day featured strong winds and light rainsqualls, not exactly the weather you want for underwater photography. So Jo and Dick Gushman and I took the skiff out about a mile to make a dive on a small patch reef just inside the main reef northeast of Enewetak Island. This patch reef lay in about 20 feet of water against a white sand bottom. It consisted of a mound of coral 8 to 10 feet high and about 25 or 30 feet in diameter.

Patch reefs (as the name suggests, they are isolated from other reefs) are exciting places to visit, because they hold more than their "share" of fish species. This one in particular, being far from other corals, supported a larger-than-normal population. Many of the fishes that hold close to patch reefs during the daytime forage abroad over the surrounding level bottoms at night, so that their feeding area may in fact be remote from their "home." The patch reef provides the essential shelter from predators that allows these animals to conduct their freewheeling lifestyle.

The flat bottom area can support only a fixed number of roving predators, no matter how many reefs there are. During the daytime these predators congregate over patch reefs, and if there is only one reef for a long distance that reef will be booked full. This is the principle behind the success of artificial reefs as fish attractors. By dumping a substantial amount of material—large rocks, automobile tires, whole automobiles—into an area that lacks reefs, fishes can be drawn from great distances to take advantage of this strange, but nonetheless effective, shelter. Building an artificial reef in a region that already has reefs does little to increase fish populations. But in areas of reefless, featureless bottom, as off much of the coast of California, the construction of artificial reefs (which attract algae, invertebrates, and finally the fish themselves) has delighted countless fishermen.

At this reef, the most conspicuously abundant inhabitants were several species of squirrelfish and several of cardinalfish, both of which are nocturnal in habit and seek shelter but not food during the day. This particular patch was just right for them, made up as it was largely of a branching finger coral which formed a perfect sort of bramble thicket. These animals often hover just outside such a shelter, diving into it only if threatened by a predator. Because of the steep side of the reef and the level sandy bottom that surrounded it, we were able to walk around it and observe the fish at eye level. There were several cleaning wrasses removing parasites both from the resting fish and from some of the plankton feeders that happened to be there for the day. On one side of the patch reef I found two small pipefish that were entwining themselves about the coral branches and appeared to be picking at the polyps of the coral animals with their long bite snouts. To the best of my knowledge, pipefish have never before been seen feeding directly on coral.

On the sandy bottom around the reef, a number of gobies lived in burrows with snapping shrimps. For some reason, the shrimps were inactive today and even though, by sneaking up close, we could see them inside their burrows, none were coming out with an armload of sand, as they usually do.

Such patch reefs as this make very good subjects for ecological study because they form a complete, discrete community unto themselves—the fish sheltering there disperse to feed, by day or night, and return after feeding to the same spot—although such a study would apply only to the workings of patch reefs, or artificial reefs, or similar structures on flat bottom. The results would tell us little about the rest of a coral atoll—the barrier reef, the lagoon bottom, exposed beaches, and so on. One of the problems which has arisen in the study of reef ecology is that there are many kinds of habitats, and few ecologists are familiar with all of them. Too many scientists come to a reef to study what they think is the "reef"—generally a zone from the reef top (the breaker zone) to the back reef where the bottom slopes into the lagoon. They observe the workings of this zone and assume that they have investigated the reef as a whole. What they have actually done is to study one narrow zone which is, in terms of flora, fauna, and water circulation, quite different from other zones.

The patch reef we visited today, for example, may look in superficial ways like parts of the main reef, but its isolation and the absence of primary food producers (green plants) reduce the biological status of a patch reef to something very much lower. The only plants that harness the sun's energy are small bits of algae on parts of the dead coral and, of course, the algae contained in the skeletons and living tissues of the corals themselves. But this plant material is largely unavailable to the fishes and other animals, so in terms of food chains it is a dead end.

The image of a "food chain" represents a simple way of getting across the idea that most kinds of organisms serve as food for other, "higher" kinds. At the end of this "chain of existence" are the ultimate predators on which nothing else normally feeds. Notable among these are human beings and sharks.

Although biologists may speak in terms of food chains, they tend to deal in concepts that more readily lend themselves to numerical manipulation. One such concept is "biomass," or the total amount of biological material in a given place. We may speak of biomass in the form of a pyramid, with a huge abundance of tiny, "lower" organisms at the bottom and a small number of "higher" organisms at the top. At the very bottom, in marine environments, are the one-celled phytoplankton—the primary food producers that are able to manufacture starch from the energy provided by the sun. Immediately above the primary producers in this biomass pyramid would be the tiny, but slightly larger, zooplankton that prey on the phytoplankton. Vast numbers of such predations occur every minute all over the world, and although these are acts performed anonymously and invisibly, they are more important to the operation of the biosphere than the falcon's swoop upon the sparrow or the cheetah's pounce upon the gazelle.

One inviolable law of the biosphere is that, for a number of reasons, many "low" organisms are required to produce a few "high" organisms. For one thing, if predators ate all their prey, they would be committing species suicide. Also, the transfer of energy from prey to predator is not very efficient, so a predator must eat a good many prey during its lifetime. But this is not to say that there are more plants than animals in the ocean at a given instant. The Russian oceanographer V. G. Bogorov has estimated that the total mass of plants in all the oceans is 1.7 billion tons and that the total mass of the animals is twenty times that. This seems at first to be a paradox, as though the horse outweighed the grass it eats. It does not, of course, and the reason for the seeming imbalance lies in the short life of the oceanic plant and the long life of the animal. In the production of new living stuff each year, the plants outgrow the animals about ten to one. More than 99 percent of all this growing takes place in the great up-welling zones of the oceans, such as the coast of Peru and the fringes of Antarctica. There the constant replenishment of seawater nutrients from below leads to enormous and continuous algal "blooms" that provide a vast stand of vegetation. Countless invertebrates—worms, crabs, shrimps—"graze" upon this vegetation and proliferate as seemingly end-less clouds of wriggling creatures. Among the commonest are crustaceans known as krill, which may form continuous rusty brown banks 30 feet deep and several miles in extent. Krill serve as the staple food in the diet of baleen whales; the stomach of a single whale may contain a ton of krill. The total weight of a whale has been calculated as equivalent to a trillion planktonic plants. But these plants may live only a few days, whereas the whale has been eating for years.

Although there is far more animal biomass in the ocean at any given time than plant biomass, it was clear that at this patch reef there was not enough plant matter to account for all the large fish we saw. The fish were drawing their energy from a much larger area—indeed, from the coral reef/atoll system as a whole. They were feeding on prey throughout the surrounding level bottom areas as well as on plankton coming in on the ocean current. That is a very large area indeed, and is not even confined to the atoll itself. A study of this particular reef community would yield a totally different picture from a study of the main reef top, where plant life seems to be most abundant and fish less so.

The largest gap in our knowledge of coral reefs seems to be the fore reef, offshore from the breakers, where the bottom slopes away from the island and the seas are usually heavy. This is the richest zone of all, be-cause the open ocean water makes first contact with the reef here, bearing its full load of plankton. Thus it supports the greatest number of plankton feeders, and because it receives plenty of sunlight, the plant life is luxuri-ant as well. This plant life, in turn, provides food for large populations of herbivores, such as the schools of surgeonfish we saw the other day from the submarine.

Where the slope of the fore reef, at the outer edge of the reef, be-comes essentially vertical, usually in water more than 100 feet deep all the way to the lower limit of plant growth at about 300 feet, we find a zone that is again different from any other on the reef. Here most of the animal inhabitants are, unlike the fishes of the patch reefs, not able to leave the environment to forage because there is no adjacent level bottom. Also, because the vertical face is almost completely shaded from even the small amount of light that penetrates more than 100 feet of water, plant life is sparse. Therefore, all life at this depth must be supported through the good offices of incoming plankton, either directly or indirectly. Here we find any number of direct plankton feeders: sponges, bivalves, some of the tunicates, zooplankton, corals, fishes, and various crustaceans. Then there are the predators that feed upon these direct plankton feeders. So despite the absence of any appreciable plant life on the lower, outer reef faces, we find large, rich populations of animals entirely supported by plankton.

Well back in the lagoon, far from the pounding surf, the opposite situation exists. Plankton of any kind is scarce, and virtually no oceanic plankton can be found. The bulk of the oceanic plankton has been consumed before it can reach that point. What we have are lagoon plankton, creatures that normally stay within the confines of the placid lagoon. Consequently, plankton feeders are rare here—rarer than any place on the reef. Frequently there are grass beds in shallow lagoons that support large populations of herbivores, but in deep lagoons, where the bottom is too far from the sunlight to allow the growth of rooted plants, and where the plankton are scarce, we find an impoverished semidesert with few organisms of any kind.

The level sandy bottoms of such lagoons, however, can be deceptively rich. Despite the absence of primary producers (plants) and, indeed, the apparent absence of any life at all, specialized and complex food chains have evolved in such environments. The lack of good shelter from predators dictates that the links of these chains be quite small—animals that can "disappear" at an instant's notice among the bits of shell and rock that may protect them from a passing carnivore. But this limitation is not crippling; many lagoon bottom dwellers are able to disappear by burrowing into the sand or mud of the bottom itself.

Among the fishes there is a goodly assortment of eels that burrow in the sand. Unlike the garden eel, many of them do not live in tunnels. Instead, they range freely, "swimming" through the loose sand itself. A number of these sand swimmers have neatly pointed snouts that seem to have been honed in a pencil sharpener. They also tend to have poorly developed eyes—the merest black dots along the small snout. A lot seem never to emerge from their sandy surroundings either by day or by night. They apparently find their food in the form of tiny creatures that live a very specialized, interstitial existence among the grains of sand of the lagoon bottom.

The possibility of making a living in this manner is not as farfetched as it may sound. Plant productivity on and among the sand grains can be quite high—just not in the macroscopic mode we are accustomed to. Instead, the plants are microscopic diatoms and other algae, the merest scum that forms on the surfaces of the sand, giving it a yellowish cast. A variegated herd of invertebrates has evolved the ability to exploit this scum. The sea cucumbers, for example, ingest the sand *in toto*, digest all the digestible material (which includes both detritus from above, the interstitial animals, and the scum itself), and excrete the "clean" sand. (Earthworms perform an equivalent operation in garden soil.)

A large number of burrowing sea urchins do likewise. In some areas of sand bottom we've found large sea biscuits, a kind of burrowing urchin 6 or 8 inches in diameter and several inches thick. Populations of these urchins may have densities approaching one per square meter of bottom. During the day they burrow into the sand; some species go to a depth of 6 or 8 inches, while others, resembling sand dollars, simply cover themselves with sand. At night they emerge from hiding and crawl about on the surface of the bottom, eating the sand sea-cucumber-style, digesting the edible portion, and passing the rest out their alimentary tracts.

Farther up the food chain, various species of fish, mollusks and crabs, and even large turtles feed on these burrowing urchins, when they can find them. Some of the crabs have devised a particularly clever way to get past the spiny defense. Using a set of claws that are shaped like hooks and act like can openers, they simply chop open the shell, snip the muscle away from the sides, and lay back the two valves to feast on the soft internal organs. The beautiful, large helmet conchs also feed on these burrowing urchins. Despite the softness of their large, fleshy feet, they simply crawl atop the spiny urchin, crush the spines down, and drill a hole through the outer shell with their filelike radulae. Then they consume the soft innards through the hole they have made.

The fishes of these sandy zones tend to be of two types (excluding the predators that forage by night from the shelter of the patch reefs; these cannot be considered true members of the bottom community). One type includes plankton-feeding forms, such as the garden eels, jawfishes, and some of the gobies that make burrows on the bottom, hover above them to pluck plankton from the water, and dive into them if predators approach. The other type, by far the commoner of the two, seems to feed on the interstitial animals that derive their existence from the microscopic algae and the detritus that settle from above. This category includes the pencil-nosed eels, the tiny dragonets, various species of minute gobies, small flounders, and a broad range of smaller fishes. The fishes may also draw their energy from the bottom creatures in a less direct way—by eating small crabs and shrimps that feed on the bottom.

A glance at the lagoon bottom by day from a boat, or even from the better vantage point provided by scuba gear, would reveal just rippled sand and, occasionally, a passing fish or slow-motion sea cucumber. Only by diving at night have we been able to observe the true richness of the bottomland. It seems that many of the inhabitants of this specialized environment seldom come out of hiding, and when they do, it is at night.

The lagoon bottom is relatively impoverished compared with the dense populations of the reef face itself, but we learn from it the lesson that a reef is more diverse than many of us think. The incoming ocean current brings oceanic plankton (energy) and phosphates and other ions (building materials). With these gifts, corals and their symbiotic algae are able to construct huge and beautiful natural sculptures and endure the pounding of the sea for many years—and then, gradually, like all life forms, die. As they die, this same sea, with its pounding and its bath of dissolving chemicals, reduces the limestone of the coralline structures to sand and mud, and these particles, along with bits of shell, bone, and teeth, are carried behind the reef, coming to rest on the lagoon bottom, vast blankets of sand and silt. If one looks at a reef ecologically, then, one sees a whole assemblage of related communities. The deep reef face, the main reef, the lagoon bottom, and the patch reefs are all related both by the moving seawater and by the roving predators—jacks, snappers, sharks—that range throughout the atoll, feeding on its inhabitants wherever they go.

Interrelations within atoll environments can be surprising. The symbiotic algae of many of the corals, especially those of the patch reefs, are nourished wholly or in part by the feces of the fishes that live there. The reef fishes have foraged far from the reefs, capturing plankton in the water that would be unavailable otherwise to the coral. These fishes have gathered the plankton, digested it for their own use, and then defecated a nitrogen- and phosphate-rich fertilizer that nourishes the somatic algae of the coral.

10

THE REEF AT NIGHT

IN many habitats on earth, animal and plant activity is distinctly different at night from normal daylight activity. In desert regions, for example, most animals sleep during the heat of the day, emerging in the cool of the evening to forage and hunt. In tropical forests, nighttime brings out large numbers of snakes, cats, insects, and primates whose eyes are extra-sensitive to allow nocturnal vision. The coral reef is no exception, and even though there is no difference in water temperature, the coming and going of the sun do affect the behavior and distribution of phytoplankton and other organisms sufficiently to produce a drastic change in the cast of characters. So we came equipped to try to observe and photograph the secretive routines of the night creatures of Enewetak.

Typically, our first night dive was delayed by what had become almost a routine at any time of day: equipment failure. We got out two of our new diving lights, from which we didn't expect any trouble; these lights are fourth- or fifth-generation tools that grew out of our original night diving work in Florida. The type that we're now using is being produced commercially, and the ones we had came from the first production run. We put them together ourselves, and they perform extraordinarily well. We had only two of the new ones, however, so we had to fix up one of the older models as a droplight for movie work, using a 650-watt movie flood in it. The new ones we rigged as headlights on plastic football helmets, not for floodlights but to help us find our way about, pick up things, and so on.

The old light gave us a lot of trouble. It hadn't been used for a year, and some of the parts were frozen. We broke a couple of screws and fit-tings before we could get one sealed and functioning. Finally, at nine-thirty, we made our dive with a full moon shining overhead. We dived directly beneath the boat to a patch reef there, turned on the big movie light, and—nothing. Back to the surface we went, only to find that the plug on the boat had been knocked loose. Meanwhile, on the bottom, Dick Gushman was heading for the light and reached to pick it up just as I plugged it in, so he got the full 650 watts of light right in his night-adapted eyes. It took him awhile to be able to see his way about again.

I jumped back in and went down to see what else was swimming around. The dominant fishes were the various species of squirrelfish, sol-dier fish, and cardinalfish. All the wrasses and parrotfish and damselfish were inactive, just resting here and there on the coral as though put to sleep by a magic spell. There were also some large surgeonfish, about a foot long. They would remain here, immobile, until dawn's first light began to rouse them for another day's work. Such fishes are said to be "diurnal" (this term originally meant "daily" but has come to mean "daytime" as well, in contrast with "nocturnal").

It was amusing to come across a large anemone that Jo had found during daylight some days earlier. The diurnal clownfish that habitually seek protection within the anemone were nestled among the tentacles, motionless and asleep. We didn't see the cleaning shrimps, so we don't know where they bed down at night. Around the surrounding sand and silt bottom we came across a number of sleeping goatfish. This is a small fish that has two chin whiskers like those of a billy goat. It uses these whiskers as sensory probes to search the sandy bottom for small burrowed organisms. As it rests on the bottom at night, it takes on a pattern of mot-tled salmon pink, which makes it very hard to see against the sand. We also saw several species of snappers out prowling the sand bottom for the small invertebrates that venture out of their burrows at night.

All in all, the situation was very similar to that found at night on the reefs in Florida. The general routine at most coral reefs seems to fall into a common pattern with respect to fauna. The invertebrates—all the corals, shrimps, crabs, anemones, and the like—tend to be primarily nocturnal animals, inconspicuous during the day, very active after dark. The fishes themselves are divided according to their feeding preferences. The herbiv-orous fishes—surgeonfishes, parrotfishes, and some of the herbivorous blennies—are all primarily diurnal. The large carnivores that eat other fishes, although they may feed at any time, are most active around dawn

and dusk and so are called crepuscular feeders. The carnivores that feed
on the crabs, shrimps, and other small invertebrates are, of course, active
when their prey is feeding—at night. The plankton feeders fall into two
groups. Some, like the damselfishes, some of the wrasses, and some of the
herrings, are diurnal feeders. Others, like the other herrings, the cardinalfishes, and some of the squirrelfishes, are nocturnal.

All these feeding schedules make good sense. Most carefully designed are those of the plankton feeders. Plankton is constantly flowing
across the reef in the great oceanic currents. To make maximum use of
this free food supply, the reef must function twenty-four hours a day. Because a single animal cannot operate on such a demanding schedule, there
are day and night shifts.

On the other hand, the animals that feed on the plants of the reef or
on the sessile invertebrates like corals and sponges—prey that can't leave,
hide, or run away—can most easily feed during the day, when they can
see best. The food that is there today will be there tomorrow if they don't
eat it today. The schedule of the invertebrate feeders is simply determined
by the nocturnal activity of the invertebrates themselves.

The big predators feed at dawn and dusk for a reason that may not be
obvious at first. A well-known tactic of terrorists, bank robbers, and pris-
oners who would escape is to strike during the changing of the guard.
Confusion reaches a peak at such a time, and neither the tired guards
going off or the groggy, slow-moving guards coming on are at their best.
Likewise, neither the diurnal nor the nocturnal animals of a coral reef are
at their best at dawn or dusk. Some of them have been feeding all day and
are slowing down; others have just emerged from sleep and are not alert.
The big predators take advantage of these changes to single out the
unwary.

We spent about thirty minutes on the bottom and then ascended.
Toward the last moments, the movie floodlight went out for some reason
that was not at all obvious. Several times we turned off our headlamps and
noticed that the light of the full moon was bright enough to enable us to
see the whole lagoon floor around us as well as the boat overhead. There
was also a fair amount of phosphorescence in the water, so that whenever
we moved, we set off a little trail of sea-glow.

WE made half a dozen night dives during our stay at Enewetak, and
it was always exciting to cruise among "the second shift" and see
just how different it was from the daytime shift.

A couple of nights later we rigged up our diving lights and went down at around nine-thirty to a small patch reef about 50 feet directly beneath the boat. The moon hadn't emerged from a bank of clouds along the eastern horizon, so it was quite dark when we dived. I had the 650-watt floodlight rigged on the arm of a movie camera, and as soon as I reached the bottom, I was in the midst of considerable activity. Snappers were foraging for smaller, unwary fish; parrotfish were gnawing on coral. Surgeonfish and butterflyfish rested in the coral, and anemone (clown) fish were dozing in the safety of anemone tentacles. But most of all, I was immersed in plankton. Each time I stopped momentarily to film the fishes, great clouds of plankton would swarm around the light like insects, blocking out the view and making it impossible to photograph. Most of the plankton were shrimps of some type, half an inch to three-quarters of an inch long. Sometimes the problem became so bad that the entire floodlight was blacked out. Even wearing a headlight was trouble; if we stopped for too long, our heads were immediately coated by a seething mass of planktonic creatures, which got in our hair, our ears—everywhere. Jo has a special problem with her long hair; sometimes after a night dive it takes her many minutes to comb out all the fish, polychaete worms, shrimps, and other creatures that have become entangled in it.

After about ten minutes of filming and fighting the plankton, a short circuit developed in the movie flood, burning the wire in two. So I went back to the surface, pulled up the power cable to the big light, and returned to the bottom just to look around with the headlamps. Dick and Jerry had the self-contained lights, so Jo and I just swam in the darkness, looking over their shoulders. The moon had begun to come up above the clouds, and we could see well enough to swim without bumping into things; there was also enough light coming down from the floodlights on deck to help a bit. There was a lot of phosphorescence in the water, and whenever we moved, we set off little showers of sparks from our hands and feet.

The large anemone beneath the boat began to close up when I put the bright movie flood on it. It completely withdrew its tentacles and rolled them inward, ungraciously leaving the sleepy little clownfish trying to snuggle up on the outside of their host. In the beam of the diving light I was able to pick up one of them and hold it in my hand, look it over, and put it back on the anemone (could that be much worse than the eviction it had just suffered?).

At another spot Dick Gushman found a parrotfish sleeping in a mucous bubble. Parrotfishes make this bubble as a protective envelope. It provides some early warning against the moray eels that prowl around rocky areas at night, looking for sleepy fish to eat. If a moray or anything else touches this mucous bubble, the parrotfish explodes out of it. The existence of the bubble may also make it more difficult for the moray to detect the sleeping fish in the first place. The bubble looks like a large ball of gelatin, more or less oval in shape. The fish we found was a beautiful green-and-blue combination, and sound asleep; when we tried to pick it up gently without disturbing it, it burst away across the coral. When the bigger parrotfishes do this, they work so hard that you can actually hear their tails making an audible thump at the end of each stroke—*b-r-r-r-r-r-r-p*. Sometimes this is followed by an abrupt *brrummp* as the fish crashes into the coral in blind flight. They are quite confused after being awakened like this. Some of the larger parrotfishes, too big to be eaten by a moray, don't bother making a bubble, and if you pick them up gently at night, they may be too baffled by the light to do anything.

We have been on the lookout for one species of western Pacific parrotfish that we haven't seen yet at Enewetak. This is the large bump-headed parrotfish, which reaches a weight of several hundred pounds. I have seen whole schools of them in the Indian Ocean, where they reminded me of a herd of grazing buffalo working their way across the coral reef. I could hear the loud crunches as they bit into the coral rock. I saw one small coral head where they had been feeding that had been deeply gouged by their teeth. They were not eating the rock itself, of course, or the coral animals. They are herbivores—hence the grazing analogy—and they were after the algae that grow in symbiosis with the coral. Most parrotfishes are so strong they are able to grind away the algal stubble left on the rock after the surgeonfishes and other herbivores have grazed off the longer algae. The parrotfishes go for the base of the algae itself, down in the rocky surface—the cleanup crew of the herbivores.

A WEEK or so later, we went up to Pole Pinnacle off Jedrol Island and decided to try a night dive there. The creatures we were seeing at night would be different with each locale, just as they were in the daytime, so we wanted to make as many night dives as we had time for.

At around eleven in the morning, when the incoming current had cleared the water, we put the sub over the side, and Jo and I went around the pinnacle and off to the southeast about half a mile. We came back in to the reef and parked on the sandy bottom at a depth of about 100 feet. The water was clear, and we could see the pinnacle towering above us all the way to the surface and the shadow of the *El Territo* on her mooring. I got out to take some pictures of this scene, holding my breath (I was breathing off the sub's air system). While I was out, I noticed a colony of garden eels nearby; because I was not making any bubbles by breathing, I was able to swim unusually close to them. I could see that the species here has a black spot on its side and another black spot on the side of the neck. I had discovered that garden eels had not been reported previously from the Marshall Islands. Sometimes your best observations come by chance like this, and they are always a happy surprise.

A short distance away we spotted a large *Cheilinus* and, since I am still trying to get a specimen of this species to examine its stomach contents, we chased this one with the sub. After 100 feet or so it dived into a hole in a clump of coral (did it know it was there all the time?) where I couldn't follow; I got out and peered around the coral heads, but I couldn't even see it.

Soon what must have been a large eddy of cloudy lagoon water swept by, cutting visibility to 40 or 50 feet, so we went up to the surface to see where we were. We were about half a mile away from the reef. By this time we had been down at 75 or 100 feet for twenty minutes, and I didn't want to return to the bottom; at that depth we would have had to go into decompression when we got back to the boat. So we ran along just beneath the surface, struggling to steer a straight course. This wasn't easy in the muddy water. The little automobile compass that I had put in the submarine was inadequate—I learned on that trip just how inadequate. It kept binding, not pointing in any direction. For longer submerged trips we were going to need a larger marine compass. When we came to the surface again, we were 100 yards or so beyond the boat, so we went back down and this time missed it by 50 yards. The third time I managed to see it from underwater, and we pulled alongside.

With a night dive planned, we didn't want to put in any more bottom time. If we did, we would have to decompress afterward. So we took the afternoon off and worked on equipment; late in the afternoon Jo and I took Marissa and Varrina to Medren Island for a swim on the beach. While Jo was giving some swimming instruction, I wandered around the island and looked into some of the abandoned buildings. Most of the equipment had been removed, although the electrical supply warehouse had piles of fittings for electrical conduits, junction boxes, and connections. I was again astonished by the corrosion of these buildings. They were all corrugated metal. Most of them had aluminum siding, which endures well near the sea, but many had iron or steel frames that were completely rusted away. And this was well inland, a quarter of a mile or so from the offshore side of the island, among trees and shrubbery. Still the sea air carries its corrosive burden of water and ions right across the island, eating away with dauntless persistence at the works of man.

We went back to the *El Territo* about six-thirty, had dinner, and then prepared to go down. I lowered the Rebikoff camera into the water with a 650-watt floodlight, connected by a cable to the ship's power supply. Jo took her Beaulieu with a small battery-powered light for close-up work. I wore a battery-powered headlight for general observation, and Jerry carried a similar light to help Jo find photographic subjects. We jumped in and settled down on the sandy bottom at a depth of 100 feet just beneath the boat. Up above, the decklights were on, and a huge cloud of plankton had already gathered near the surface. They appeared to be some kind of small reddish crustacean, and they turned the near-surface water into a reddish soup. Fortunately they preferred the lights topside to those we were using, and we were not bothered by them this time.

We had some more problems with the floodlight (a short burned out one of the leads) and then with Jo's battery-operated light (malfunction unidentified), so Jo did some close-up filming with high-speed Ektachrome in the light of just her headlight, while I put the Rebikoff on the bottom, useless, and swam around, looking at the reef at night. The big schools of *Caesio* that hover out from the pinnacle during the day, feeding on plankton, were now scattered all over it, their orderly ranks in disarray, resting individually among the coral nooks. They were blinded by the light and darted about in confusion. The dominant species was 8 or 10 inches long and had a red belly and a blue back. The soldierfish, by contrast, were out and active. By day they school and shelter far back under coral ledges and in caves; now their bright red forms could be picked up all around us as they fed upon plankton both around and away from the pinnacle.

On the bottom, one of the first things I spotted was a large crown-of-thorns starfish (*Acanthaster*), a coral predator that achieved notoriety recently when it was said to be sweeping unchecked like a scourge across the reefs of the Pacific. Newspapers reported, with more than a trace of panic, that as much as 90 percent of some reefs had been destroyed by this plague, and volunteer cadres of dedicated frogmen were busily slaying the beasts one at a time, by hand, in an effort to stave off what looked like impending disaster for the coral reefs of the world.

In all the dives that we had made at Pole Pinnacle up to this point, we had seen only two *Acanthaster*—one on each of two different occasions. The animal apparently is nocturnal in many cases, holding back among the shelter of rocks and coral during the day. As soon as I saw this one, I started looking for them more earnestly and found ten in an area covering only about a quarter of the distance around the pinnacle. This was undoubtedly not all of them, so I would guess that there are probably between 50 and 100 *Acanthaster* on this one small reef. This suggests that the animal is much more abundant than previously supposed. But in spite of this abundance, there doesn't appear to be any extensive damage to the coral here at least. During the daytime I've noticed white patches where one of these starfish has fed, but certainly the rich coral growth of the pinnacle as a whole is intact. The top is a solid, virtually untouched bed of living corals. Tonight I went up, after finding these ten starfish, to see if any others were feeding there, but there were none. All the individuals I could find were down around the sides at depths between 50 and 100 feet. From my own limited observations, therefore, I would guess that the recent starfish scare was generated by a combination of a few localized cases of depredation and an overreaction to the discovery that populations of these rather unappealing creatures are larger than we had suspected.

Elsewhere around the pinnacle I spotted old friends from the Caribbean, especially among the small nocturnal invertebrates. Virtually all of the Pacific species of fishes seem to be different from those of the Caribbean, but many of the invertebrates seem to be the same. One of the favorites I came across is a small brittle starfish, whose little arms I saw protruding from holes in a rock. Most brittle starfishes live either freely in the sand bottom or on sponges (or *in* sponges) or lying under rocks. But this particular species lives in minute holes in the solid coral rock face, invisible except for its arms, which are apparently filtering the water for plankton. The arms are lightly banded, a couple of inches long, and they each have a chain of luminescent organs. If you touch one of them, these organs fire off their tiny lights in series, so that a line of luminescence races up and down the arm. It continues to glow as long as it is agitated; I plucked one of the arms from a starfish and rolled it between my fingers for several minutes, during which time it continued to shine.

As I turned my headlight across the coral and rocks around the slope at the base and sides of the pinnacle, I could see glowing red pinpoints;

these were the eyes of the coral shrimps that come out at night. A particularly abundant species is the little humpback shrimp, which is usually two to four inches long, bright red with paler markings. It has two large, prominent eyes, which are very reflective, and a pronounced hump on the tail, almost a bustle. This is the same species we have in the Caribbean, and until marine biologists changed their own habits slightly, it was thought to be rare. When we started using rotenone to collect fish we discovered not only that rotenone kills shrimps, too, but also that there are far more of them than anyone suspected. We also began diving at night, with reliable lights, and found that although the little humpback shrimp is a rare and cryptic fellow in the daytime, it is abundant at night. At Enewetak it turned out to be even more abundant than in the Caribbean.

I also saw another species of shrimp that I didn't recognize at all. It was about 3 to 4 inches long, bearing long arms, legs, and pincers; its body was covered with leaflike appendages, probably some form of camouflage, and when I touched it, the shrimp darted off among the coral where the unicorn surgeonfish were resting. This species forms the big schools seen off the pinnacle during the day, but now all were hunkered down like legless rhinos, dozing. I couldn't resist approaching one of the surgeonfish that was confused by the light and grabbing it by the rigid horn. The fish was outraged by my presumption and darted away. Jo blinded another with her light; the fish swam right into her leg, butting her with its horn.

We ran into some other old friends that were wearing their nightclothes. The striking species of *Naso* we saw courting the other day—the males with the blue eye mask and the yellowish marks on the tail and the very pale head—did not show the pale head at night. That seems to be a daytime feature appropriate only to courting situations. Another fish that had changed radically in color pattern was the Moorish idol. It had shed its strikingly beautiful daytime colors for a uniform almost entirely of black.

One of the most interesting predators I saw tonight was a cornetfish, an elongate, tube-mouthed creature about 4 feet long with a streamer of 8 or 10 inches extending from its tail. For all that length it was only 2 to 3 inches in diameter, slightly flattened along the sides. Its mouth was about 6 inches long, making it one of the most improbable-looking predators that swim. Completely toothless, it seems suited to nothing more than perhaps sucking bananas. Around the lips it has some gritty, sandpaper-like tissue, but nothing you could really call teeth. Nonetheless, the cornetfish swallows some large prey whole without difficulty; I remember opening one in the Caribbean and finding a goatfish 6 or 8 inches long in its stomach, along with half a dozen other small fish.

When I swam near this cornetfish, it performed a feat of swimming that astonished me. Like many of the members of the night shift, it was confused by my headlamp, and as I started to grab it, the fish suddenly shot backward for a distance of 5 or 6 feet. It then turned and darted off forward again. Its long body is so serpentine that it seems to be able to throw a reverse sine wave into it, moving backward almost as fast as it can move forward. Many fishes can back up slowly, with the cautious aid of their pectoral fins, but I've never in all my time underwater seen a fish, using whole body motion, *swim* backward with such speed.

It was a dark night, without moon, and the amount of starlight that penetrates 100 feet of ocean is small. When I turned off my light down there, it was black indeed; the only evidence that there was anything but blackness on earth was a spot of light on the surface around the *El Territo*, and the tiny sparkles and stars of the luminescent but unseen organisms I was disturbing as I moved in the water. I didn't see any of the sharks that we see during the day; they were either avoiding our lights or foraging in other parts of the atoll.

THE next night dive began with an unprecedented burst of temper on my part.

The day started out well enough, right where we had ended the previous one—tied up to Pole Pinnacle. It was bright and sunshiny, with moderate trade winds, an eye-opening contrast with the inky depths that had surrounded me the night before. Jo and I ran up to Runit Island to look over the craters of the A-bomb tests. Dick and Jerry stayed on the *El Territo* to keep an eye on the children and to work on some lights for diving that night. Jo and I climbed to the top of the tower on top of the bunker on Runit, and we could see from there the craters on the north end of the island. It was a spectacular view that bright day, with the breakers indigo-blue offshore, the turquoise and other shades of the reef and the lagoon and the vegetative green of the islands running along the spine of the reef itself. We stood there for some time, just gazing at the scene. Then we climbed down, and I took the skiff up to the north end of the island and landed on a beach about 50 yards from the nearest crater. The flora immediately around the crater, and even on the mounds of earth thrown up by the explosion, appears to be typical of the flora throughout the area: no strange, twisted mutations of shape or color.

The craters themselves (there was a pair of them) were about 150 yards in diameter, separated by about the same distance. Around the edges of the craters were large areas of reef rock tossed into mounds 10 to 12 feet high. The craters looked very much like those in pictures of craters on the moon thought to be dug out by the impact of large meteorites. Instead of moon rock, of course, the excavated material was sand, chunks of coral, shells and hard parts of reef animals. There was none of the glassy material you might expect to find if there were siliceous (silica-rich) sand around; when the calcium carbonate sand of the reef is melted by impact or, as in the case here, by explosion, it forms not glass but a sort of cement that bonds the outer surface of the mounds together into sort of a rough, but rigid, conglomerate. There were also, not surprisingly, various pieces of metal here and there, structural steel, pipes, and other remnants of the test apparatus. These chunks of metal are still sufficiently radioactive so that it would be dangerous to handle them or be in contact with them for any period of time. The sand itself, however, is nearly inert, so that most normal dealings with the sand, short of rolling in it or carrying handfuls of it or eating it, are safe enough. At least I didn't worry about walking through it.

The outer side of one crater is exposed to the reef flat; in other words, it is linked directly with the open ocean by virtue of a channel of water a foot or so deep. The depth of the crater itself is about 20 or 30 feet. The bottom is covered with sand and silt, and generally, it resembles any number of rock pits where I've dived in the Florida Keys. I put on the scuba gear and went into the crater to get a closer look. Along the rocky sides were various species of surgeonfish, damsels, small groupers, cardinalfish, puffers, triggerfish, herring, snappers, gobies, butterflyfish, and almost every variety of reef fish you would expect in an environment that *hadn't* been A-bombed. Away from the sides, the bottom of the crater was covered with algal scum and pocked by the burrows of various burrowing creatures—worms, shrimps, a few small mollusks, and so on. This niche, too, resembled the Florida rock pits. Although visibility was poor—only 6 or 8 feet—I spent about an hour swimming around in the crater, watching the fish and filming some of them in order to illustrate that life persists in these craters. Overall, the flora and fauna seemed to be just what one would expect for the area, and I for one was surprised that none of it appeared to be suffering in any way from the effects of radioactivity.

In the afternoon we moved on up the island chain in the skiff to a couple of other islands we wanted to visit. One was Alembel, where there was also a tower left from the days of testing. This tower was in bad shape, however, and we decided it was too dangerous to climb because of the corrosion. We then went on to the next two islands, Lojwa and Bijile, which are joined by a causeway, or wooden trestle. This trestle crosses a channel 15 feet deep and several hundred yards wide. The wood is badly decayed by now, and the only man-made object we saw on Lojwa was a small aluminum shed that had probably been used by some of the biologists from the Enewetak station. In the channel by the bridge we saw a group of six leopard rays swimming in loose formation, silhouetted against the white sand bottom, which at that depth appeared a brilliant turquoise. They circled majestically for some time directly below us—a striking sight. The grace and imperturbability of these primitive creatures seemed to demonstrate for us just what little effect the forty-three nuclear explosions appear to have had upon the islands, even upon the area adjacent to the test site and even within the bombed-out craters themselves.

A LITTLE after three we left Bijile Island and headed back to the *El Territo*, where we arrived around four. As we pulled up to the ship, Jo realized that she had lost her watch, so we got a cold drink and, since the children were up from their nap, took them and went back where we had just come from to look for it. At the bomb test site I went ashore quickly while Jo idled the boat offshore; we both seemed to recall that she had had it on her arm after we left there, but we couldn't be positive. I didn't see it in my brief look around, so we headed on up to Alembel, where we had walked back into some of the brush to get near the base of the tower. Jo searched there while I searched in the water where we had got off the boat. I was underwater when I heard her yell, and as I popped up, I saw that she was holding the watch high.

B EFORE our night dive, I completely disassembled the movie flood-light that had been giving me so much trouble. Then I put it back together, dropped it 100 feet to the bottom, and turned it on for about fifteen minutes to be sure it was functioning. Everything seemed ship-shape, hunky-dory.

After supper, around nine-thirty, we started getting our gear on for the dive. When we were just about set, I lowered the Rebikoff camera with the light by means of the power cable. I plugged it in without turning it on, started to put on some more gear, then looked over the side again, and the light was on. Since I hadn't turned the friggin' thing on, this meant that either it had shorted to turn itself on or the switch had bumped something on the bottom. So I had to hurry to get in the rest of my gear and swim down there before it either burned out or burned up, depending on which it was. When I reached the bottom, I could see it was bubbling from electrolysis, so I knew it had shorted. As I put my hand out, I could feel an electrical field in the water around the light, so I knew I couldn't touch it without getting a bad shock. I just disconnected it from the camera and left it there. At about that moment it went out, so I had to swim all the way to the surface and haul the goddamned thing up.

It never helps to get mad at machinery, but the lights were beginning to push me over the edge of sanity. It didn't seem to matter how thoroughly we checked them out (and one of the things I know about myself after half a lifetime is that I am thorough). There seems to be a malevolent nature in some inanimate objects that blossoms near the sea; *in* the sea, it really bears fruit. This was about the fifth straight time that movie light had fizzled and when I reached the surface, I had almost made up my mind to smash it against the side of the boat. I knew that wouldn't rid us of the malevolent genie, but it would at least take away one of its playthings.

I decided not to, and went back down with just my headlight and my hand net to do some collecting and looking around; Jo's portable movie light worked without problems. When I got to the bottom, I came across a large crown-of-thorns starfish, pried it loose from the rocks, and put it in the collecting net. I also collected the piece of coral it was feeding on. From what I've seen here, it seems that these *Acanthaster* prefer one type of encrusting coral. I moved along and soon came across another one, which was not feeding, just crawling along, and I also collected it. I wanted to use it both for bait and for some experiments to find out if any predators will take a crown-of-thorns.

I also picked up a beautiful cone shell that was out crawling around. These animals are quite venomous, so I was very careful, using my heavy glove to grab it. Normally, during the daytime when the cones are closed, we pick them up with our bare hands by the back of the shell. But when the animal is out it might be able to strike with its venom apparatus, and I didn't want to take any chances. I also collected some of the small *Caesio* with the little hand net I carry. I wanted to take them back for Mikka. He hadn't been feeling very good because he had eaten some of the larger fish we'd caught on the rod and reel, and they had apparently been slightly toxic. These small *Caesio*, which feed on free-floating plankton, are not likely to be.

After I had collected the *Acanthaster* and the Mikka food, I began just to look around. I noticed a species of squirrelfish that I hadn't seen at night before. It was unusual because although it was red like the other squirrelfishes, it also had a very reflective iridescent turquoise mark on its back—a clear stripe on the posterior portion. I turned off the light to see if the mark might also be luminescent, but it didn't show at all without my light. Many of the cardinalfishes have a similar iridescence at night: their scales reflect light all over the body. But this specific mark on the squirrelfish was unusual; it is hard to imagine what "use" it might have, since it shows only at night and only when light is directed at it.

While I was prowling around, Jerry and Dick were with Jo, who was photographing a large *Acanthaster*. She wanted someone's hand in the picture for purposes of scale, so she motioned to Dick to put his gloved hand next to the starfish. He obligingly did so, and just where he touched the spines of the starfish there happened to be a hole in the glove. One of the spines punctured his finger, and it bled profusely, though it apparently didn't hurt very much. This spine seemed to be more effective as an anticoagulant than as a toxin. Even though it was a small wound, it kept bleeding for quite a while.

When I got back to the surface, it was raining. Jo and Jerry and Dick had just come up, and Jerry and Dick were putting on fresh tanks to go down again. They had spent most of their time on the side of the pinnacle in only 50 feet of water so they wouldn't need to decompress yet. I had spent most of my dive at the bottom, 100 feet down, so if I made a second dive, I would have to decompress. Instead, I watched Jo feed Mikka the smaller of the *Caesio*. He really enjoyed it. The last I saw of him, he had eaten from the head all the way down to the midsection of the body, spreading a mess of scales around him on deck.

As I was putting the cameras and lights back on charge and squaring things away, Dick and Jerry came up from their second dive. While Jerry was standing on the back platform, he yelled, "Hey, there's a squid back here," and I looked over the stern to see the strangest-looking squid I've ever seen. It had just two very long arms and no short ones, and I suspected it might be an octopus free-swimming in the water. But for an octopus to be swimming around on the surface in 100 feet of water is unusual behavior, to say the least, and the more I looked at it and the way it was darting around, the more I thought it must be a squid. I called to

Dick to hold it in the light to keep it mesmerized while I ran and got a net. I found one and passed it to Jerry, who scooped it up, immediately transforming the creature into a regular octopus. It had been holding four of its eight arms on each side, so tightly pressed to one another that they appeared to be just two very long arms. Whom can you trust out here? I put it in a bucket of water on deck and turned around to straighten up some other gear. When I turned back, it had crawled out of the bucket and was sliding along the steel deck. I tried to push it loose, but it stuck stubbornly on the deck, so I put a swim fin down in its path and it slithered right along onto it. Then I picked up the fin, octopus and all, held it over the side, and let it ooze off into the ocean.

A NOTE about all this underwater photography we are doing: The fact that we are spending so much time at it is remarkable enough, if you remember the old days. For many years, recording an image of anything underwater that was in focus and properly exposed was considered a rare triumph. But over the last two decades the development of reflex cameras, fast lenses, and fast color films has changed that. Exposure is all but taken for granted, and we are now able to concentrate on composition and subject matter. Telephoto lenses are available, so that we can observe and record the activities of shrimps and other small creatures that are beyond the range of the naked eye. These small creatures are among the most interesting, and the ability to observe them without disturbing them is essential. In the past, the routine was to use a wide-angle lens, affording the greatest depth of field (and the best chance of getting the subject in focus) and the greatest proximity to large objects. But this big-picture approach gives you little idea of all the myriad individual dramas being played out. Now we are finally equipped to watch these. When water visibility is 100 feet or more, which is not uncommon at Enewetak, we can put on a medium telephoto lens, drop back 5 or 10 or 15 feet and zero in on a shrimp digging a hole or a clownfish hiding amid the tentacles of a sea anemone. This ability, along with the ability to watch an act again and again, has made underwater photography one of the most powerful tools available to the marine biologist.

THE next time we tried a night dive was four days later, up at the concrete ship. I had decided to give up on the movie floodlight that had brought us so much grief, and I replaced it with a headlight. I tested it for about five minutes and, like everything else, it worked while I tested it. The surprise was that it also worked throughout the whole dive, so it looks as if we got that problem solved. I planned to send back for some more of the new headlight housings for my movie floods.

I saw several beautiful specimens of *Caesio* just hovering around the coral and resting. One had rainbow striping with blue on the back, red on the belly, and a green stripe down the side—quite spectacular. The other was larger, about a foot long, with a heavier body, and was a brilliant, luminous blue all over. Then I spotted a number of the unicorn surgeonfish we had seen on previous dives at night but hadn't been able to film. These showed a white head at night and seemed to be a different species. So I went down with the powerful movie flood, mesmerized them, and was able to get some good close-up shots of these strange-looking animals.

Over the sandy bottom I noticed a very large species of goatfish. These peculiar fishes have a way of getting at the bottom-dwelling invertebrates they eat by day or night. The chin whiskers, which it drags through the sand, act as sensory antennae, and when the antennae send back a "crustacean" or "worm" alert to the fish's brain, it immediately starts to grub about until it finds it. Goatfishes have piglike little faces that seem appropriate for this rooting activity. Most of them are only 7 to 10 inches long. The one I saw tonight, however, was about 2 feet long and probably weighed about 10 pounds. The chin whiskers were nearly 3 inches long. One of the stranger features of goatfish—at least of one species in the Pacific that I know about—is that the brain produces hallucinations in humans if eaten. If this property holds true with the large species I saw tonight, it would have been a real mindblower.

Out in force tonight were the various species of squirrelfish, including one that has gone to extraordinary lengths to make a living. This is a species of *Myripristis*, found hovering in midwater and around the sides of coral heads, where they feed on plankton. Most of the close relatives of this genus, such as *Holocentrus*, feed at night on invertebrates found on the bottom. The mouth equipment suitable to this task is a long, pointed snout and a mouth that faces forward. The *Myripristis*, by contrast, is a deep-bodied fish whose upturned mouth gives it a bulldog appearance. Its eyes are also larger than those of the species of *Holocentrus*, and well up on the top of the head. It is not easy for the *Myripristis* to feed on plankton at night because it is not easy to see it. This is not a problem for sponges, basket starfish, feather starfish, tube anemones, corals, and other animals that simply filter-feed at night just as they do in the daytime. But for a predator that has elected to grab nocturnal plankton one by one, some fine adaptations are called for. Apparently, what the species of *Myripristis* do is to peer upward toward the surface, which is faintly brighter than the surrounding ocean by virtue of incoming starlight. A moon, of course, helps immeasurably. As a choice bit of plankton swims above the waiting fish, it is dimly silhouetted against the surface, allowing the fish to see it with the large eyes and strike directly upward with the underslung mouth.

On several of the coral clumps I saw a very strange little starfish. It was a tiny thing only about an inch or so across the arms, one of which was much enlarged beyond the others. Jo found them also, and surmised that the first one she saw was a mutant, or perhaps an animal that had been injured. But then there were more, all with the one long arm, so it seems to be the normal arrangement. When I showed mine to Jo, she pulled back the sleeve of her wet suit and revealed another that she had tucked away. We didn't see any of the crown-of-thorns starfish tonight, which was surprising. A friend of mine told me that last winter he saw about a hundred of them alongside the concrete ship. There's a good deal of coral around that may have been devoured during the population buildup of these creatures, but what happened to them is a mystery. Perhaps a predator got to them, or perhaps it was just a spawning aggregation that later dispersed in the normal course of events.

The most interesting things we saw tonight were a series of deep-water myctophids that darted about in the blackness, bumping into us and our headlamps. The myctophids, or lanternfishes, are probably the most abundant kinds of fish in the sea, with the possible exception of the herrings. They are fishes of midwater, and they spend their days at depths of 1,000 or even several thousand feet. At night they rise above this— some even come all the way to the surface—in pursuit of the plankton they feed on. Like many deep-sea fishes, they are black and bear a series of light organs along the side. In the dark, they look like miniature ocean liners bearing lighted portholes. They are easily attracted at night by a light in the ocean, but here inside the lagoon it is surprising to see them. The concrete ship is about a mile from the edge of the atoll, which means that these myctophids are coming all the way in on the ocean current to feed in the lagoon—presumably to return to the deep ocean before dawn, since I can't imagine them staying in the lagoon into the daylight hours. The maximum depth of the lagoon is only about 200 feet, and I've never heard of these creatures hanging about in such shallows.

The myctophids have deciduous scales—that is, the scales come off at the slightest contact. As they darted about tonight in the dark, we would see clouds of bright silvery scales bloom suddenly whenever a fish hit a light or bit of coral. This silvery effect is all the more remarkable because it comes from a black fish. The trick is that beneath the pigmented layer of epidermis is another layer of highly reflective material that is as shiny as chrome plating. When the scales are knocked loose, this plating catches light with a startling visual explosion.

Jo spent a lot of time with her lights turned off, and she saw a small fish doing some parasite cleaning. She couldn't identify it in the dark, but the observation is most interesting: no species of reef fish is known to clean at night. The one she saw is not the daytime cleaner, *Labroides*, but something else. She also saw a fish that had two glowing areas on its body and that looked like a squirrelfish. After all the years I've spent diving I sometimes feel as though I've just begun to know the creatures that live around coral reefs. And the reef is doubly mysterious at night, when creatures that are familiar in the daytime may change their behavior and even their patterns and colors, so that you must learn to know them all over again.

Later that night, back in the *El Territo*, when I was reciting the day's events to the tape recorder, the "clicks" of snapping shrimps came clearly through the steel hull. It sounded as though someone were frying bacon.

A FEW weeks later we invited three biologists who were visiting the laboratory to make a night dive with us. They were doing some work on squirrelfishes, but they had never had a chance to see the animals feeding at night, which is when they make most of their noises and exhibit most of their interesting behavior. The biologists were very pleased at the chance, and we all went down after dark.

The wind this evening was from the southeast for a change, so the boat was above different patch reefs from the usual. They are really smaller than patch reefs—just coral mounds about 8 feet high and 18 feet in diameter. One of them was right beneath the boat, and as we came to it, there were a number of squirrelfish feeding, so the biologists were quickly in touch with what they wanted to see.

The silty sand bottom made it difficult to photograph, because every time we settled down great clouds of silt would billow out beneath us and blot out the view. A number of small snappers, as well as feeding cardinalfish, were prowling over the sand. I moved over to an adjacent patch of coral and spotted a large crown-of-thorns starfish feeding on coral. I reached down to flick on the floodlight and got nothing, so I had to go back up to the surface; as I suspected, the plug on the boat had come out of the socket, and I had to put it back in and go all the way back down. The starfish was still busily feeding, so I turned on the light and shot 50 feet or so of this grazing episode. I tried to pull it loose by carefully grasping the tip of one of the arms, but these starfishes are very soft-bodied, and the tip of the arm pulled right off. I tried another arm, with the same result, and finally gave up and moved around to the other side of the coral head. The squirrelfish people came over and saw one of their squirrelfish and managed to scoop it up in a hand net. While they transferred it to a plastic bag, I moved back to where I had had the tug-of-war with the starfish (I only wanted to move it) and saw that it had moved of its own accord out of the coral depression. I got the shot I wanted without having to argue anymore with the beast; as it left the depression, it left behind a large white patch on the piece of coral where it had been feeding. This patch, the scar of eaten coral, stood out clearly and made some dramatic footage of what the starfish can do.

When I moved back to the first coral patch beneath the boat, I found that Jo was having trouble with the small movie light. It was growing dim for lack of juice, so I took the big 650-watt light off my camera and transferred it to hers. She turned it on, and since she was shooting close-ups, she had more than enough light. She quickly finished the roll on her camera, and we swam up to the surface just as the rest of the people arrived. It turned out the power cord on the light had fouled on the coral, so I had to go back down. I dived, and freed it, and when Jerry Condit had pulled it out of the way, I pulled off my light and gazed into the darkness beneath the boat. I could see the shadow of the hull above and the dim outlines of scattered coral patches. It is an eerie sensation to float suspended in almost complete blackness. My only company was the half-seen shadows of fish moving in front of my face.

Adrift from my normal experiences, I pondered those of the creatures around me. They have lived with the same problems for the past 50 million years or more and have learned to cope well with their surroundings and their neighbors. With all the brilliant daytime colors and clouds of small schooling fishes gone, I seemed to be much closer to the essence of the reef and the reef community. The scene around me, invisible but at the moment dominant over my frail existence, seemed infinitely old. As I swam slowly up through clouds of silvery bubbles, I seemed to be suspended in time, a mere datum point in eternity. All the efforts of man— the now-distant bomb tests, the whole culture and history of the Enewetakese, whole civilizations—seemed to belong in that tiny moment with me. On either side of that moment, the ancient cycles and lives of the corals and fish around me seemed to extend in time forever.

When I reached the surface, I found that one of the two squirrelfish that had been collected was in difficulty. The fish had been brought to the surface rather rapidly, and their swim bladders had expanded. As a result, they were suffering what amounted to a mild case of the bends. One of them, unable to compensate for the extra volume of gas in its swim bladder, was swimming belly up, unable to right itself. The other was struggling to stay upright, swimming hard to stay underwater. It seemed that the second one would probably be able to resorb the gas and recover, but the upside-down fish probably wouldn't, without help. We got out a hypodermic syringe, slipped the needle into the bladder, and let out the excess gas. The fish was then able to right itself, and although it looked a little groggy, we agreed that it now stood a good chance of surviving.

Fish, like humans, have to obey the laws of pressure. Unfortunately, they are often forced against their will to break these laws. If a fish with a large swim bladder is brought to the surface from a considerable depth— several hundred feet, say—the swim bladder expands to such an extent that it everts the stomach out through the mouth and blows it up like a huge red balloon trailing along outside the animal. This will kill the poor creature unless it is relieved, and sometimes nothing can be done if the gas has expanded that much, although often it is possible to save it by letting the excess air out with a large syringe and pushing the stomach back into the fish through the mouth. The fish then swallows its stomach. This would seem extremely uncomfortable, but it may not be as bad as it sounds. A shark, for example, can voluntarily throw out its own stomach, swim around for a time tugging the stomach along with it, and then reswallow it. This happened frequently with the small lemon sharks I once tagged in the waters off Florida. Many times we would catch a shark, put it in the bait well, and then look in a little later to find that it was swimming around with its stomach trailing from its mouth. Sometime later we would look in again, and the stomach would be back inside where it belonged; the sharks never seemed to have suffered from the experience. In fact, this trick is probably a special adaptation that has become essential to a beast with such flamboyant feeding habits as the shark. As scavengers, they occasionally eat something that is too rotten or too bony for even a shark to digest. Stomach eversion is a good way to get rid of the offending meal and to wash out the stomach at the same time.

11

THE PEOPLE OF ENEWETAK

THE wind roughened during the next few days, bringing rain and gray skies, so that both the lagoon and the reef were stirred up and cloudy. We were unable to get good photographs, even though there was no problem swimming around the reef beneath the rolling waves; the colors seemed dull, there wasn't much light, and we had the uneasy feeling that whatever we did would have to be done again later. At the same time it was a bit of a relief to do nothing for a while. I spent long hours lying in my bunk, recharging my own batteries, listening to the rain rattle down on the steel deck above.

The weather reminded me very much of the same time of year in Florida. September is usually the month of the heaviest rain, as well as hurricanes. As a matter of fact, I heard on the radio yesterday that a hurricane had smashed into the eastern part of Honduras and then continued on into British Honduras, passing through the same area we were working a year ago. In the Pacific, hurricanes are called typhoons, although they both are grouped under the heading of cyclonic storms.

Hurricanes and typhoons—cyclones—form where they do for very good reasons: in simple terms, they are like energy-release valves between the tropics and the higher latitudes. If the entire world received the same amount of energy from the sun, there would probably be no cyclonic storms. As it is, however, the equator receives far more sunlight than the poles, and thus more energy. This is easy to understand by examination of a globe: incoming sunlight strikes the equatorial regions at more or less a right angle, while it barely skips over the surface of the polar regions.

"Sunlight" is really a complex mixture of energy and particles that we can define as electromagnetic radiation. This includes infrared light, visible light, ultraviolet light, X-rays, and other kinds of energy, including cosmic rays. When this energy strikes the earth, some of it reflects back into space and some of it is absorbed as heat, both in the atmosphere and in the ocean.

If we examine this situation in light of the cliché "Nature abhors a vacuum," we can guess what comes next. The poles don't get "enough" energy, and the tropics have to get rid of some of their "extra" energy. The energy transfer from tropics to poles takes place in two ways. One is by oceanic currents, such as the Gulf Stream and the Japan Current, which move warm water away from the equator. (Remember that both the Atlantic and Pacific oceans have major currents of this type in both hemispheres and that these currents are prevented from moving away from the equator at right angles by the Coriolis force, set up by the eastward rotation of the earth.)

The second way to transport energy away from the equator is by atmospheric means, chiefly cyclonic storms. The process of storm formation is still imperfectly understood, but the whirling motion of cyclones imitates the rotation of the earth. By loose definition, a cyclone may be any disturbance varying in size from a dust devil, waterspout, or tornado to a low-pressure system or a fully mature tropical cyclone. Cyclones are circular rotating storms ranging in diameter from 60 to well over 1,000 miles. Their winds blow at speeds of from 65 to more than 200 miles per hour, and a 20-inch rainfall during the passage of a single storm is not uncommon. The energy they carry is so great that we can attempt to estimate it only in terms of nuclear explosions.

In 1960 a memorable hurricane, Donna, struck the Florida Keys, passing directly over my parents' home. I was in Italy at the time and remember hearing a news report that a bad hurricane was headed for the Keys in the vicinity of Turk's Island. I was eating dinner in a small restaurant, and I recall thinking that right at that moment the Keys were probably being blown away. A few days later I got on a plane to fly back to the States. Lying on my seat was a Miami newspaper, carrying a front-page picture of a bridge near my house that had been completely washed out. I knew then that the damage must have been considerable. When I got back, I found that the eye of the storm had passed right through the area, leaving a brand-new scene for me. All the leaves had been stripped from the trees; the ground had been washed so clean that only the white coral rock was left, gleaming brightly. I needed sunglasses just to look around. The waves had been thrown across the island where my parents' home is, washing my grandfather's house away completely and half flooding my parents'.

Within a couple of weeks, however, surprising changes had begun. The leafless trees were showing new leaves (with the exception of the mangrove trees; when these trees lose their leaves, they die). Broken tree limbs had begun to sprout branchlets, and green buds were appearing throughout the wreckage.

The reason for the death of the mangroves is to be found in a peculiar specialization they have developed. Because the mangrove grows with its roots in salt water, it is dependent on its leaves to excrete salt. Without them, the tree can no longer get rid of the salt and it dies. Fortunately, the rising seawater during the storm covers and protects many of the smaller trees so that their leaves are saved. These trees survive and help repopulate the area.

As soon as the water calmed down, I went out to Alligator Reef to see what the effect of the storm had been on the sea life. The entire top of the reef had been scrubbed clean by the surging sand and rubble. Much of the coral had been ground away, and the rock was now largely a polished-looking white—an alien and chilling aspect that one might imagine on another planet.

Within a few weeks, however, just as the trees were sprouting new buds, the whole reef began to turn a pale tan-yellow as algae quickly took hold and masked the deathly whiteness. Surprisingly, the fish fauna seemed to be little affected, apparently having moved during the storm into deeper water, where they waited for it to pass. I saw all the usual species doing the usual things. To complete the resurgence, the coral itself, even though much of it had been broken as well as scoured, began to grow again very quickly. All in all, I was astonished at how fast the reef managed to heal itself and begin the process of rebuilding.

The hurricane did leave its mark in one way that could not be so rapidly reversed. Tremendous quantities of silt had been stirred up in the shallow waters of Florida Bay and deposited throughout the reef. On the shallower parts of the reef the waves and currents removed the silt fairly quickly, but in deeper water it simply settled and lay. I dived to 90 feet and to 150 feet, and the closer I got to the bottom, the closer the water came to resemble soup. In the last foot or so the water seemed to merge imperceptibly with the bottom in a heavy, almost colloidal mass of minute particles of carbonate rock that blanketed everything and, of course, killed much of the deep coral. It took four or five years for most of that silt to clear away. For the first several years of that period diving was just not the same. Every time we touched anything in the deep reef great clouds of silt would billow around us, making photography very difficult and the diving unpleasant.

In time the reef did recover and return to its old clean condition. This is to be expected in a world where storms are regular occurrences; all natural systems must be capable of regenerating if they are to survive more than a few decades. The coconut trees are one of the best examples. The trees in our yard were knocked flat by Hurricane Donna, but those that had not been uprooted entirely began to pick themselves up again within a year or two. This seems to be an impossible trick for a tree, which has no muscles. But apparently, by differential growth or some other phenomenon, a coconut tree can partly right itself after being blown over. Although the trunks were flat on the ground, enough of the roots on the downwind side were still attached to the soil to keep the plant alive, and gradually the trees lifted themselves several feet off the ground. Then, as growth continued, the growing part of the crown began to curve upward. Today they are still, although bent out of shape, growing upward.

Bad hurricanes and typhoons tend to occur once or twice a lifetime. Since I've grown up in the Keys, we've had many hurricanes pass over or near us, but only one really bad one. The previous hurricane that caused real destruction was in 1935, and no one knows when the next one will be. We are aware that many natural phenomena (droughts, ice ages, great storms, and so on) happen at more or less regular intervals, and we still do not know why. These periodic phenomena often limit the functioning of the rest of the natural world. A good example is the forests of the Keys or New England, where a great storm strikes on the average of once every fifty years. The size of the largest trees in both these regions is limited by this cycle, because every fifty years the largest trees are knocked over. The effects of this destruction are most evident when you visit an area that does not have big storms. Coconut trees are again a good example. In the Keys we never see a coconut tree more than 60 or 70 feet tall, whereas in places like Tahiti or the Seychelles, where typhoons almost never strike, coconut trees commonly exceed 100 feet in height.

I T was impossible to lie securely in my bunk amid the howling wind or, indeed, to do anything at all on Enewetak without thinking about life as it used to be for humans on the atoll. We were constantly reminded of the contrast between the rich assembly of life underwater and the poverty above, and a storm always served to heighten the contrast. While we ate food that had been frozen or preserved or tinned, transported by us in our elaborate ship or flown at great expense of energy across half the world, the native Enewetakese had to rely upon the few crops that could be grown on land and the many, but elusive, creatures that dwell in the sea.

Until the advent of the white man in the Marshall Islands, the Enewetakese maintained a precarious existence through their own ingenuity, self-reliance, and toughness. These qualities allowed them to meet the challenge of the atoll environment, which is highly restrictive in comparison to that of the high volcanic islands of the Pacific, such as Fiji, Samoa, and the Hawaiian Islands. Most anthropologists agree that the Enewetakese, like other peoples of Micronesia, are descended from hardy sailing pioneers who sailed eastward from Indonesia centuries ago. There are no good dates for the time of settlement; in the words of the people themselves, "We were there from the beginning." The Marshallese language is part of the large Malayo-Polynesian language family that extends through a huge expanse of largely empty territory, from Madagascar through Indonesia across Micronesia, Polynesia, and parts of Melanesia.

The people themselves are relatively short in stature and slender in build, with brown skin, brown eyes, broad, flat noses, straight to curly black hair on their heads and little on their bodies. Because of Enewetak Atoll's relatively isolated location, in the northwestern region of the western of the two island chains making up the Marshallese archipelago, the Enewetakese had little contact with other populations before the advent of the Europeans. Thus their language and culture grew separate from those of other Marshallese, and they thought of themselves as the unique "people of Enewetak" rather than as part of a larger civilization. Isolated in this way, on a pinpoint of land, with a tiny population of only several hundred, the Enewetakese must have felt a relationship to the physical universe unimaginable to anyone today.

As we would expect, their culture was adapted in specific ways to their ecological setting. They were skilled navigators (an art that has been lost with the advent of motorized vessels). They remain skilled builders of sailing canoes and must surely rank among the world's best fishermen. They have also shown themselves to be socially adaptable—a convenient attribute in the eyes of the various traders, missionaries, and colonial governments that have dominated the islands over the past century. They have been quick to adjust to diverse outsiders; with each adjustment, however, they have lost some of their own unique character. Today the controlling government, that of the United States, would clearly be most pleased if the Enewetakese would blend comfortably into American ways of life.

Like other Marshallese, the people of Enewetak exercised a traditional pattern of settlement and exploitation of natural resources. First, the people of an atoll resided on only one or a few of the largest islands rather than occupy the entire atoll. Secondly, the people were very mobile, dividing their efforts between nonintensive agriculture and various fishing and collecting patterns throughout the environment. They routinely visited every island of consequence, making copra and collecting coconuts, breadfruit, pandanus, arrowroot, and other vegetable foods when they were ripe, as well as clearing brush and planting when needed. In addition, they made special expeditions to catch fishes, shellfishes, and turtles and their eggs. Clearly, such persistent exploitation of the environment is necessary only because that environment yields so little. Without supplements from the outside world, this way of life can support only a small population.

Before the advent of the nuclear testing program, when the Enewetakese were carried off to the atoll of Ujelang, they lived as two separate communities—one each on the two largest islands of the atoll. One community lived on Enjebi Island, on the northern rim of the atoll (the top of the acorn), and the other lived on Enewetak Island, across the lagoon at the very bottom of the acorn. Although members of the two communities intermarried and cooperated in certain activities, each was very careful to retain its own identity. And though they were "the people of Enewetak" to everyone in the outside world, at home they belonged either to the driEnjebi—"the people of Enjebi Island"—or to the driEnewetak—"the people of Enewetak Island."

Not surprisingly, the sociopolitical structure of the two communities was identical. Each group was ruled by an iroij (chief), who handed his title down to his son. Although each chief had authority over one of the two domains into which the atoll was divided, they consulted each other on questions regarding the atoll as a whole and the atoll's relations with the outside world. For purposes of governance, the acorn was divided neatly in half, the Enewetak people controlling all the islands from Kidrenen and Ribewon counterclockwise to Runit, and the Enjebi people controlling the islands from Billae and Alembel counterclockwise to Biken.

This neat arrangement was disrupted with the advent of World War II and the invasion of the atoll by U.S. military forces. Enewetak and Enjebi islands themselves were devastated by fighting between American and Japanese forces, and all the people from both islands were resettled by the U.S. Navy in a crowded village on Aomon Island, smaller than either of the original settlements. Because Aomon was within the traditional domain of the Enewetak chief, the Enjebi people understandably felt uncomfortable and after a few months moved to adjacent Bijile Island, which was part of their territory. Nonetheless, the two communities, no longer separated by the broad lagoon, had effectively become one. This artificial resettlement pattern was perpetuated with the move to distant Ujelang Atoll, which has only one sizable island, Ujelang Island, where the entire population lived. The people carefully observed the existence of a dividing line down the middle of the compact central village, the Enjebi and Enewetak peoples occupying houses on their respective sides of the line. Gradually the groups divided the land on the island and later divided the lesser islands in the atoll.

After the move to Ujelang, American planners sought to move the Enewetakese into a more "democratic" way of living, drawing up a master plan by which each atoll population under American control would be ruled by an elected council of elders, headed by an elected magistrate. Early descriptions of this plan went largely unheeded, and during the initial years on Ujelang the traditional political structure of the Enewetakese remained as it had been, dividing line and all. But by the early 1960s signs of change were appearing. Both chiefs were old by then, and some of the younger men had attended American schools or had otherwise absorbed the flavor of American life. Some decisions about community life began to be made by majority vote. In the late 1960s the old Enjebi chief died; he was succeeded by his younger brother, who was also old and frequently ill. These events made possible a modification in the entire system of governance over the next few years, featuring the election of a magistrate and a council of twelve, six from each community, to govern the entire population. This occurred in 1968 and signaled the beginning of the end of the old division. A few years later the council was elected from the population as a whole, rather than half from each group, so that it has become truly representative.

Although the demise of the old system is a sad turn of events for the older residents, the conditions of life have changed. For better or worse, the Enewetakese have now been weaned on a cash economy, dependent for their food upon the money they earn from copra and other products. Many centuries ago, when there was no one to buy such products, their existence depended upon food gathering, and such food gathering, in turn, depended upon the division of territory on which to gather it. An equal division of the scarce land resources was of utmost concern to each community and family and individual, so that an equal opportunity to make a living was available to all. The Enewetakese, like other Marshallese, adopted the unit of the *wato*, a parcel of land commonly stretching across an island from lagoon beach to ocean reef and varying in size from about one to five acres. Food sources from all possible ecological zones, both terrestrial and marine, were thus equally available to all. Boundaries consisted of slashes on coconut trees or sometimes ornamental plants or large boulders.

These *watos* were usually divided evenly among all the children of two parents, so that a child received some land from both father and mother. As the child grew up, he worked the land with his parents until they died. The children, in turn, passed the land to their children. This system differed from most other Marshall Island communities, where land was inherited on a strictly matrilineal basis.

Although all the households on the atoll were located either on Enewetak or on Enjebi Island, usually upon the land of the husband of the family, every individual held the rights to land on islands away from the main settlements. Every piece of land in the atoll was held by someone, except for a single *wato* on Enewetak Island that was donated to the church—a conservative Protestant mission forming a central part of life.

Today the agricultural resources of Enewetak Atoll are practically nonexistent, the *watos* are barren of food-bearing plants. There are very few coconut trees that bear fruit, and no edible varieties of pandanus. The only surviving "crop" consists of a negligible amount of arrowroot. Before the war, the *watos* were thickly planted with the main vegetable crops— coconuts, pandanus, arrowroot, and breadfruit—and, to a lesser extent, bananas, squash, and papayas. Breadfruit, taros, and bananas were rare, but the people have learned to cultivate these plants on Ujelang and will probably bring them back to their native atoll. A number of terrestrial plants are also used as medicines, both internal and external. The best-known include the ubiquitous *Tournefortia,* the shrub *Scaevola frutescens,* and the leaves and shoots of coconut plants, pandanus, and bananas.

In contrast with this bland terrestrial menu, the seafood eaten by the Enewetakese is richly varied. It is a safe generalization to say that they eat everything that swims, crawls, or burrows beneath the sea, with a few exceptions: sea cucumbers, rays of all species, and pufferfishes, which are poisonous. The people are also on the lookout for the poorly understood phenomenon of fish poisoning (ciguatera), which occasionally affects species as diverse as red snapper, mullet, blue parrotfish, bass, pink parrotfish, and moray eel.

The heads of fish are considered delicacies, and the internal organs (heart, liver, brain) are also eaten. The intestines are not eaten, but the intestines of turtles, after being cleaned and washed, are considered a good meal; they are either baked or boiled. All kinds of shellfish are collected and eaten, and everything but the "black part" of clams is part of the diet. Other favorites include coconut crabs (other species of crab are used only for fish bait), all species of birds and sharks (which the Enewetakese learned to prepare from the Carolinians during the German occupation of Micronesia), and porpoises, which are considered a delicacy throughout the Marshall Islands. The Enewetakese have learned to capture these intelligent mammals by a method familiar enough to warrant its own name—*jubuki,* or the "surround" method. Whenever a porpoise or school of porpoises was spotted entering the lagoon, usually through the southwest passage between Biken and Kidrenen islands, the men would set out in their sailing canoes and herd the animals toward a beach. When they got close enough, some of the men would jump out and bang two stones together underwater, frightening the animals so that they would become disoriented and beach themselves. The people would also eat whales that became accidentally stranded.

In general, the Enewetak people prefer to eat their food fresh or sometimes preserved by sun drying, salting, or smoking. By contrast, the natives of the island of Truk like their meat slightly "high," as it begins to spoil. The Enewetakese have picked up some eating habits from the Trukese through contact while attending school on Ponape. Some of the Enewetak people now eat dogs, for example, as well as the intestines of pigs, after cleaning and washing them. They have also learned to eat the heads of pigs, which previously were discarded along with the intestines.

12

QUESTIONS
OF SHARK BEHAVIOR

AFTER a few days of a hard blow I was getting restless within the confines of the *El Territo* and was glad when the wind dropped slightly to moderate strength. We jumped at the chance to get out, and decided to take the submarine for a dive around the concrete ship off Jedrol Island, near Pole Pinnacle. There was a pretty good swell rolling in through the pass, so launching the sub was a little more tricky than usual. We do this with a crane, and when we pick up something as cumbersome as the skiff, we are maneuvering the equivalent of a 1,500- to 2,000-pound wrecking ball. As it dangles on the end of the cable, the slightest roll of the ship can send it into a motion impossible to stop. The submarine is only slightly more controllable than the skiff, weighing 1,200 or 1,400 pounds instead of 2,000, but Jerry and I are able to handle it fairly well by hanging onto each end.

We got it safely out over the side and dropped it in, and I jumped over after it. We had already placed our cameras and diving gear in the sub, so when Jo jumped in behind me, we flooded the ballast tanks and submerged as quickly as we could to get below the surface chop. As soon as we were under, we headed toward the edge of the bank on which the concrete ship rests. This bank is about 20 feet deep across the top and a quarter of a mile or so long, being roughly triangular in shape, with the apex of the triangle pointed toward the deep pass. There was a pretty stiff current running, and we cut across it at a diagonal. Unknown to us, Dick and Jerry had noticed as we submerged that one of the control cables on the rudder had come loose. But they had no way of warning us, so we blithely disappeared beneath the surface and cruised away. For the moment, the cable remained on the T bar that controls the rudder, because of a kink in the line.

We reached the edge of the bank in a couple of minutes and began our descent. The sides of the bank are steep, and we motored down this slope to a depth of 150 feet. I wanted to get up high enough to see the stern of the ship and actually pass under it. We did so and found the usual group of plankton feeders hovering out from the stern. I took several shots with the fish-eye lens of the still camera, and we went back down the slope. Just above the bottom the top canopy unsnapped and swung open. This happens periodically, so we were going to have to arrange a better catch to hold it down. Jo had some difficulty getting it latched again, and I stopped the sub to help her. We were slowly sinking, and just as I got it fastened, we touched bottom.

This presented a small problem. Because we were still on a slight incline, I couldn't plane upward from the bottom, so I started to back up. I went for a distance of 30 feet and then gave it a hard right rudder. That way I hoped to turn away from the slope, pick up speed, and begin flying forward again. When I gave it the hard right, however, the cables went limp, and I knew that something had come loose on the rudder. Again we stopped, and again we settled helplessly to the bottom.

By this time we were off the slope and down on level floor at 150 feet. I opened the canopy and took a couple of breaths off the submarine's regulator—I wasn't wearing any scuba gear—and swam back to the rear of the sub. There I discovered what had happened: the cable clamp had slipped, and the cable had come out of the T bar so that we had no rudder and no means of steering back to the surface. We could, of course, blow our ballast tanks and come up, but we would have no propulsion and the current would carry us away. Dick and Jerry could come to get us, but that would be a lot of trouble and would also disrupt the dive. I didn't want that to happen, so I swam back to the regulator, took a breath, and thought about it for a moment.

I went for another look at the cable to see if I could force it into the rudder. As I was trying that, I turned around and noticed a whitetip shark just on the other side of the sub, but it was moving away. As I was taking another breath, Jo tapped me on the shoulder and I looked in the other direction, and there was a gray reef shark, a small one about 4 feet in length. It, too, was moving away from us at a distance of 30 or 40 feet, so I went ahead and took a few more breaths off the regulator and flippered back to the end of the sub. I tried to tuck the end of the cable back into the clamp, but I couldn't do it. So I swam back to the regulator again for some more air and tried to figure out a way to loosen the screws in the clamp and refasten it. I didn't have anything I could use as a screwdriver. Then I remembered that I had a small piece of elastic that I had used with a small hook to help hold the canopy down, and I untied it and fastened the cable through the T bar, lashing it with the elastic so that it seized up firmly.

On one of my excursions back to the sub air regulator, Jo tapped me again and pointed above us, where there were four or five leopard rays cruising. She got out the camera to film them. They were some distance off, but to the eye they made a beautiful sight, sailing gracefully like a fleet of delta-winged aircraft against the blue sky above.

When I finally got the cable lashed, I got back in and closed the canopy. We started up and planed off the bottom for about 100 yards, when we came to the triangular point of the bank, which extends outward and downward at a very steep angle where the channel divides. The triangle is swept by strong currents that split at the apex, where there is a large number of fish hanging against the current to feed on the plankton. There were whole schools of plankton-feeding butterflyfish, a large number of unicorn surgeonfish, several species of snapper, and a large school of Moorish idols. Just as we rounded the point and started down the other side, we spotted a small gray reef shark about four feet long; it may have been the one that we had seen a few minutes before when I was working on the sub. We headed at it in the submarine, and when we were 40 or 50 feet away, it began the first portion of the display. It was swimming in awkward-looking S fashion, moving its head from side to side. As we came closer, the movement became more exaggerated until finally the shark was swimming fairly fast. We went along at a good rate also, both of us moving with the current, and we gained on it little by little. It began to arch its back and turn the pectoral fins downward—the second distinct portion of the display. It darted off to the side in an attempt to escape, but we turned and circled and kept right on top of it. As we pressed it hard, its movements became almost spasmodic: the back became severely arched, the head turned upward toward the sky, and the body assumed a down-facing attitude of about 45 degrees. The pectoral fins turned ever more sharply downward, wobbling back and forth, so that the fish was virtually disabled by its display.

Meanwhile, Jo had the side window open and the camera up and was filming the whole remarkable episode. We circled around and around the shark as the display continued, practically bumping into it, moving within two or three feet; its only response was to move slightly out of the way. The only explanation for this incapacitation that we could think of was that the shark was just small enough, and we were just large enough, that it was inhibited from attacking. Hence the display itself proceeded into a totally exaggerated phase without reaching its normal conclusion of aggression. From moment to moment I expected it to show some displacement behavior, such as rushing off to attack the bottom or attacking some nearby fish, thus releasing the aggression it apparently would have liked to release against us but could not because of our size. It continued to thrash about for some time, and we continued filming. Finally, I decided to see if I could collect the fish with the bang stick to look at its stomach and see what it had been feeding on. We circled around, and I poked the bang stick out the window, still steering the submarine with one hand. I managed one shot, but it was just a glancing blow, insufficient even to detonate the cartridge. By the time we got straightened around from that charge, we had lost it. We found the shark a short time later, but by then we were beginning to get low on air, and I wanted to see more of that side of the slope.

The water was flowing at two or three knots, and we went sailing down-current for a time, exploring, and then turned around to come back. The current was so strong, we discovered then, that we could move at only about one knot against it. By the time we had crept back to the apex of the triangle and taken some stills of the local fish, Jo signaled that she was running out of air. We immediately turned and started back up the slope and across the top of the bank to the *El Territo*. The current was so strong that I had to face up-current and hold the sub steady while Jo got out and swam to the stern platform. Then I ran the sub to the bow where the crane was, blew the ballasts, caught the cable, and snapped the clasp tight. We lifted the sub, and on deck I checked for a problem I had begun to sense; on the way back the motor had seemed to miss, as though there were a momentary break in the electrical circuit. I took a quick look around at the connections and noticed that when the two scuba tanks had been put in the back, they had shoved against the connection between the battery compartment and the motor compartment, pushing it to one side and breaking the watertight integrity. We had been running the sub with seawater in contact with the electrodes; as a result, one of the pins had been eaten off completely by electrolysis.

The sea had struck again. Let me regale you for a moment. This problem developed into a monster that took the rest of the afternoon to correct. To remove the waterproof connector and drill up the old pin, we had to take the connector out of the motor housing. In order to do that, we first had to remove the motor itself. And in order to do that, we had to remove the transmission, propeller, and rudder system. The transmission, or reduction gear, runs in an oil bath so that when we pulled that apart, we ended up with a large puddle of oil on deck, which we had to clean up. Then we had to take out a series of screws to get the transmission apart, then another series of screws to get the motor out. When the motor was out, we could finally unscrew the waterproof electrical connector, which unscrewing was followed by the real chore we had started out to do— drilling out the corroded pin, making a new one on the lathe, threading it in, and putting the whole affair back together.

That evening, I went over the vigorous display behavior of the little gray reef shark in my mind and found it not at all easy to understand. Various animals arch their back in display—the domestic cat is one of the most familiar examples. This arching, plus forcing the back hair to stand on end, supposedly makes the animal look larger and more fearsome. However, when a shark arches its back, the animal doesn't look any bigger—at least not to me—and I can't see the benefit of it. I can even imagine some dangerous disadvantages. There are some sharks, such as the bull shark, that feed on other sharks. If a large bull shark had come in while this shark was putting on its display, and the presence of the larger bull shark had served to exaggerate the display, as our submarine did, the reef shark would have been immobilized and unable to avoid an attack— easy pickings. Of course, it may be that in the case of a bull shark the reef shark would simply speed away. It may be that the display is offered only to other members of its own species, and perhaps other species that don't feed on sharks, and perhaps (now) submarines.

The display does not appear to be territorial. By this I mean that the shark does not seem to be defending geographic space. Instead, it behaves as though it were protecting a personal space, a living room, a sense of privacy. The shark begins its behavior irrespective of geographic location, so that it may serve to some extent to keep populations of this species dispersed, to avoid overcrowding.

We saw today an aspect of these sharks we had never noticed before. As the shark twisted and turned within a couple of feet of us, we were dazzled by beautiful iridescent colors flashing on its side. Many writers and divers have remarked upon the beauty of sharks—their streamlined forms, solid, muscular bodies, the ripple of muscles as they move, and so forth. But I've never found any mention of this iridescence. It seems to be a diffraction phenomenon, like the rainbow effects produced by the fine lines of a diffraction grating. It may be that the very fine tips of the teeth of the dermal denticles of sharkskin break up the light at various angles into its basic colors. As the shark turned, this would produce the rosy and greenish and other hues that we saw flashing in the sunlight. Close up, the chromatic display was strikingly beautiful, especially when combined with the shark's swimming virtuosity. The colors are not visible unless you are very close to them; it is possible they have not been mentioned simply because it is rare for a human to get that close to an excited shark—and live to describe it.

13

WHY I DO SCIENCE

I T is easy to list the disadvantages of working at such a remote location as Enewetak. Take just being there, for example. The next day I had to go ashore to call the University of Hawaii for permission to stay at the island past the regular closing date for the laboratory's summer session. Then there are the logistical problems. That day was "plane day," a nickname which just by itself tells you a good deal about our degree of contact with the mainstream. Our first two shipments of film, sent weeks before, still had not arrived—a miscarriage not at all easy to make right from here. Then there was food. Jo had ordered a list of supplies from distant Kwajalein Atoll, including frozen food, fresh vegetables, and various dry goods. I met the plane at noon to pick up the supplies and hurried back to the boat before the food could thaw in the heat. On the same plane a half-dozen laboratory visitors left; this reduced the population to three at the lab, plus two more camping out on an island where they were studying coconut crabs.

But there are advantages to working here that may outweigh the hardships. The most obvious is that it is one of the few places in the world where we could do what we are doing in relative comfort. More subtle, and perhaps more important, is the effect of near-isolation on your perspective. When bits of news arrive from the outside world, they arrive in isolated form, uncluttered by a whirl of events competing for your attention. I don't know how much of this is illusion, but it seems easier to think clearly about them at a distance.

Take the article in *National Geographic* that arrived today, about the so-called Tektite undersea habitat. The object of that program is to put some people on the bottom of the ocean in 50 feet or so of water so that they can study marine life—roughly the same goal as our own. The article described the Tektite 2 program, run in the Virgin Islands, and I found myself strongly disagreeing with the whole idea behind it. Supposedly it was justified on the basis of its technological inventiveness and the medical and psychological information gathered about humans living under, literally, pressure. The idea of Tektite is that divers work, sleep, and eat for several weeks in and around a spaceshiplike capsule on the bottom of the sea without ever decompressing. The air pressure inside Tektite is the same as ambient water pressure outside. The article made a great effort to dramatize the strain on scientists—both men and women—of living together in a hostile environment. This was much the same justification used by NASA for the manned space program, and it was no coincidence that NASA was a major sponsor of Tektite.

Technologically, however, the program offered nothing that Ed Link, the various Sealabs, Jacques-Yves Cousteau, and several English, Russian, and German groups have not already accomplished to varying degrees. All have experimented with air-supplied habitats in shallow water. Likewise, nothing new of a physiological nature emerged; there were no real problems, just as there had been none in previous programs. Psychologically, even the premise seems false. To an experienced diver— especially a diver who is also a marine biologist interested in the rich life around him—the shallow, clear, warm water of the tropics is anything but a hostile environment. I might even go so far as to say it is far more relaxing and benign than many of those to which we are exposed on land, particularly in large cities.

But the real argument about this program, in my mind, centers on money and how we divide our research funds. Tektite itself cost more than a million dollars, and the operation of the program cost several million dollars beyond that. Very little of scientific importance was achieved in relation to this vast expenditure. Nothing was done that could not have been done at a tiny fraction of the cost from an outboard skiff with scuba tanks. By way of illustration, in an adjacent bay of the same island Dr. John Randall of the University of Miami spent three years studying marine biology in that fashion and produced a stack of publications a foot high, many of them containing really basic information on the ecology and biology of marine animals.

Once you are inside such a habitat as Tektite, there is little advantage other than the fact that you don't have to leave. However, at a depth of 50 or so feet, where Tektite was sitting, a person can work six to eight hours a day without decompression or with only minimal decompression, depending upon the breathing mixture used. The Tektite aquanauts did not average any more working time than this and generally put in considerably less. For a small fraction of the money spent on Tektite, program managers could have bought and outfitted a small research vessel that could move from reef to reef, or even stay in one place as long as desired, and the same number of scientists could have spent the same amount of time underwater doing the same work. And there would have been a permanently available ship, instead of the Tektite habitat, which has to be brought up and expensively refurbished after each mission, involving the expense of ships to move it from place to place.

It seems that if enough money is spent on a program, it automatically becomes self-justifying. A friend of mine who participated in the Tektite program pointed out to me that for each five-man team, which stays on the bottom for twenty days, the cost is in the neighborhood of $250,000, not counting the initial cost of the equipment. For this sum, each man could have had a $50,000 grant for a year or more. Defenders of the program rebut this argument by saying that without it the money simply would not have been available to anyone.

And that, unfortunately, is the hard truth. If asked how he chooses his subjects of study a cynical scientist might answer that he simply goes for the available grant money. I am often asked what I study and why, and neither question is easy to answer. The second carries value judgments and is by far the more difficult. We scientists are surrounded by an infinity of ignorance, so that almost any subject is "suitable" for study. At a place like Enewetak, even the basic life history of virtually every species is unknown, not to mention anything of its physiology, behavior, embryology, locomotion, and so on. If a scientist's job is to investigate the unknowns of our physical universe, then the variety of jobs just for marine biologists at Enewetak alone is practically limitless.

You could argue that there are two kinds of scientists. The first are the professional, career-oriented scientists to whom any "problem" is adequate for study as long as it serves to move their career along. A problem is useful if it results in information that can be published—an accepted criterion for success in professional science. A reputation in the field of choice is established by the production of a sufficient number of good-quality publications, through which academic professorships and perhaps jobs in industry are won.

The second category includes scientists who are motivated less by the desire for professional rank than by curiosity. The world around us is at the same time familiar and mysterious. We know that grass grows, that fishes swim, and that coral builds reefs, but we do not know why. Examined in this light, the world presents an infinite number of challenges. If we are driven by curiosity to accept them, it matters a great deal which one we choose; in any one lifetime, we can hope only to push a little beyond the doorway of any one problem.

And here is where we must make philosophical or esthetic judgments. The practical value of any scientific study is often slight in relation to the whole subject of which it is a part. Of the things I am presently studying, only two have some immediate practical application. The first, the behavior of sharks, is of interest to me and other divers from the practical point of view of safety, since sharks constitute a constant potential hazard in the environment where I work. The second, the crown-of-thorns starfish, has been described as a predatory threat to whole coral reefs and therefore to the islands protected by such reefs.

However, these practical questions are tiny in relation to my broader motivation to spend whole days underwater peering at fishes. I must confess that I am only a little concerned with the utility of any information I may gather. I would expect that my work will produce some data and observations that can be published and that will be of interest to other people studying similar problems. But much more important to me than utility is an understanding of the world around us. If I can contribute toward the deepening of that understanding, both among professionals and among nature lovers, I will have done something truly worthwhile.

Esthetically, my impulse is straightforward. I am simply pleased by the products of nature, whether flowers or sunsets or mountains or reef fishes, and firmly believe that I work in one of the most pleasing environments on earth. The variety of color and pattern here on the reef at Enewetak, and on most other good reefs I have seen, is at the same time soothing and invigorating. So much the better if we learn to understand some of the functions of these colors and patterns.

However, my overall objective in studying the structure of the fish fauna of coral reefs (my overall interest, if that is not already apparent) was chosen largely on a philosophical basis. And here many of the practical goals go by the wayside. The findings in this line, such as they are describable, may not even be of importance in themselves—they may just lead to more questions. But that result in itself is a triumph; indeed, one could argue that there is no higher result. After all, what use is a result that ends with itself—that gives rise to no further study, that does not expand? Philosophic dead ends are the thing to be avoided. I try to seek problems that implicitly pose further problems or perhaps throw light on problems others are studying. If it is a particular aspect of the physiology, behavior, evolution, biochemistry, or genetics of a fish, for example, it should ultimately tell us more about ourselves, the distant cousins of fish. Our own natures have evolved from fishiness, changing slowly over eons and changing even now. Insights into the nature of past change tells us about the present; the nature of the present tells us about the future. We as individuals are connected in an eerie way to an unbroken chain of organic evolution extending back in time many millions of years. We came from our parents, who came from theirs, who came from the earliest humans, who came from the earliest mammals, and so on back through reptiles, fishes, invertebrates, and one-celled organisms, into the secret misty concoctions of primitive life.

Well, that's heavy, but we are very much a part of trying to answer these remote mysteries even with our work on fish at Enewetak. Each fish here is, after all, connected to the "great chain of being" described so eloquently by the late Joseph Wood Krutch. And each fish here evokes the basic questions that have taunted philosophers through the centuries: What am I, where did I come from, and what is the significance of my being? The more we can learn of our basic nature—a nature linked to that of fishes and reptiles and chrysanthemums—the more we can contribute to answering these questions.

A broad study of coral reef fish populations is not as remote from such questions as it may seem. Coral reefs can be considered without exaggeration one of the most complex products of evolution, providing us (me) with a perfect laboratory for studying the long-term esthetic results of specialized evolution. An investigation this broad is inevitably open-ended, pointing the way to other areas of research and perhaps even defining whole new areas of investigation. It also demands that the student deal with a great breadth of information, which I find a stimulating challenge. Every animal and plant that lives here must fit into the broad biological structure we know as the reef; conversely, every animal and plant tells us more about the nature of that structure. We learn about the whole from its parts and about the parts from the way they define the whole.

And this, with your indulgence, leads me to my own tentative and imperfect understanding of the nature of God. This recalls the questions of what am I and what is my significance. A way to approach these questions is to examine the nature of consciousness: how is it that I perceive what I perceive? Philosophers have never satisfactorily answered this question, and science hasn't really tried to. But science has recently begun to give us insights into the nature of the problem at least.

I have said that each one of us represents an unbroken chain of organic beings extending through geologic time to the immortal first cell (well, immortal so far anyway). This might be described as a biological continuum.

You may already see what I'm getting at. If there is a biological continuum, it is only fair to suppose there is a continuum of consciousness. Many of the major stages of evolution (cockroach, oyster, horseshoe crab, coelacanth, lungfish, spiny anteater, opossum, and so on) are still represented on earth, so that today we have at one point in time many, if not most, kinds of organized living matter, from simple viruses (barely living!) through one-celled plants all the way to the highest mammals.

Although the only consciousness we can truly know is our own—we cannot speak even for a spouse or offspring—I think we are ready to assume that other human beings are at least conscious on some similar level and that so were our immediate ancestors (that is, perceiving, apprehending, and using a degree of controlled thought or observation). We might also conclude safely that the ancestors of our ancestors had some degree of consciousness also. Granted this inference, we can see that there is no sharp dividing line between a beast that is conscious and one that isn't.

Nor is it clear where consciousness begins or leaves off in our own bodies. From our knowledge of neurophysiology, we know there is no particular spot in the body or in the brain that functions as our "consciousness center" and that, if removed, leaves us "consciousnessless." If we remove enough, certainly consciousness will cease to exist, but there is no particular cell or group of cells that embodies the thing. The changes we make in the body or the brain may alter consciousness, but they don't eliminate it; the total entity seems to be involved.

When we examine consciousness in terms of evolution, it seems to be an inherent property of matter—not something that has been superimposed upon it. But this property of consciousness can be brought out to a greater or lesser degree by the way that matter (water, oxygen, hemoglobin, sodium, protein, and so forth) is organized. And by changing the organization, we can change the consciousness. In fact, we don't even have to change the organization. Experiments during the space program, in which a human being is submerged in water of body temperature and deprived of normal sensations of vision, hearing, touch, temperature, and even gravity, have shown that the mind quickly begins to desert its habit of rational thought in preference for what we know as hallucinations or other nonrational imaginings. This desertion can occur in as brief a time as fifteen or twenty minutes. So consciousness seems to be a tenuous thing, dependent on the environment of the being as well as on the being itself.

We can even extend this consciousness if we wish. By turning on a transistor radio, we can become aware of events far beyond what we normally perceive. Or we can strap on a scuba tank and enter fishy realms that are not "normally" a part of human experience. We can send a television camera to Mars and bring the appearance of a foreign planet into our consciousness. Mars is joined to us in this way, made a part of our earthly existence. So perhaps consciousness is not only an inherent property of matter but also an inherent property of the organization of matter in the universe, brought into focus at various points we call individuals: you, me, a dog, a cockroach, a virus—all different levels of consciousness. But there is no indication that we can draw a line between the focal points that are conscious and those that are not.

What this ultimately leads to, it seems to me as I rock beside the pier at Enewetak, is a more sensible vision of God than that of the Old Man sitting on a golden throne. In my own vision, I and the cockroaches and the fishes and the corals are part of the universe in a way that binds us together. The information coming together in the halls and journals of science these years seems to me to indicate that consciousness is truly universal and that we as humans are part of this universal whole. This binding is not something that we can believe or disbelieve, we do not pledge our faith in this system; it simply is.

14

COLLECTING FISH

I HAVE mentioned how slight is our knowledge of coral reef fishes and of coral reef ecology in general. We have only begun, thanks to scuba, underwater photography, and other techniques, to gain access to the undersea environment and the creatures that inhabit it. And until we are well acquainted with those creatures, we cannot hope to understand the principles they live by.

One way to learn about marine animals is to watch and photograph them. These visual records tell us a good deal about color patterns, schooling behavior, approximate size, interspecies relationships, feeding habits, and the time of day they are active. But for other kinds of study—actual food eaten, reproduction, differences between and within populations, body chemistry and structure—there is no substitute for a "fish in the hand." Thus a certain amount of collecting is necessary, especially at this primitive stage in learning about coral reef fishes. At Enewetak, we also wanted to get some fishes to use as shark bait, since there had been a bit of a lull in our shark observations and we wanted to lure them in by means of their acute sense of smell.

So we started out the next day to do some collecting, for both purposes. Before we actually got to it, there were several delays and detours. We had been told of good numbers of sharks around an old tower going by the code name of Mack Tower or Photo Tower Mack, so we left the concrete ship after breakfast and headed northwest across the lagoon for about seven miles. The tower was there all right, about 70 feet tall, set on pilings in about 15 feet of water. Ten feet above the water was a wooden platform about 40 feet square with a tin shed on it. Above that rose a steel structure with a small tin house at the top.

On the way across the lagoon Jo decided to inflate the children's wading pool and put some fresh water in it; there would be no beach for them to play at today. Before she could do this, however, she had to rectify another one of Mikka's atrocities: the otter had used the wading pool for chewing practice the last time it was inflated, and several spots had to be patched and glued before it could be filled. While Jo was working on it, Mikka came out and crawled under her legs to get a good view. He loves to lie between Jo's feet when she's doing something like that; if she's kneeling down, he'll snuggle up underneath her the same way. Meanwhile, the children took off their clothes and had a splash party with the hose.

We tied up to the tower and shut down the engine. I took a camera and climbed up for a look around; after all, it was called a photo tower. The original means to the top was apparently a small elevator cage, but since there was no longer any electricity, I had to creep up an old ladder attached to the outside. The rungs of the ladder, like everything of metal, were badly rusted, so I had to test each one as I climbed. Most of the steel parts of the tower seemed to be only a few years from complete collapse.

I finally reached the top. There was a stunning view, much more striking for being in the middle of the lagoon, in an area where there was no other way to get this high for a look around. I could see the islands all the way around the atoll, starting from the southern end at Enewetak, along the chain to the north, up to the large island of Enjebi at the northern peak of the acorn, and then around to the few scattered islands of the northwestern and southwestern sides. To the east, the line of islands and the reef made a continuous white line on the horizon; the white sand beaches of the islands were linked by long lines of white breakers. On the western side, the leeward side of the atoll, there were no breakers. So all I could see were the islands themselves and, just on the horizon, little green smudges where the water was shallow.

If there are any sharks here, this will be an excellent place to work. You can climb the tower, attract the sharks by chumming with bait, and easily count the number for a good distance around. You could even see how quickly they come in and try attracting them with underwater sound emitters or bait fishes. The tower is set just at the high point of a patch reef, which extends nearly 100 feet in each direction. I didn't see any sharks, however, so I made my way back to the *El Territo* and prepared an explosive charge to use in the afternoon.

After lunch, we went out to the far side of the patch reef and dropped the charge over. As soon as it exploded, we put on our gear and went into the water. It had exploded on top of a mound of dead coral with algae growing on it, and the area affected by the bang was surprisingly small—only about 4 or 5 feet in diameter. There were no sharks anywhere to be seen, but there were *Caesio* floating stunned and dead for an area of 10 feet or so. There were also some jacks grabbing the damselfish that had been killed. I picked up a few of the damselfish and held them out, and the jacks came right in and ate from my hand. I moved gradually down the sloping bottom away from the affected area to see if any sharks were coming in. During the International Indian Ocean Expedition, where we used explosives to collect some of the larger reef fishes, sharks had come in to eat some of the individuals killed by the explosions. But although some of the men at the base at Enewetak said they used to catch as many as twenty or thirty sharks a day here, none appeared to be in the area.

I did look around a bit, however, because we hadn't been this far out in the lagoon before. There were some siganids, or rabbitfishes, so called because their mouth-and-head profile is distinctly rabbitlike. Two siganids of one species were swimming together; they were bright yellow, about a foot long, and had a black bar on the side of the head reaching the eye. There were also some small gray siganids in large numbers around the base of the tower. And I found a different species of *Caesio* here, with a yellow stripe instead of the blue stripe we were used to.

I moved on down the slope to a depth of 60 or 70 feet, filmed a few of the smaller fish around the coral, and then went back to the area where the dead fish were. Still no sign of sharks. I decided to take back some *Caesio* for Mikka to eat, so I picked up a sling spear and strung some of the dead fish on it by slipping the point through their gills and out the mouth. I loaded the five-foot shaft almost from one end to the other, picking up most of the fish; all were about six inches long. I swam to the boat and passed the spear up to Jerry, telling him I got them all with one shot; you just have to wait till they line up right, I said.

Then I went down again to examine the tower itself. Beneath it lay a tangle of wreckage, steel beams and girders at various angles. There weren't as many fish as I expected; in Florida there are large schools of barracudas and jacks seeking shelter under similar structures, such as lighthouses. But here the natural coral cover is apparently so abundant that the addition of this extra bit of artificial cover didn't seem to make much difference.

One interesting thing I did see was a large tangle of stainless steel cable about half an inch in diameter. It had been used to haul the elevator and now hung uselessly in a big loop and snarl. The cable was in perfect shape, but the portion below the waterline was festooned with coral growths, some of them as big as a fist. At one point where the loop of the cable crossed under a beam lying near the bottom, the cable seemed to have cut several inches into the solid beam. Apparently what had really happened was that the cable was gently rubbing the beam, owing to the moving water, continually erasing the rust that formed on the surface. As more rust formed, it too would be rubbed away, exposing fresh metal to the seawater. The cable and the ocean were working in concert to achieve what seemed like a trick. I've heard of similar situations caused by sea urchins on steel pilings. The urchins cling to one place, and by moving their spines, they sweep away the rust as fast as it comes, maintaining a fresh, clean metal surface. In a matter of six months these pilings are pocked with urchin-sized holes.

Our collecting effort wasn't much of a success in terms of attracting sharks; all we really got was some negative knowledge (that no sharks came in) and a supply of otter food. The collecting of fish by means of explosives or chemicals is often criticized by conservationists as indiscriminately destructive. Such wholesale slaughter is unwarranted, they say, for the sake of only a few specimens. Let me try to explain. It is true that used on a commercial scale, either explosives or poisons can drastically affect the environment. But for scientific collection our objective is usually to sample every living thing in a small area, and for this purpose both techniques can be well controlled.

In actual practice, a marine scientist like me will go into an area, look around, and see a certain number of species of fishes. But he knows there are many species he doesn't see, and he wants to find out what they are. He can fish for them with hook and line and may get a few of the large carnivores. Or he can set a trap for some of the smaller free-swimming species that are out feeding. Or he can drag a trawl through the area, and if it has a sandy or muddy bottom, he will get a number of fishes that are normally scattered, camouflaged, and not seen. None of these techniques really gives much idea of the total population, and the most careful visual survey leaves out many individuals and even whole species. But if the biologist can put out some poison, usually rotenone, he will probably find two to three times the number of species that can be seen by swimming around and five to ten times as many as he can get by all of the techniques mentioned above—with the possible exception of trawling the bottom, which is quite effective. Rotenone, made from the toxic derris plant, is used widely by ichthyologists because it is not toxic to corals or to higher animals, such as man. It is even possible to eat rotenone-killed fish, which I have done myself. This is common practice in many islands of the South Pacific, where natives used derris plant derivatives to catch fish. Likewise, rotenone normally poses no threat to birds that might eat rotenone-killed fish, or to sponges, crabs, shrimps, and other invertebrates, although a heavy enough dose will kill some of the crustaceans. The poison itself also has the advantage of breaking down rather rapidly in the environment, so that in a matter of a few hours, at most, it is no longer dangerous. And as it diffuses away from the affected area, it is diluted and does not affect fish down-current.

At Alligator Reef in Florida, where we collected with rotenone for ten years at the same spot, we found no measurable effect on the fauna. After a collection episode, fish moved in from surrounding areas within a few weeks. In fact, the larger fish come in within a matter of minutes; the smaller, less mobile species take longer. If rotenone has a fault, it is that the action is a bit slow. It spreads to form a cloud in the water, and many of the faster-moving fish—parrotfishes, jacks, groupers—have time to escape. While you get many species you have never seen, you miss some of the most common residents.

This is where a small explosive charge has its place. Properly used, an explosive affects only an area with a radius of 10 or 20 feet, bringing an instantaneous sample of the larger, hard-to-get midwater species. One case where explosives proved invaluable to us was in studying the life history of the gray snapper on the Florida reefs. This fish feeds at night, so that to study its feeding habits we had to take samples at dawn; during the day most of the stomachs are empty or contain unidentifiable remains. The other reason to sample at dawn was that the fish reassemble then from their feeding forays into tight schools. To kill some of them with rotenone would require a large amount of poison, which would kill many other creatures we had no desire to take. With an explosion we could set a delayed fuse and sink the explosive into the middle of the school. The school would open up as it entered from above and then close again—just as the charge went off. In this way we could discriminate, taking only the species we were after at a known point in time. In order to prove that the gray snapper is a nocturnal feeder, and to show its seasonal changes in feeding habits, as well as changes when the species moves from one area to another, we had to study about 1,000 stomachs, and we never could have done it without the explosive technique.

Using explosives to kill fish reminds me of some work I once did in

the southeastern part of Panama (Panama is geographically confusing because it runs east and west—not, as most of us think, north and south;
this was the corner on the Pacific side, facing South America). In 1961 I
was there on an expedition and saw that a number of the local inhabitants
have only one hand. Apparently what happens is that they use dynamite
to kill fish from their dugout canoes. This is illegal, but there is no one to
enforce the law in the jungle. So they go ahead and do it until a stick or
half a stick goes off in their hand, taking the hand and the lower portion of
the arm with it. At this point they decide to give up fishing, since they
can't afford to lose the other hand. Why the dynamite should go off in
their hands I don't know, unless they are using very short fuses for some
reason, but the fishermen seem to accept the risk of such an accident as
simply an occupational hazard.

At this atoll, one aspect of explosive work puzzles me. Normally, in
any area where explosives have been used for construction or other purposes the sharks quickly learn that explosions kill fish, and they become
conditioned to rush in as soon as they hear one. I was hoping that would
be the case here—there has been a lot of explosive work around Enewetak
Lagoon over the years—but it doesn't seem to be. We began to spear
some of the larger fishes and chop them up as bait for the sharks.

15

THE GHOSTS
OF EXPLOSIONS

MY mind kept returning to the nuclear program inflicted upon
Enewetak. The ghosts of explosions seem to hang over the islands, maintained by the faint radioactivity still present in some areas. We
motored down to Runit Island today, where the two big bomb craters are,
and tied to a buoy offshore. I went ashore just for an hour or so to take
some additional still pictures around the craters, walking the half mile
from the pier to the north end of the island. There is a dirt road leading
there, which the people from Scripps have been using for trucks, so it was
fairly smooth and clear of brush. About 75 feet from the edge of one of
the craters we discovered a large concrete bunker. It seemed to have been
buried completely by the blast and then uncovered by a bulldozer. It was
probably an instrument bunker to monitor the blast, and there was a small
door on the side about 3 feet square, made of heavy steel, that had been
designed to open outward. Nonetheless, the force of the blast had blown
it *inward*, past its ledges and sills, for a distance of 8 or 10 feet. There the
entrance tunnel, as in all these bunkers, makes a couple of right-angle
turns. The door hit the wall at the first of these turns, took a large chunk
out of the concrete, and lay crumpled on the floor where it fell.

By contrast, the outside of the bunker was in remarkably good condition. The surface of the concrete was not burned or chipped; in fact, the
marks of the wooden form molds could still be seen plainly, even though
it sat only 300 or 400 feet from ground zero. Some small bushes and
grasses covered the area, and about 300 feet from the edge of the crater
grew a palm tree that seemed to be in normal condition. I can't imagine

that it stood there during the blast; it must have sprouted since. But it doesn't appear to have been inhibited in growing in ground which I understand is quite radioactive.

THIS apparently scant effect of nuclear explosions on the life of an atoll was noted almost immediately after the first test explosions on Bikini Atoll, just 165 miles east of Enewetak. During the early months of the atomic age there arose a fear of radioactivity. This is understandable, in view of the fact that the second and third nuclear explosions in history (the first was the test shot at Alamogordo, New Mexico) were used to kill thousands of people in the Japanese cities of Hiroshima and Nagasaki, bringing the Second World War to an abrupt end. There flowed from these events a tremendous curiosity among both the military, who suddenly found themselves with an all-powerful but poorly understood weapon, and the public, who feared that this weapon might be dangerous to friend as well as foe. It was therefore judged desirable to detonate an atomic bomb in an area that was both too remote to harm humans and comfortable enough to monitor the finest details of the explosion and its effect on the surrounding environment.

The specifications of the planners called for a site within the control of the United States, uninhabited (or subject to evacuation without great hardship on the inhabitants), within 1,000 miles of a B-29 aircraft base (in expectation that one bomb would be delivered by air), free from storms and extreme cold, and having a protected anchorage at least 6 miles in diameter to hold a large fleet of target vessels as well as support vessels. The site also had to be remote from cities and to have predictably uniform winds from sea level to 60,000 feet and predictable water currents not adjacent to inhabited shorelines, shipping lanes, or fishing areas.

Sites in the Atlantic, the Caribbean, and the Pacific were studied, but quickly eliminated in favor of those in the Pacific. The planners easily found isolated dots of land set in great reaches of otherwise empty ocean, in the warm and stable climate of the trade wind zone. Bikini Atoll— 2,500 miles west-southwest of Honolulu, within reach of the military support facilities on Kwajalein Atoll to the southeast and Enewetak to the west and sheltering a tiny group of only 162 Marshallese—was the choice.

Bikini, discovered in 1825 by the German explorer Otto von Kotzebue, closely resembles Enewetak. It is an atoll roughly oval in shape, exhibiting many of the classic characteristics of atoll growth: strong reefs to windward, protected lee entrances, a lagoon about 190 feet at maximum depth, and a nearly continuous necklace of islands joined by stretches of sandy reef. The largest of the twenty-six islands is named Bikini Island, 2½ miles long and ½ mile wide, containing about 540 acres of dry land. The lagoon is 26 miles long, from east to west, and 15 miles wide. It covers 243 square miles, as compared with a total land area of 3.4 square miles. The highest point on the atoll was a dune that towered all of 23 feet above the reef flat.

Bikini escaped most of the violence of World War II, but the events of Operation Crossroads, as the bomb tests were called, were to make up for those years of peace. Operation Crossroads was a joint scientific-military operation of unprecedented size. In the spring and summer of 1946, as the operation began, Joint Task Force One took to the northern Marshalls no fewer than 250 naval vessels of various types. About 70 of the ships and smaller craft were anchored in the target area of the lagoon. In addition, there were more than 150 aircraft for transport, liaison, observation, and drone use and some 42,000 military, scientific, and technical personnel. Extensive oceanographic, biological, and geological surveys were carried out by thousands of scientists as a previously unheard-of atoll became the theater for a vast range of scientific studies.

Although the biological testing seems crude to us now, it was thorough for the time and provided the first rough evidence of the effects of radioactivity on living creatures. Animals taken to Bikini included 200 pigs, 60 guinea pigs, 204 goats, 5,000 rats, and 200 mice. More relevant to our own work here, a group known as the Applied Fisheries Division caught, both with rotenone and fishing lines, 1,926 fish to be used as controls to indicate the state of affairs before the two explosions. After the first test 1,819 more fish were taken; after the second test an additional 1,407 were caught, providing material for measuring radioactivity and for studying the effects of irradiation.

At about nine o'clock in the morning of July 1, 1946, Test Able began with the air drop of an atomic bomb from a B-29 aircraft named *Dave's Dream*. The bomb burst as planned at an altitude of 500 feet, though about 1,500 feet to the west of the battleship *Nevada*, the intended bull's-eye. The attack transports *Gilliam* and *Carlisle*, each about 450 feet in length, quickly sank—the *Gilliam* within one minute and the *Carlisle* about forty minutes later. The destroyers *Anderson* and *Lamson*, 338 and 344 feet respectively, also sank—the *Anderson* almost at once. The Japanese light cruiser *Sakawa* went under after burning for twenty-four hours. The hull of the aircraft carrier *Independence* was buckled and wrinkled, the remnants of her superstructure tangled, and the 600-foot flight deck broken in several places. Another carrier, two cruisers, and several destroyers were badly damaged; other ships escaped with only moderate damage. Surviving ships were hosed down to reduce their radio-activity, and radiological patrols scouted the target area. By two-thirty that afternoon the lagoon was declared safe for all ships, and by evening eighteen of the target ships had been boarded by teams recovering scientific instruments and test animals that had been placed throughout the target fleet. The questions in everyone's mind: how long would the effects of the explosion last, and how dangerous would they be?

Test Baker, a device exploded underwater rather than in the air, had a different scenario. On July 25 the bomb was suspended from a small landing craft to a depth of 90 feet—halfway to the lagoon floor. Elaborate arrangements had been made for measuring water pressure and wave height. Neal Hines (in *Proving Ground: An Account of the Radiobiological Studies in the Pacific, 1946–1961*, University of Washington Press, 1962) describes the explosion:

> The air burst of July 1, despite the damage it had inflicted, scarcely had prepared observers for the wrath of sound, light and volcanic shock that erupted within the lagoon. At the moment of explosion a giant bubble, brilliantly lighted within by incandescent materials, burst from the surface of the water to be followed by an "opaque cloud" which quickly covered about half of the ships of the target fleet. Within seconds the cloud had vanished and a hollow column 2,200 feet in diameter and containing some ten million tons of water rose from the surface of the lagoon to a height of more than a mile. The 26,000-ton battleship *Arkansas*, broadside to the LSM 60 but more than 500 feet away, was lifted and upended in the column before she was plunged to the bottom. At the base of the column was a tumult of foam several hundred feet high, and the descent of the water back into the lagoon set up a base surge from which rolled waves eighty to one hundred feet high. The waves subsided rapidly as they proceeded outward, and the highest wave recorded at Bikini Island, three miles away, was seven feet, not sufficiently high to pass over the island or to cause damage there.

Many of the remaining target ships were sunk, radioactivity in the lagoon waters was intense, and the target ships still afloat were drenched with radioactive substances as the tremendous pillar of water crashed down. After the first few days, however, the radioactivity in the water began to diminish. It began to appear, instead, among the living organisms of the area—a phenomenon that gave rise to the intense interest in radiobiology there (and on Enewetak) that persists to the present day. All kinds of algae were found to be highly radioactive, as were fish and other animals that fed directly on the algae. By mid-September the radioactivity within the waters of the lagoon had dropped to low levels. This drop was attributed to a combination of factors: dilution, radioactive decay, and, to an unexpected extent, uptake by organisms. Giant clams collected at the northeastern rim of the atoll, near Bikini Island, contained considerable radioactivity in digestive glands; clams at the western end had only trace amounts. Coral samples that had living polyps had taken in more radioactivity than samples from the same location where the corals had died. Fouling organisms on ships' hulls, such as barnacles, continuously built up activity as a result both of absorbing isotopes directly and of eating radioactive plankton.

Clearly these events called for more investigation. Because biologists had had little idea of what would happen, they were not surprised to find that radioactivity had spread to this variety of marine organisms. Similarly, they had no idea what the long-term effects would be. In the introduction to the published reports of the Bikini blasts it was written that "certain questions necessarily had to remain unanswered, either because post-test radiation made desired inspections hazardous, or because the questions were concerned with long-range effects. For example, the problems of how long and in what ways abnormal radioactivity affects the flora and fauna of a region could not be solved immediately." The introduction went on: "It is too soon to attempt an analysis of all of the implications of the Bikini tests. But it is not too soon to point to the necessity for immediate and intensive research into several unique problems posed by the atomic bomb. The poisoning of large volumes of water presents such a problem."

This problem seemed sufficiently grave that the Navy Department and the War Department agreed to conduct a Bikini Scientific Resurvey during the summer of 1947, just a year after Operation Crossroads. The resurvey was initially administered by the Armed Forces Special Weapons Project, then by the newly formed Atomic Energy Commission. The resurvey force totaled about 700 military personnel, crew members, and technicians and some 80 scientists trained in geology, biology, fisheries, radiobiology, radiochemistry-radiophysics, engineering, and aerology.

Most of these scientists came from the nation's top institutions and represented the best technical talent the country had to offer. The purposes of the mission included not only the collection of biological specimens but also the recovery of specific instruments from the target ships and the inspection of the structure of these ships, the retrieval of water and bottom samples and cores, and radiological studies of the lagoon, the surrounding islands, and all forms of life.

Even though the resurvey did not attract the kind of global attention of Operation Crossroads, members of the survey crew were acutely aware that the results of their work could be every bit as important as the detonation of the bombs themselves. In the memories of many of them was the image, reproduced in newspapers and magazines around the world, of that mile-high column of water that had erupted from the lagoon during Test Baker. Even those who were seeing the atoll for the first time could visualize that memorable column as it hung like a ghost in the mind's eye. Everyone on the resurvey expedition knew that what was found would provide a first, if tentative, answer to the question the world was already asking: would a nuclear war render the earth unfit for life? The discovery of high levels of widespread radioactivity would point toward a yes; the absence of dangerous quantities would soothe millions of anxious people.

The first findings seemed to be soothing. The day the resurvey crew landed and took the first measurements, the Navy issued a press release describing what they found:

Geiger counters indicated some radioactivity on the beach. However, CDR. E. S. Gilfillan, Jr., N.S.N.R., technical director for the project, said the amount recorded was not dangerous. Stronger amounts of radioactivity were noted on life rafts and other gear cast up on the beach. It is believed some of this material may have been blasted loose from ships of the target fleet last year. . . .

Ten days later the Navy information office put out more dispatches meant to calm a worried public:

One year later the scientists and military personnel now engaged in an intensive six week resurvey of Bikini Atoll can find few visible effects of that blast. Except for activities of the 700 man Bikini Scientific Resurvey Task Group, Bikini is the same placid palm ringed lagoon on which King Judah and his subjects sailed in outrigger canoes. . . .

Fish and other forms of marine life still inhabit Bikini's teeming tropical waters. On the island, coconut palms, pandanus, papayas, and other forms of vegetation threaten to obscure man-made installations left from last summer. . . .

Fears of catastrophic damage, at least, were allayed. But there persisted an uncertainty about long-range effects: perhaps the radioactivity was working some subtle genetic mischief that could be detected only by collecting thousands of organisms over a period of many years. The radiobiology group did its best to tackle this problem during the resurvey, establishing some fifty-five collecting stations throughout the atoll, where the scientists captured plankton in nets, bottom-dwelling organisms in dredges, large fish by hook and line, and hundreds of small, miscellaneous types of creatures by snatching them from tide pools and lagoonal coral heads and beaches. Altogether the group gathered 5,883 specimens, including snails, sea cucumbers, corals, birds, amphipods, lizards, insects, sea urchins, comb jellies, sponges, coconut crabs, and, of course, fishes. Many of the organisms were reduced to ash in a small furnace, and the ash measured for radioactivity; others were taken back to the United States for study. Overall, the data indicated a very wide and rapid distribution of radioactive substances among the creatures living in and around Bikini Lagoon. Most of the samples gave off low amounts of radioactivity, but very few gave off none.

Easily the most tangible effect of Tests Able and Baker was found in the mud beneath the site of the Baker blast. This lagoonal mud contained a good deal of radioactive matter. The average thickness of the contaminated layer was about 5 feet, the diameter of the coating was about 300 yards, and the total mass was estimated at about 500,000 tons. Yet the organisms that lived in and on top of the mud bottom seemed not to have been affected.

In the popular imagination, perhaps the greatest fear about the explosions on Bikini was that they would cause widespread genetic mutations, producing generations of freaks among plankton, hermit crabs, coconut palms, sharks—a menagerie of biological horrors. Yet no evidence could be found to justify these fears. In the words of the "Report of the Technical Director, Bikini Scientific Resurvey":

At Bikini more than 1,000 species of organisms have been exposed to radioactivity, and many have reproduced through at least one generation. A careful search of the area by competent biologists, including ichthyologists, botanists, invertebrate zoologists, and entomologists, in the course of which tens of thousands of specimens were examined, failed to reveal definite evidence of aberrant forms.

All in all, the scientists (particularly the biologists), who left Bikini after the six-week resurvey, felt they could breathe a little more easily. Neal Hines, in *Proving Ground*, offers this reassuring summary:

There was so much of Bikini without apparent disturbance, and so few instances of possible deviation from the expectable, that any questions tended to appear academic. Practically everywhere Bikini seemed too normal to be otherwise, and might, in fact, have been scarcely distinguishable from any neighboring atoll except for the presence of the shacks and towers on the principal islands and the litter of sun-scoured flotsam on the beaches. . . . Certain corals were discovered to be dying on the reef between Bikini and Aomon Islands, corals that had been known to be healthy shortly before Test Baker, yet it was not possible to determine whether these coral clumps had been injured by radioactivity, by oil from the ships of the target array, or—although improbably—by the fresh water of heavy rains during exceptionally low tides. Whitaker's studies of the sea urchins and other invertebrates led to the observation that the specimens examined in the shipboard laboratories—whether taken from places showing no more than normal background radiation or from the most radioactive of Bikini's reefs—were healthy, abundant, and reproducing normally without evidence of aberration or ill effect. One specimen of an unknown species of sea urchin, a specimen brought up by the Navy divers from the flight deck of the *Saratoga*, was by far the most radioactive invertebrate studied, a Geiger counter reading of its shell and exposed viscera producing a reading of twenty times background. This sea urchin, it was believed, had spent its whole life on the sunken vessel—one of the ships which after Test Baker had been described as a "radioactive stove"—yet dissection disclosed ovaries filled with full-sized eggs altogether usual in number and character.

WHILE the Bikini Scientific Resurvey was under way, the new Atomic Energy Commission was quickly coming to grips with the unique role it was about to play in the world: the development and improvement of nuclear weapons. Essential to this task were not only the money and manpower of a soon-to-be-great bureaucracy but also a place to test new bombs, or "devices," as the bureaucratic idiom would have it. It had become clear that Bikini was not suitable, lacking sufficient land area or a good site for a major airstrip. The AEC needed a long-range proving ground that was both accessible and yet remote from human population centers. By the summer of 1946 only five nuclear devices had been detonated: one at Alamogordo, New Mexico; two over Japan; and two at Bikini. There was much to learn not only about the performance of new devices but also about protecting people—and life in general—from both short- and long-term effects of radioactivity. On December 2, 1947, President Truman approved the selection of Enewetak as the new proving ground, and the 136 people living on the atoll were moved to Ujelang Atoll.

Preparations for nuclear tests on Enewetak began in December 1947, involving a civilian and military force that reached a peak of 9,800 persons. Three tests were planned for the following spring in a quasi-secret program known as Operation Sandstone. Unlike Operation Crossroads at Bikini, Sandstone was not displayed to the press or other members of the public; observers were limited to members of the Joint Congressional Committee and representatives of the AEC and of the military. The tests were to be done under conditions as close as possible to those in a laboratory, which involved laying almost a million feet of submarine cable to and from the hundreds of instruments that would monitor every aspect of the explosions. Each device was set on a 200-foot tower. The first went off on the island of Enjebi at 6:17 A.M., April 15; the second on Bijile at 6:09 A.M., May 1; and the third on Runit at 6:04 A.M., May 15. The largest explosion was the second test, which released an amount of energy equivalent to that of 49,000 tons of TNT.

No formal biological sampling was planned to accompany Operation Sandstone, but a small effort was made nonetheless by fisheries biologist Lauren Donaldson of the University of Washington. On May 16, the day after the detonation on Runit, Donaldson and a small group of volunteers spread rotenone along the reef at a point a mile and a quarter north of the test target. The collection point was chosen because it was outside the area of greatest fallout but still within the general fallout pattern. The fish and invertebrates killed by the rotenone were preserved in formalin solution, then in alcohol for return to Seattle.

The specimens were so few in number—there were 118 samples—

that Donaldson took them all home in his suitcase. However, this small amount of tissue samples was significant in showing just how fast radioactive particles found their way into the bodies of marine organisms a mile-and-a-quarter from the blast point. In the stomach of a black surgeonfish, for example, a fish that feeds only on algae, the radioactivity on May 22 was at a level of 55,980 counts per minute per gram of wet tissue (as measured by a sensitive radiation counter). A "normal" background count is around 40. A sample from the gut of a red-striped squirrelfish gave a count on May 23 of 32,542 per minute. An oyster gave a count of 14,004. Other samples of muscle, bone, liver, and skin also gave high counts, indicating a considerable degree of penetration by radioactive products.

At about this same time the members of the Bikini Scientific Resurvey were drawing up a report urging that the survey work be continued. "Biological studies," said the report of the University of Washington Fisheries Laboratory, "are of necessity long time, complex projects. The Bikini biological studies are so very complicated that only through *continuous* long time effort can we hope to understand the basic principles involved."

Bikini itself was of more immediate concern than Enewetak because its inhabitants were yearning to return to their home. The United States had originally told them that they would be on Rongerik, a nearby but much smaller atoll, only for the duration of Operation Crossroads. Now, after fifteen months, they were running short of food and short of patience. But the Navy decided too little was known about the biological effects of the radioactivity in the mud of the Bikini Lagoon and elsewhere. The people were therefore taken to the Marshallese island of Kili, which had ample room to grow crops but no lagoon for fishing. It was clearly a half-good solution. But would Bikini be even worse? No one could say for sure if the residual radiation was dangerous, and in this uncertainty Kili seemed the more prudent choice.

Out of this uncertainty grew the Bikini-Eniwetok Resurveys of 1948 and 1949. A small but carefully chosen band of specialists—including experts in zoology, botany, biostatistics, marine algology, fisheries, and radiology—reached Bikini on July 3, 1948. The survey group, numbering twelve scientists, took 187 specimens of fish and additional samples of sea cucumbers, slugs, clams, oysters, sponges, snails, sea urchins, and plankton. The plankton in particular were taking on increasing importance, because they were proving to be active transfer agents, ingesting radioactivity from one place and carrying it to others. This was especially important in the case of the still-hot mud at the bottom of Bikini Lagoon. Plankton were able to retrieve radioactivity from the mud and spread it to fish and other predators that ate the plankton. One peculiar circumstance was the discovery of slightly higher than average radioactivity in a part of the lagoon where little leftover activity was expected. Scientists calculated that the lagoonal waters should have been replaced by new water from the ocean eighteen times since Test Baker, sweeping out most of the radioactivity. The cleansing of the lagoon basin clearly was being retarded by the radioactive mud.

There was another bit of evidence of the longevity of radioactivity in the lagoon despite the flushing effect of the ocean. When the survey ship anchored in the lagoon, twelve eight-foot floats made of scrap wood were lowered into the water in and near the blast area; fourteen days later the floats were retrieved, and the organisms that had begun to accumulate there removed. These hydroids and algae had significant amounts of long-lived radioactivity, presumably brought from the bottom mud. Thus even newly introduced objects could be contaminated by residual radioactivity. Samples at every test station contained small amounts of radioactivity, as did living and dead land vegetation. It was clear that life at Bikini Atoll was proceeding in an environment that was no longer what it had been before the Age of the Bomb.

Much the same situation was found at Enewetak, where the survey group went next. Fish were found to have taken radioactivity into their stomachs; other kinds of organisms were also affected. Off the shore of Enjebi Island a group of scientists swimming with face masks could clearly see the area of kill, represented by dead clams and corals. Within this same area, however, algae were alive and growing. The lowest form of life seemed to be the toughest.

The resurvey was continued in 1949. The group began with two weeks' work on Bikini, moved to Enewetak for ten days, and went finally to Likiep for five days of sampling on an atoll that had not been exposed to radioactivity. Again, there was a good deal of detectable radioactivity, and yet life, for the most part, was unchanged. On Bikini, the ambient radioactivity was still being replenished by the "hot" mud at the bottom of the lagoon. Geiger counter readings on Likiep were around 21 per minute; land readings at Bikini were around 30 counts per minute, rising to 60 per minute in living vegetation and 120 in dead leaves and coconut husks. Most surprising were the dry leaf bases of the palms, which were producing counts of up to 8,000 per minute. Another interesting discovery was that large carnivores—barracudas, groupers, snappers, mackerels—taken with deep-sea gear far from the blast points had significantly radioactive livers. Presumably this came about because these fishes fed on smaller fishes coming out of the lagoon, but few people expected to find so much activity three years after the tests in animals at the end of the food chain.

On Enewetak, fifteen months after Operation Sandstone, the first cases of deformed plants were found. Some specimens of one species of grass on Enjebi had flattened, spiral, truncated stems. They appeared to be suffering from dieback, in which young stem tips turn yellow and a withering sickness moves through the mature leaves to the stems and roots. A botanist in the survey group concluded that seeds from this grass and another plant, *Portulaca oleracea*, had probably germinated successfully, but the seedlings were gradually being killed by the radioactivity in the soil. He also found bare patches that were presumably too hot for plants as far as a mile from the blast crater. Stem abnormalities, atrophies, cancerous tumors, and unusual leaf color were also found, but where tumors appeared, radioactivity in the tumor tissue was low. Also, some deformed palm trees with curling, spiraled fronds could not be traced to radioactivity.

What did appear clear was that the differences in radiation effects between Bikini and Enewetak were due to the different location of the bombs. The two Bikini bombs were triggered respectively above the lagoon and below the lagoon surface. At Enewetak all three shots were on towers located on islands. At Bikini the lagoon mud was affected most severely; at Enewetak the explosions produced bare terrestrial patches of wasteland.

B Y June 1952 the United States had detonated, both in Nevada and in the Pacific, thirty-two atomic devices of one sort or another. The Soviet Union had detonated three more, bringing the world total to thirty-five. At the time this testing was proceeding, the United States and other countries were wrestling with the scientific and moral problems of developing what was variously known as the fusion bomb, the superbomb, and the hydrogen bomb. It already had been shown that in theory such a bomb was possible, given an initial burst of energy great enough to fuse four atoms of hydrogen into one atom of helium. This burst could now be provided by an atomic bomb, and between 1945 and 1950 this possibility was discussed on many levels, both public and private. By 1952, with the Korean conflict under way, the pressures of military opinion and advances in nuclear technology had moved the AEC to schedule the first explosion of a hydrogen device. Operation Ivy, which included that explosion, was planned for Enewetak Atoll, which returned once again to the center of the nuclear stage.

Operation Ivy consisted of two shots—Test Mike on November 1 and Test King on November 16. Test Mike was a hydrogen bomb, and biologists would have only six days to assess the radiological effects before they had to clear the area for Test King. The Applied Fisheries Laboratory scientists picked seven sampling stations around the rim of the atoll for pre-test and post-test collections. Six of the seven were the same as stations used in the 1948–49 resurveys; the seventh was near Bokombako and Bokoluo islands, just two to three miles downwind from the site of the detonation, Elugelab Island.

Planners of the operation took the precaution of ordering a complete evacuation of the atoll, so that military, construction, and technical personnel all watched the explosion from a distance of 30 miles. Even so, the sight was awesome. When Test Mike was triggered at 7:15 A.M., the mushroom cloud was of a size and energy greater than any yet seen on earth, boiling upward into the stratosphere to an altitude of 130,000 feet in just fifteen minutes. In place of Elugelab Island was an irregular crater about a mile in length and 200 feet in depth, a nuclear excavation right to the basement rock of the atoll, as deep as the lagoon bottom. Although the crater was partially filled by the backfalling mud and sand, it can still be seen today between Bokinwotme and Bokaidrik islands on the northern rim of the atoll.

The ships bearing the Enewetak force stood offshore until the next morning, when the safety engineers declared the atoll safe for humans. By the afternoon of November 2 the biologists had begun to revisit the seven stations spread around the rim of the atoll. At first, on the southern rim, the collections seemed familiar, and the biologists could detect no changes. Then, working northwestward, they arrived at Biken Island and saw the first obvious biological effects of the blast. There, 14 miles from the Test Mike crater, the trees and brush facing the blast site had been burned and shriveled by the heat. Many of the birds were sick, and some were reluctant to fly.

At Runit Island the next day there was little vegetation to study, owing to previous bulldozing and clearing, but radioactivity levels were high. On the following morning, radiation at the station between Aomon and Bijile was still too intense to allow a landing, so the survey party went instead to Alembel and Lojwa to set rattraps and collect several shore-birds. The next day, the last one available, the party went all the way to Enjebi, where the sense of desolation was far more powerful. The rein-forced concrete building, constructed for the test, had been ruptured and shaken; no living animals and only the stumps of plants could be seen. The body of one bird was found. The party moved westward past the Mike crater, which was now about 90 feet deep, to Bokombako and Bo-koluo islands. The former, which had borne a heavy stand of coconut palms and a sizable population of birds, was now stripped clean of both plants and animals. Palm trees had been burned all the way to their roots. The situation at Bokoluo was similar. The radiologists had counted on making collections from among trees and the birds, but all they could do was to dose some fish with rotenone in the adjacent shallows and head back south preparatory to evacuation for Test King.

All the specimens were frozen and shipped back to Seattle for analy-sis. As the results began to come in, it became apparent that the radioac-tivity produced by a fusion bomb was far greater than that of a fission bomb. The post-test samples of plankton—foraminifera, snails, copepods, worms, eggs—contained 200 to 300 times as much radioactivity as the pre-test samples. The pattern of distribution, however, was hard to under-stand. The planktonic sample taken from Ikuren, the island farthest from the test site, was more radioactive (140,000 disintegrations per minute per gram) than the samples from Alembel (100,000 dmg) or Biken (71,000 dmg), both of which were closer to the blast. Among the four types of algae collected (five species of blue-green, fourteen species of green, three species of brown, and seven species of red) no one kind showed greater amounts of radioactivity than the others, and samples from all the islands near the blast seemed to have absorbed about the same amount. The aver-age count from all samples taken at Bokoluo was 5,200,000 dmg; at En-jebi 4,000,000; and at Aomon 3,600,000. But despite this heavy contamination all the plants appeared to be in good health.

A total of 237 fish specimens were taken at the seven stations, and the amount of radioactivity in them closely paralleled the distribution of radioactivity in the algae. The activity was greatest just downwind of the test site—at Bokoluo—as revealed by counts from muscle, bone, skin, and liver tissue. A surgeonfish taken at Enjebi before the blast had a radioac-tivity count of 30; a surgeonfish taken after the blast had a count of 110,-

000. Similarly, a pre-test blenny from Enjebi had a count of 850, while a post-test fish of the same species had a count of 340,000. All over the atoll, fish were taking in radioactivity as they fed on smaller creatures that had been exposed to fallout after the explosion.

An even more sobering discovery was that both birds and rats, neither of which live in the water, had ingested radioactivity varying in the same way as that in the algae and fish. This was surprising because the birds, especially, feed over a broad area which is not necessarily correlated with their "home." Nonetheless, the birds and rats that showed the highest amount of radioactivity were those either close to the test site or just downwind of it. Noddy terns and sooty terns had picked it up by plucking small fish from the ocean; shorebirds, like golden plovers and ruddy turnstones, by eating insects and small crustaceans along the waterline; and rats, by eating the seeds and fruits of plants. All these creatures had become radioactive within days, sometimes even hours, of Test Mike.

Such results as these created an impulse to expand and refine the biological investigations on Enewetak. By 1954 this impulse had produced a modest one-story building that was given the name Enewetak Marine Biological Laboratory. Although the building was small, its very existence indicated that the administrators of the nuclear program were finally convinced of the importance of biological studies. It had become apparent that the effects of irradiation and fallout could be understood only in the context of the living creatures that ingested and transported radioactivity. The nicest physical calculations of terrestrial and marine dispersal were meaningless unless they included movements of the animals and plants of the area. And it was obvious that these movements were poorly known.

In 1954 the Pacific proving ground was expanded again to include Bikini, where facilities for airplanes, ships, and men were constructed. The next series of tests, Operation Castle, caused the first human casualties of the nuclear test program, bringing even greater urgency to the task of understanding the behavior of fallout. The first Castle explosion, Test Bravo, was much more powerful than Test Mike of 1952 and at least 750 times more powerful than the atomic bombs of Operation Crossroads eight years previous. Bravo's mushroom cloud reached a height of 100,-000 feet, where an unexpected jet-stream wind carried much of it eastward over the inhabited atolls of Rongelap, Ailinginae, and Rongerik, as well as over a Japanese fishing vessel, the Fukuryu Maru No. 5. More than 200 Marshallese and 28 American military personnel were exposed to mild radiation on the islands; 23 Japanese, unaware that the snowlike ash that landed on their clothes and on the ship was highly radioactive, suffered much more severe effects. Although only one of the Japanese died, the illness of the other fishermen and the discovery of radioactivity in tuna and other fish touched off widespread panic in Japan and a strict inspection system for fish caught near Bikini. The Japanese people, for whom the memories of Hiroshima and Nagasaki were still fresh, experienced an epidemic of anti-Americanism and nuclear paranoia that did not subside for many months.

The Castle accident provoked interest in the behavior of radionuclides in the open ocean, and there followed several Japanese and American midocean surveys and several underwater nuclear tests, including one shot detonated at a depth of 2,000 feet off California. In 1958 a device was exploded 500 feet below the surface of the ocean just southwest of Enewetak. The spread of the nuclear by-products was traced by the USS *Rehoboth*, equipped with sensitive radiation monitors. That was the last year of testing on Enewetak. By then the public had become considerably alarmed over the prospect of strontium 90 fallout, which was eventually found to be contaminating even the milk of human mothers. Public pressure in response to this revelation led quickly to a suspension of atmospheric testing and, in 1963, to the test-ban treaty with Russia.

Enewetak's decade of nuclear testing had ended, with results almost as variable as nature itself. Investigations by biologists during that decade had raised more new questions than they had answered, but radioactivity was no longer the sinister stranger it had been when the tests began in 1948. There had been several practical discoveries that have since proved invaluable to biochemists. Radioactive isotopes, because they are easily identified, can be used to trace the movement of substances through an individual organism or through an ecosystem. It was also discovered that radionuclides can move "uphill" from water to land (as when a tern eats a fish that has ingested radioactivity) or "downhill" from land to water (as isotopes are leached or washed by rainwater). Scientists concluded that each release of radioactive products sets up a biological reaction that varies widely according to the special environment of the place.

They also were forced to conclude that some organisms seemed much more resistant to the effects of radiation than laboratory tests indicated. After Test Mike, for example, a small population of rats on nearby Enjebi was found, against all expectations, to have survived. Also, three years after the termination of tests on Enewetak, grasses and other vegetation had already returned to the once-barren and highly radioactive shot islands. As Neal Hines concludes:

> The Laboratory had developed a confidence during the years in the healing powers of the natural environment. Members of the field teams had examined the effects of nuclear blasts. They had seen islands swept clean, water churned, and the damage created by heat, pressure and radioactivity. Yet they failed to find in the natural environment evidence of gross population or morphological change definitely ascribable to the effects of residual radioactivity alone. They realized that changes probably did occur, but neither in the ocean nor on land were examples discovered, and nowhere that they had studied the long-term effects of radioactivity as a separate phenomenon was there evidence that normal regrowth was not occurring.

The resilience of terrestrial life forms seems especially remarkable on Enewetak, where the environment is bleak and life opportunities rare. Similarly, the rich underwater communities, where one might imagine all sorts of disruptions to be possible, seemed to be just as stable in their diversity as they are on atolls without any exposure to radioactivity. The general durability of natural systems on Enewetak and Bikini has done a great deal to assuage our fear of nuclear obliteration.

16

THE CHANNEL BETWEEN
JAPTAN AND MEDREN

THE next morning we left Mack Tower and headed southeast across the lagoon toward the deep eastern channel between Japtan and Medren. A moderate trade wind, which had built up the sea during the night, was blowing. I had noticed that the pier on the western side of Japtan Island had practically no surge, making it an appealing dock site. Once again it was calm there, so we tied up to explore the northern branch of the channel.

Before lunch I made a dive just under the boat and around the end of the pier on the sandy bottom where it slopes to the channel. (Jo's sinuses were bothering her, so she didn't come.) Around the end of the pier is a good deal of junk; one item in particular attracted me—a 55-gallon oil drum with one end cut out. This is good cover for fish, and when I looked inside, I found two beautiful lionfish. It was too dark inside to photograph them, so I resolved to come back later with a light.

Farther on I saw a pair of sea cucumbers that were about two feet long and five or six inches in diameter. Remember that these vacuum cleaners of the lagoon make their living by inching along the bottom and ingesting the surface layer of sand, along with its film of algae and detritus and small creatures, digesting the organic portion of this mixture and passing the clean sand on out the anus.

So far so good, but there's a catch to this peaceful way of life. This animal also breathes through its anus, for which it has an organ called the respiratory tree. It draws water in through this tree, extracts oxygen, and pumps the water back out. This "breathing" can be seen clearly as the anal opening pulses open and closed, open and closed. The catch is that there's a fish that has learned how to take advantage of this breathing system. Some species of pearlfish, of the family Carapidae, have adapted to life within the respiratory trees of sea cucumbers; some also live inside the body cavities of clams, sea urchins, tunicates, and starfishes. One species, at least, lives inside the pearl shell, where specimens have been found embedded in the shell wall—hence the name. Most are from six to eight inches long, and sufficiently transparent that it is possible to watch their internal organs in action. Pearlfish sometimes come out at night to prowl around, returning to the host during the day. I've observed in the West Indies that a pearlfish finds its way into the sea cucumber by finding the opening with its nose, then curling its tail around to insert it right next to the nose. The fish then straightens its body, forcing open the anus, and backs inside. There it does considerable damage by feeding on its host's internal organs.

I turned the sea cucumber over to see if it had any parasites on its underside. It is common to find a small snail—one of the few parasitic mollusks—clinging to sea cucumbers in a relationship that goes back millions of years. There was no snail, but there was a small, flattened polychaete worm about an inch and a half long and perhaps three-eighths of an inch wide. It is obviously adapted to hanging onto the underside of the sea cucumber; as soon as I rolled the sea cucumber over to photograph it, the worm flexed its body and rolled around toward the "new" underside. I had to hold it with one hand while I took some movie footage with the other.

After I finished the roll, I went back to the boat for a close-up lens and a light and returned to the lionfish in the drum. Many lionfishes, also called scorpionfishes, are highly venomous. The dorsal spines are shaped like a hypodermic needle and may be five or six inches long. The spines are hollow and bear poison glands at the base. If a diver bumps into one of the spines with enough force that it penetrates the skin, the pressure forcing the spine downward causes the poison to be injected with painful and sometimes even lethal results. And scorpionfishes are so cleverly camouflaged against the background that it is quite easy to touch or step on one without ever seeing it. Most of these animals have a zebra-stripe pattern of white and red or white and brown, with feathery flaps on the trailing edge of each spine. The pectoral fins are also enlarged, with the tip of the rays being free and expanding into a large winglike structure. Altogether, they are strikingly beautiful. They are also unafraid of larger creatures because of their toxicity; their unusual color patterns may serve to warn other marine animals away. They are so fearless that they will not move even on the close approach of a diver; it's up to the diver to avoid contact. In the Indian Ocean once, a scorpionfish came out of the reef and followed me like a puppy, swimming within a foot of my face mask and gazing into my eyes. I had to be careful not to swim into it as it hovered behind or above me while I was working.

The pair of lionfish in the drum held still as I turned on the movie flood and filmed them, even turning and posing in front of the camera. After five minutes one of them ventured outside, moving over to a coral head, so I quickly put on the daylight filter and followed it with the camera as it cruised about.

I went back to see if the second lionfish was still in the drum, and beside it I noticed a small goby that lives in holes on the bottom. This species wasn't living with a shrimp; apparently it makes its own burrow. It is often seen spitting out sand and appears to feed by taking a mouthful of bottom material, passing it through the gills, and filtering out the edible parts. This particular goby was hovering above a hole which happened to be the neck of a beer bottle buried in the sand. As I approached, it dived into the bottle in a bid for safety. I reached down and pulled the bottle out, and I had a goby in a beer bottle. It seemed to be disturbed when I brought it into the light, and darted around, stirring up the sand that was in the bottle. So I dug a hole and put the bottle back the way it was.

After lunch Dick and I made an excursion in the submarine across the channel to the bank off Jedrol Island. The channel between Japtan and Jedrol is only about 50 feet deep, and for the first half of the way we saw just sand bottom with occasional clumps of coral. But from the middle of the channel onward, the clumps became increasingly thick until finally it formed a jungle of platelike coral, a coral that grows from a central stalk to form a flattened disk as much as six feet in diameter. It looked like a forest of giant toadstools. I also saw two *Balistoides conspicillum*, the big-spotted triggerfish. This is one of the rarest triggerfishes, and also one of the most toxic if eaten. It is spectacular in color and design, wearing a basic chocolate brown broken by a greenish saddle, shocking white circles from the midline downward, and garish yellow lips.

About three-quarters of the way across I came upon a small reef whitetip shark, *Triaenodon obesus*, about 5 feet long, and turned the sub and chased him. As usual, he kept just out of reach, circling at a distance of 15 or 20 feet. I broke off the chase after a couple of minutes and moved toward Jedrol.

Even though Jedrol is in the lagoon, it is in the open middle of a deep channel, so that ocean waves come rolling in to break on its shores. As we got into 12 or 15 feet of water, we started surging back and forth with the rhythm of the large breakers above our heads, so I turned around and started on a course back toward the outer tip of Japtan. We were slightly farther out to sea on this diagonal, and the coral was, if anything, more profuse. About halfway back I spotted a gray reef shark and started after it. It, too, was about 5 feet long, but unlike the whitetip, it began to display when we were about 30 feet away. The shark swam in exaggerated fashion and then, as we closed in, began to arch its back, raise the head, and lower the pectoral fins. As we kept coming, it slowed almost to a stop and continued the display. We circled so close that we could easily have touched the shark with a stick 4 feet long.

While we were pestering the shark, trying to provoke an attack, we spotted the biggest *Cheilinus undulatus*—giant wrasse—we had yet seen. It came at us like a small bulldozer, lumbering slowly along through the coral. It appeared to weigh about 200 pounds. But our circling apparently frightened it, and it dived suddenly over the edge of a coral ridge and down a hole of some sort.

The shark, too, disappeared, and we motored across the channel to Japtan. We went around to the lee side, where the water was mysteriously muddy; we could only see 10 feet or so. But the cloud was small, and as we broke out of it on the far side, we discovered the cause—a large school of the tamest bonefish I've ever seen. The school consisted of at least 100 four- to five-pound bonefish which had undoubtedly been grubbing around on the bottom, stirring up mud. This fish is, of course, one of the most sought-after game fish in the world, and it is usually shy; I've never even seen one underwater before except on a hook and line. These individuals, however, were quite comfortable associating with us—so much so that I stopped and put on my scuba tank, picked up the camera, and spent some time with them, filming and milling about. The school would go into the muddy area, and I would go in with them; then they would come out into the clear water, all the while circling around me at a range of only 6 or 8 feet. They even waited for me to go back to the sub and get the still camera, which I then proceeded to use on them.

So much for the good news. When I was filming the bonefish, the camera had stopped at just over 380 feet on a 400-foot roll, so I knew I had a problem that had occurred before. This is the sort of breakdown that is the most maddening of all because it is the result of incompetent manufacture. I can accept a certain frequency of breakdowns on any mechanical equipment as a natural phenomenon. But human sloppiness is especially hard to accept. This particular camera uses daylight load spools rather than the cores that most professional cameras use. This means that we can load film in the boat in bright sunlight and that the cameras can operate as fast as 512 frames per second. Most film suppliers don't carry this type of spool, and they have to order it from Kodak. But when we were getting ready to leave, our film supplier, instead of ordering the right ones, decided to use spools he had on hand, winding them on himself. Unfortunately he made two errors. First, he taped the end of the piece of film to the spool with a piece of masking tape. This means that when you get to the end of every spool, there is a piece of masking tape that comes off with the film and goes into the film gate, jamming the mechanism. The pull-down plugs then proceed either to tear the film to shreds or to jam and blow a fuse in the drive mechanism. Secondly, the spools he used were old, and some of them were bent. This is the third time that film has begun to pile up on the outside edges of bent spools. In the first two cases the film ran right onto the end of the roll, so that when we pulled the camera apart, all the film was instantly exposed to daylight and ruined. In this case I knew what to expect and opened the camera in the dark of one of the heads amidships. I wound it all by hand back onto the spool, but it was torn in several places. We won't know how much, if any, of this roll is good for many weeks. Unfortunately the bent spools don't look any different from good spools since the difference is only a few thousandths of an inch. It seems that I shall have to test each take-up spool before I put it into the camera.

L AST night, after finishing my notes, I made a dive beneath the stern of the boat. Of course, I checked the 55-gallon drum to see if the lion-fish were home, and, as I expected, they were not. But there was a new tenant, a large pufferfish about 2½ feet long that would have weighed about 15 or 20 pounds. As I peered inside the drum at the puffer, I saw that a number of small, clear-bodied, glasslike shrimps were running about on his body. That was new to me, and I think to the scientific world at large. It seems to be an undescribed species of parasitic cleaning shrimp that operates after dark.

The shrimps were afraid of lights, so I couldn't photograph their ac-tivities. As soon as I put a light on them, they would leap from the body of the pufferfish. When I turned the light off, they would climb back on, and so forth, on and off. So I headed toward the surface to get a small net, passing a number of little cardinalfish with beautiful iridescent blue-green colors on the way. One of the lionfish was hovering around another drum, and on yet another rusted drum I saw a large colony of beautiful bright-yellow sea anemones that seemed to be fully expanded to catch plankton in the dark.

After I finished the roll of film, I swam back to the boat, left the camera, and got a fine-meshed hand net to catch some of the shrimps. We biologists have the unfortunate habit of collecting even the rarest of creatures if we think they are in some way exceptional. This habit has arisen out of our natural skepticism: we are loath to take someone's word on a question as fundamental as the discovery of a new species. Even motion-picture film won't do; often the differences between the known and the novel are so fine as to be resolvable only in terms of millimeters or fractions of a gram.

I made a swipe inside the drum and captured several of the glasslike shrimps, but left most of them inside. There seemed to be about twenty, and I took four or five to be preserved in formalin for examination by a shrimp expert.

The corner of my eye caught a small, shiny object on the bottom. It looked like a piece of tinfoil, but I had to rule that out since we don't throw our garbage overboard, and besides, I had an immediate suspicion that the thing was alive. If that was true, it was living dangerously. Any creature that stands out against its background, as this one did, has a better-than-average chance of being eaten. It turned out to be a young squirrelfish that had just come in from the ocean wearing its oceanic camouflage—blue back and silver belly. When seen from below, it blends with the sky; from above, it disappears within the blue of the water. This species of squirrelfish has a false pointed nose in front of the snout and a streamlined body. It discharges eggs in the open ocean, where they presumably drift for some time. They hatch in the sea as well, and as the larvae develop, they may continue to drift for hundreds or thousands of miles. When they reach a reef, which this one apparently had just done, they settle down at the bottom and overnight change their entire coloration, which this one was presumably about to do.

I scooped it up in the hand net, and by a black spot on the fin I guessed that it was *Holocentrus sammara*; but because none of the rest of the "normal" reef pattern was showing, it was too soon to tell. I brought it up in a gallon jar of seawater, along with the shrimps, and by the next morning it had transformed into a typically brown-striped, brown-bodied *Holocentrus sammara*—just as I thought it would. The speed and extent of this transformation are amazing—and also essential. Without it the life of this squirrelfish would be as short as it is amazing. A shiny fish against the varied background of a coral reef would stand out like a beacon to predators.

B EFORE leaving Japtan Island, Dick and I made an excursion in the submarine. I wanted to go across the channel again where we had seen the *Cheilinus* and the gray reef shark. We didn't see any sharks on the way over, but the expedition turned out to be an active one indeed. We reached the large area of plate coral, and I tried to set the sub down on the bottom so we could photograph. The bottom was so covered by these plates—five and six feet in diameter—that there was no open sand to set down in and, if we had landed, not enough space to take off again. So I picked a large plate of coral slightly higher than the others and tried to land, birdlike, on top of it. I thought that then we could take off easily as from a perch. But there was so much surge from the sea that the sub wouldn't stay on this perch, and I had to fire up again and leave. We finally found a spot of rubble bottom near the edge of the plate coral forest and set down there. I got out with the camera and photographed a large school of parrotfish. A reef whitetip shark glided by without paying us much attention. Meanwhile, the surge was raking the sub back and forth and working it toward the plate coral, so I had to go back and take off again.

We had gone only a short way into the middle of the channel when I spotted a whitetip. I went after it with the sub, but as usual, it started moving quickly away. I circled and saw a large *Cheilinus* and started to follow it. There was a fairly strong current flowing, as I could see by the bits of weed and debris drifting by, but I had no idea how strong until later. The water visibility was not exceptionally good—about 60 or 70 feet—and the *Cheilinus*, swimming with its pectoral fins and an occasional boost from the tail, was making about the same speed we were, or a little better. It kept out at the limit of visibility; I would almost lose it in the haze, then it would slow a bit, and I'd spot it again. I had chased the fish like this for several minutes over a distance of several hundred yards when out of the haze loomed a large mound of coral, 20 feet high and perhaps 40 feet in diameter. The *Cheilinus* slowed, and I started to gain on it. As I did, I saw it turn on its side and slither into a cavern within the coral mound.

We pulled the sub along the bottom right next to the cavern, and I jumped out with the bang stick to see if I could capture the fish. As I did, I realized how strong the current was. Even though I was partly in the lee of the coral mound, I could barely make headway against it, dragging myself hand over hand along the coral toward the cavern. When I reached the entrance, I saw a fairly large grouper of about 50 or 60 pounds, but it disappeared down a side channel. I shoved my head up inside where it was fairly dark and could see the *Cheilinus* lurking near the roof about 10 feet above me behind a clump of coral. Its head was hidden, but I had a clear shot of its middle, where I hit it with the bang stick. The fish didn't move. I turned around and called for Dick to bring over the second bang stick; I wasn't sure it was dead. It was possibly just shocked momentarily, and might recover shortly in a maelstrom of flying fins. Then clouds of blood began to boil out of the holes in the coral, and a small whitetip appeared and circled the area. So Dick came over with the second barrel, and I asked him to stand guard over me. I did this by slipping my mask down over my mouth and then putting the mask against his ear and shouting. I told him I didn't want a shark grabbing my legs from behind while I was trying to get at the fish in the cave.

To enter the cave, I had to remove several large chunks of rock in the entrance. Then I wriggled all the way inside and grabbed the fish by the tail. I maneuvered it down to the entrance, where I laid it out of the current. I signaled to Dick to get the camera because I wanted a picture of the grouper. He went back to the sub, which by this time was about 30 or 40 feet away; the current had been nudging it steadily along the bottom. Dick realized the sub was getting into the current and drifting rapidly, so he fired up the motor and circled back to the original place. He parked it and brought the camera over. We started to film, but he was having difficulty holding himself against the current, and the sub started to drift off again. We stopped for a moment, and I stuffed the fish in a crevice and went back to the submarine. I got in and circled to the lee side of the coral reef and parked where there was a convenient mound of sand. As I got out, the eddies behind the mound were so strong they sucked the submarine right against the coral in a small eddy where it couldn't move.

With the problem resolved, I got out and right away noticed a gray reef shark in the area, so it seemed we were beginning to attract more company with our bloody *Cheilinus*. Later Dick told me that when I had gone into the cave earlier, one of the whitetips had come in and showed a lot of interest in my kicking legs, but with Dick standing right there the shark stopped short of a taste test.

We got back to the wrasse and got some footage of me hauling it out of the cave and stuffing it into the submarine. It seemed to weigh about 100 pounds and was about 3½ feet long and 2 feet deep through the body. The scales were each about 4 inches in diameter. As we stuffed it into the sub, a very large jack came by—about 40 or 50 pounds. It might have been attracted by the blood. We hoisted the wrasse for a few still shots and then got back in the sub and headed across the channel to the *El Territo*. We had been out about an hour and were beginning to run low on air, so we went on in, hauling the fish up by a rope through the gills so as to avoid a slimy mess in the sub; also, I wanted it on the back platform of the ship, where I could dissect the stomach to see what it had been eating.

Jo and the children were on the beach right in front of the boat. They all swam over, and Varrina spotted the rope and tried to pull the fish in. It was floating because the swim bladder had expanded when we brought it up. Marissa touched it, but didn't like the slimy feeling. I got a knife out, sharpened it, and slit the fish's stomach open. This was not easy because the scales are so tough and large. They are firmly embedded and don't push out of the way as do the scales of most fish; I actually had to cut *through* these scales.

As soon as I got the stomach out, I could feel a large lump inside. I slit it open (much easier), and sure enough, there appeared the partly digested remains of a large crown-of-thorns starfish, our old friend *Acanthaster*. So it appears that this wrasse is a starfish predator and possibly an agent in controlling starfish populations. The fish is also interesting for reasons other than its great size, huge scales, and unusual diet. The dorsal and anal fins have a large bulbous ridge of flesh along the top like a railing—a large, smooth roll whose purpose I can't imagine. The lips are very thick and blubbery and tough. Apparently they just wrap around the spines of *Acanthaster* without pain to the fish. After the lips, the next stop for the starfish seems to be the stomach. There don't seem to be any conspicuous pharyngeal teeth for grinding, and the teeth in the jaws are large, blunt conical spikes unsuited for anything but grabbing. Judging from the shape of the starfish that we found in the gut, little, if any, chewing preceded swallowing. The fish, which appears greenish overall with many small, dark, wavy lines, is prized as a food fish in many areas. With the widespread use of modern spearfishing equipment, it is easy to understand how populations of this fish can be quickly reduced. The fish itself is an unwitting accomplice, being large and conspicuous and with the habit of holing up when chased. It is an easy mark. If a good many of the wrasses are killed off in an area, predation pressure on the starfish will be sharply diminished. A *Cheilinus* large enough to eat starfish is probably five or six years old or more, whereas starfish seem to reach adulthood in about two years. Thus, if the wrasses are killed off, the starfish can increase rapidly in number before the wrasses can repopulate—if they are allowed to repopulate. In the meantime, the unusual numbers of starfish might seriously damage the coral. The system would right itself, given time, but only if the wrasse population recovered. If this little scenario is realistic, it may become necessary to protect this wrasse throughout its range in the Pacific in order to protect coral from the ravages of *Acanthaster*.

While I was dissecting the *Cheilinus* on the stern platform, four or five small blacktip sharks showed up and circled the area, apparently attracted by the smell of blood. But when I hung the carcass in the water, they didn't seem much interested. As soon as we finished lunch, we cast off from the pier at Japtan and ran on up the inside of the reef to Enewetak Island. We first tried the dock, but there was a little too much surge there for the boat to lie comfortably, so we moved out to the mooring.

This evening, after packing up the week's exposed film and taking it ashore for mailing the next day, I talked with a couple of the graduate students at the laboratory. It's good to see a new generation of biologists coming along who are oriented to working with marine organisms directly in their environment. Originally marine science came into being in the northern temperate regions, where the water is cold most of the year, so that much of the work was done in museums and aquariums and on the decks of ships. The subjects under study were not observed directly in their environment, so that the science of marine biology was largely abstract, much like astronomy or seismology. Inferences were made remotely from small displaced samples or secondary evidence of some type. With the widespread use of scuba diving gear and the development of marine laboratories in the warm tropics, where conditions for diving are not only better but hard to resist, the way was opened to study marine animals firsthand in their natural environment, thereby expanding the potential for learning about their ecology, behavior, distribution, and so on.

As this change was taking place, however, the younger divers brought up on scuba encountered considerable resentment among established biologists, who for some reason felt themselves too old to learn this new trick. In many cases these senior people even discouraged diving, regarding it as frivolous or even unscientific. By thus discouraging their students, they perpetuated their own indirect techniques of studying marine animals.

Gradually the situation is changing. Many of the students who have come into the field over the last ten years came directly from skin diving. They are accustomed to working in the environment and have a good understanding, based upon personal observation, of how marine relationships are constructed. It is really gratifying to meet some of these people and learn how sharply their attitudes differ from those of many senior biologists. Personally I think this change is going to produce some rapid advances in our knowledge of marine biology over the next few years.

17

AT THE CONCRETE BARGE

STRONG northeast trade winds blew today from the northeast, and the whitecaps were illuminated by a bright sun. In the morning we moved in to the end of the pier and took on water. We have been taking on water here frequently since it is readily available. We carry about 4,000 gallons, about 2,500 of which are in the ballast tank. We normally pump the fresh water aft to our drinking-water tank as we burn up fuel. This trims the ship at the same time that it allows us to carry more fresh water than the drinking-water tank holds. But while we're at Enewetak, loaded with fuel that we're not burning, it's easier to fill up the potable-water tank than to keep changing the trim of the vessel. This tank is amidships, so that our trim doesn't change whether it's empty or full. It holds about 1,500 gallons, but since we use it to wash down the decks and hose off underwater equipment and fill the children's wading pool, much of which can be regarded as squander, this amount lasts us only about a week.

At the same time we fill the water tank we wash off the week's accumulation of dirt. It's amazing how fast the mess builds up, even at sea. Some of the grit comes from the exhaust stacks—fine bits of carbon that drift onto the deck and smear when you step on them. Then there's dried salt and bits of rope and chips of paint and crumbs of food. Mikka in particular helps this process along. He is expert at dragging fish into inaccessible nooks, eating them, and leaving a pile of scales and bones which the rain distributes over the decking. He also seizes cardboard boxes and other paper material whenever the chance arises and shreds these into their smallest possible subdivisions.

The plane came in today, and Dick Gushman flew out on it to Honolulu to take care of some business of his own. He may meet us later in Palau, which is where we go from Enewetak. After seeing him off and completing our chores at the pier, we moved back out to the mooring. On the way we threw over some garbage, and immediately three small blacktip sharks came up and circled it. These sharks are nearly ubiquitous here, but very shy. We haven't been able to approach them at all with the sub; they move quickly away.

In the afternoon, what was left of it, we went to the sunken barge for a dive. The trade winds had stirred the water in the lagoon, so the visibility was poor, but we were taking close-ups and watching some of the smaller fish, so it didn't make a lot of difference. I wanted to film the burrow-making activity of the snapping shrimp and the goby that lives with it, using a small light to bring out the colors, I hoped without disturbing the animals. They were shy about the illumination, and I went through about ten gobies that dived into their burrows before I found one that would hold still. Shortly after I began filming it, its partner-in-housekeeping, the shrimp, came out of the burrow and embarked on some chores, so I was able to get a nice series of takes as the shrimp worked and the goby rested nearby.

After I finished shooting the gobies, I moved over to the side of the sunken barge and explored the hull. It was about six feet high, and the deck supported quite a bit of coral growth. Just at eye level there was a very large patch of stinging coral, called Millepora. The patch, which was about six feet long and three feet high, consisted of innumerable vertical tines, brittle and about the size of a pencil, sticking up a foot or more from the thickly grown base. Stinging coral belongs to the class Hydrozoa, one of the three constituting the phylum Coelenterata—the group of organisms that includes jellyfishes, sea anemones, and corals. The stinging coral is not a true coral, like the reef coral, but it does have a stony skeleton. Instead of being pocked with the little grooves or depressions where the polyps of true corals live, the surface of stinging coral appears to be smooth. If you look at it under a microscope or even with a hand lens, however, you can see the minute pores which give rise to the name Millepora. Out of these pores rise little arms, or tentacles, which belong to the animal itself. The bulk of the animal rests within the stony skeleton, guarded by the tentacles, which can give a powerful sting when touched. If you brush against it with a section of tender skin, such as the inside of the arm, the result is a pain very much like a bee sting. I once sliced a piece of skin off my finger by accident and happened to bump a piece of stinging coral at that very spot. It stung so much that it ached even in my far-distant armpit. It seems that the neurotoxin discharged from the tentacle had affected the lymph glands, some of which are located under the arm. The pain lasted for an hour or so, giving much the same sensation as the sting of a Portuguese man-of-war, which also affects the nerves.

There are, not surprisingly, very few creatures that choose to eat this stinging coral, with the possible exception of some triggerfishes that must have a taste for Tabasco. But I did notice a small translucent fish about three-quarters of an inch long, with a dark stripe down the side, that seemed to be right at home on the stinging coral. As I searched around, I found many of these tiny fish, all perched right on the branches of the hydroids with the aid of their ventral fins. It appeared to be a goby with its two ventral fins united to form a sort of disk by which it can cling even to vertical surfaces. Most remarkable, the fish seemed to be sucking on the branches. I resolved to collect some of them the following day, as it may well be a new species.

That evening we went ashore for dinner and to pick up mail, and I spoke on the shortwave radio to our contacts in Los Angeles, who told us that most of our film had arrived and been processed with generally good results. I also talked with a friend from Honolulu, who has developed an explosive powerhead for killing sharks which is apparently very effective. He came down here to help close up the field lab for the season and to experiment with his powerhead. It seems to me, however, that he has missed the real problem in defending oneself against a shark. It is not that there is a lack of weapons to shoot and kill them; there are a good many cartridge-powered bang sticks that will do the job of killing a shark at point-blank range. The real problem is in seeing the beast in the first place. The usual routine of a shark in relation to a diver is to come in and circle at a moderate distance—6 to 12 feet—and then leave, curiosity apparently satisfied. The shark stays out of bang-stick range but does not become a real threat; this is the procedure in the great majority of shark-human encounters. In cases of actual attack, the pattern is usually different. The diver or swimmer sees the shark only momentarily, if at all, before it bites. A shark making an all-out attack can move so fast that there is little or no opportunity to bring any kind of underwater gun into play. The gray shark that attacked the submarine some weeks ago, for example, whirled, turned in a 20-foot arc, and closed from behind at such speed that there was scarcely time to move. A free-swimming diver probably could not even have turned around in the time available. The real value of a powerhead is probably psychological. At least you are not totally defenseless when you spot a curious shark, and you don't have to hang helplessly in the water, wondering if this is the rare shark that really does attack. You can take some comfort in being prepared, and you might even bluff the shark into fleeing.

The principal worry of any experienced diver who knows sharks is the one you never see—a big one, like a white or a bull shark that suddenly rushes in from a blind side and grabs you before you even suspect it's in the vicinity. And the diver has far more blind sides than sighted ones. With a face mask on, the field of view is limited to 60 or 70 degrees out of 360. This means that about five-sixths of your environment is out of sight, and you are just as vulnerable with a powerhead as you are without one. The most vulnerable diver of all is one who has speared a fish that is both bleeding and making loud underwater noises—both of which can attract sharks. As a shark rushes in toward these stimuli, it may or may not see the fish; the diver makes a larger target.

Big-game and commercial fishermen commonly see sharks attack the catch near their boats, and they have reported some really atrocious shark tricks. I myself have seen sharks come in after a fish on several occasions, and when the fish has been pulled away from them, they have attacked the propellers on fairly large fishing boats. After being struck by the screws, they come charging back in again. The first blow alone would be enough to kill any reasonable sort of animal, but not a shark. I've known them to attack the propeller of an outboard and shear the pin, just as the reef shark did earlier on the submarine. In that instance we'd been chasing the shark in shallow water when it turned, and we turned at the same instant, but it got inside our circle and managed to grab the spinning propeller.

I lived through another instance of ferocious shark behavior when I was about sixteen. I was out fishing with my friend Gary Bolger in Florida Bay and we managed to harpoon an enormous hammerhead shark that probably weighed 800 or 1,000 pounds. The harpoon was rigged to come off the socket and pay out a cable and then a nylon harpoon line with a float on the end. By watching the float, you can follow the path of the shark as it pulls away from you. The shark ran out the float line, and we followed along parallel to its course in water that was about 10 feet deep and glassy calm. The shark was running fairly fast and too deep for us to reach it, so we decided to try a lance which we had made by bolting an old

World War II bayonet onto the end of a pole. We figured that it would speed up and perhaps surface, whereupon we could get a shot at it with the high-powered rifle we carried. I was running the boat from the bow, and Gary threw the harpoon/lance. It struck the shark, which immediately whirled and snapped the lance. It then whirled again and charged the boat, knocking it right out from under Gary. At the same time Gary managed to fire the rifle, which he was holding in one hand. The gun went off as he fell through the air and landed squarely on top of the shark. Even that failed to stop the shark, which thrashed back and forth, striking Gary several times with its tail. But the fish was so single-minded about attacking the boat that it ignored Gary. I got the boat into reverse and backed toward him. He was swimming like mad, reached the stern in a few seconds, and fairly leaped over it into the boat. We pursued the shark, and after a struggle that lasted for five or six miles we finally got close enough to kill it with a pistol.

In another instance, my grandfather threw a harpoon at a bull shark and missed the mark completely. Nonetheless, the shark was infuriated, ran off a short distance, and came charging back toward us. As it closed with the launch, it jumped cleanly out of the water and hit the side, carving a hole about a foot long and four or five inches high through the seven-eighths-inch planking.

I could go on and on with such instances. All these, of course, are provoked attacks. But a spearfisherman who tries to slip a spear or knife into a shark, or kill one with a bang stick, could end up in a similar situation, inciting the shark to attack the nearest, largest object—the diver. When I was a boy, my grandfather warned me often to stay away from big sharks, telling me that if I kept after them, I was going to get hurt. I can still remember that as Gary Bolger went flying through the air, my first thought was about my grandfather and what he would say when I came back home alone.

THE next day was sunshiny with only a light breeze, and we celebrated by going ashore to pick up some fresh fruit, eggs, milk, and other supplies. I also fetched half a drum of rotenone preparation from the Enewetak lab.

After lunch we went out to the barge wreck again, a few hundred yards away from our mooring. I took the microphotography rig and the reflex movie camera to film the little goby that seems to live symbiotically on the fire, or stinging, coral. I went down, and the gobies were again scattered all over the spikes. Using a full end floodlight with the micro lens, I was surprised to find that they had brilliant red eyes and were quite a pretty little fish. To the naked eye they are pale drab with a dark brownish band down each side. They cling agilely to the branches of stinging coral, either on the underside, the side, or the top. If they are disturbed, they flip from one branch to another much like a warbler in a treetop. After considerable effort I managed to film about 100 feet of these little creatures; they are so tiny that I had great difficulty holding them in focus. One of the biggest photographic problems in the ocean is lack of weight. The slightest bit of current or surge moves you easily, like a strand of seaweed. Even breathing makes for movement, as does, to a lesser extent, heartbeat. We weight ourselves heavily to shoot these close-up pictures and hold our breath whenever possible, but there's not much that can be done about the heartbeat. The best solution is usually to wedge in tightly against a rock or other fixed object, where we tense all muscles to inhibit motion. Today, however, there was nothing to wedge against, so I had to make maximum use of the rare moments when both the fish and I came to a momentary pause in our ebbing and flowing.

After I finished shooting the gobies, I went up to the skiff to get the rotenone, the collecting nets, and the larger movie camera with the wide-angle lens. While I was waiting for Jo to finish a roll of film in her camera, I swam around and filmed whatever fish life I encountered. There was a large school of *Caesio* of yet another species. This one had several yellow lines down the side and black tips on the upper and lower lobes of the caudal fin. The black tips are about the same size as the pupil of the eye. Because these tips are usually moving as the fin moves, and the pupil of the eye doesn't move, the fin serves to attract the attention of a predator more often than the eye itself. At a short distance the body of the fish also blends nicely into the watery background, offering a seething mass of black spots when an entire school is moving past. This masks the true outlines of the fish themselves and serves as a very effective visual shield against predators.

The large *Cheilinus* we shot yesterday had been hanging from a line beneath the boat; by this morning the stomach had been eaten. When we got ready to go out diving, we found that most of the rest of the body had also been eaten, so we towed the head and upper portion of the body to the wreck in hopes of attracting a few sharks. We also wanted to get it away from the boat so that when we made a night dive, we wouldn't have to worry about feeding sharks any more than necessary.

I waited for a while to see if anything would come in to eat the carcass and then went back to the wreck, where Jo had finished her filming. We set out to collect some of the gobies with the rotenone, which we carried in an old plastic bleach bottle. Jo took the bottle out of the net, swam over to the clump of stinging coral, and squirted pale clouds of the toxin up through the coral and into the algae and other growth on the side of the barge just beneath the clump. As the cloud came up, enveloping the area, the small fish moved off to one side, avoiding the poison. We waited for it to take effect but gradually realized that something was wrong. Usually the smaller fish begin to kick their way spasmodically out of the cloud, or float out dead, after only a minute or two. This time nothing seemed to happen. It is common for rotenone preparations that have been exposed to the air to break down and lose their toxicity, and that appeared to be what had happened to this batch. We waited and waited, eventually killing only a few cardinalfish. But it stunned enough gobies that we were able to catch them with our hands, brushing them off the coral and scooping them up in our little nets. We got four or five of them this way. Jo was stung in several places by the coral, while I, who spent some time actually handling the corals, felt nothing. I can remember the first time when as a child I was stung by these creatures; it itched for days. Now a sting irritates for only a few minutes and doesn't even leave a red area. Apparently I've developed an immunity to the toxin. Jo also has considerable immunity, but today for some reason it let her down.

The rotenone we were using happens to be toxic to crustaceans, so we spent quite a bit of time prowling about with our face masks just a few inches above the bottom, picking up tiny crabs and shrimps. When we had finished, we went up to the *El Territo* and got out the microscope. There were half a dozen or more species, all of them exotic-looking creatures. One was tannish brown with bright blue stripes; another was medium brown with brick-red spots that had white edges. Another tiny shrimp was uniform tan with two hugely extended arms that were about three times as long as its body. There were two small mantis shrimps, which are not really shrimps, but part of a separate group of crustaceans having arms like a praying mantis that fold back and can be shot forward to catch prey. A large mantis shrimp (some species reach a foot or more in length) can drive its spines right through a one-inch piece of wood. But these were only small ones, and there was no danger in handling them.

THE next morning we went from Enewetak Island over to Japtan under a bright sun. We tied up at the pier, and Jo, Marissa, and Varrina went with me in the skiff back to the concrete ship. Although the wind was only light, there was a larger surge than when we were there before, and it was forcing air in and out of the holes in the deck plates of the ship at a great velocity. Jo put her hat over a hole and watched it sail 20 feet in the air. I poked around the ship, marveling at the durability of the concrete. It really is an amazing material for ship construction. In one place I found a room extending well below the waterline that was still perfectly tight and dry after fifteen or twenty years on the reef. Holes had been knocked in other parts of the hull, and the little bit of ironwork was rusted away, but the concrete itself was in extremely good shape. A properly constructed cement vessel would probably last indefinitely.

From the concrete ship we skiffed over to Jedrol Island, where Jo spent some time giving the children swimming lessons while I went up to the wooded section of the island to try for some more footage of fairy terns. As always, their snow-white feathers were extraordinarily beautiful against the pure blue sky, and as always, they hovered just a few feet over my head, making it very difficult to follow them in the viewfinder of my camera. The only really reliable way to get them in a picture is to squeeze the shutter release as you fall over backward into the sand. Eventually I managed to shoot about 150 feet of fairy terns, as well as a beautiful rock crab that lives along the rocky northern side of the key. Then we went back to the ship for lunch.

In the afternoon we got the sub out for an excursion. Jo's sinuses had flared up again, so Jerry Condit and I went down. As I started to flood the ballast tanks, pushing the control levers back to open the valves, one came back and the other didn't. The valve had stuck, and I couldn't free it with my hand. We were hanging sideways as a result, and Jo got a hammer and passed it down to me. I managed to swim around to tap the lever on the valve, and we were able to flood that side.

I planned to make a series of transects of the channel between Japtan and Jedrol, and where we first went across there were some rather large and strangely eroded rock formations of dead coral, resembling the badlands of the Dakotas. We went back and forth several times, then broke off to chase a large *Cheilinus* until it disappeared in a hole in the side of a patch reef. We couldn't stop there because there was too much coral growth to be able to start up again, so Jerry got out and looked for the wrasse. He couldn't find it (it had chosen a crevice too small for humans), so we continued across the channel. We saw a small whitetip shark and went after it. It went into a large overhanging coral clump but came right back out. Whitetips have a habit of sleeping in such caves, but apparently this one did not feel secure enough with us there. We chased another *Cheilinus*, also without success, and then saw in the distance a gray reef shark. We took off after it, and as we came within 30 or 40 feet, it started to swim in the exaggerated motion that is the first part of the display. As we approached closer, it began the back arching and head turning, and Jerry shot some footage of this display as we circled it. He tried shooting from the open cockpit of the sub, just leaving the canopy open, but his resistance against the water made it hard to steer. So we had to try to get close to it and then stop and shoot film, by which time it would usually move out of range and we'd take off after it again. This happened several times, and finally we lost it.

In the next moment, however, we witnessed a scene so striking that I can still visualize it. I looked up and saw a large school of white-tailed surgeonfish silhouetted against the surface. All were in silhouette from where I was, and there must have been 200 of them in formation at a diagonal to the horizontal. Crossing immediately in front of them was another large school, this one of *Caesio*, also in silhouette and positioned in just the opposite diagonal from the *Naso*. The sky was completely obscured by the warp and woof of this fishy tapestry; the light from above twinkled and flashed as it bounded and rebounded off the glistening scales.

After the schools had passed each other, I went into the cave once more in search of the *Cheilinus*, but it was nowhere to be seen. We got back in the sub and shortly spied another gray shark. This one was about 5 feet long, not a large one, and as we approached to a distance of 30 feet, it went into the slightly exaggerated swimming routine. As we drew even closer, the shark arched its back in no more than a mild display, but then, finding itself between us and a coral head, it suddenly ran around behind us, and I thought we were about to suffer another sheared propeller pin. Fortunately all the side windows and the canopy were closed; as I turned and looked back through the window, I could see the shark bearing in very fast from the right rear, right toward the back of Jerry's head. Jerry couldn't see it because he couldn't twist around that far where he was sitting. Fortunately his head was shielded by the backward-sloping rear window of the sub. The shark charged all the way in and hit the plexiglass just above Jerry's head and glanced off at a shallow angle.

I turned the sub around and started after the shark. Jerry had heard it hit, but I wasn't sure he realized what actually had happened; I wanted to show him the animal to be sure he didn't open any of the windows. As we turned toward the shark, I reached back with my hand and pulled down tight on the canopy to signal Jerry not to open any of the ports. He didn't. We closed in on the shark again, and this time it rose slightly and then charged directly at me as though realizing that I was the one responsible for this harassment. It moved very fast during the actual attack portion of what could have been a fatal *pas de deux*—probably more than 20 miles per hour. It hit the front windshield with great energy and with open mouth, the teeth leaving furrows in the plexiglass. We circled, and by the time we completed the turn the shark had moved up into midwater 20 or 30 feet above the bottom. I guided the submarine toward it again, and the shark whirled in our direction again and charged right at the front of the canopy from a slight angle to the right. Once more it hit the front windshield just below the top where it joins the canopy. After the collision I remembered the camera, and as we circled and came back one more time, I got several still shots of the shark as it arched its back in display. It continued this behavior for at least five or six attacks—I admit I lost count in the excitement—all of which were directed at us apparently rather than at any of the various solid parts of the submarine, including the propeller, which had attracted the attention of the first shark that attacked us. I felt highly uneasy during these moments, knowing as I did that the sight of an attacking shark is usually the last sight on earth for anyone who witnesses it. Although we were well protected by an invisible shield of transparent acrylic plastic, the repeated, deliberate, mute assaults by this fearless creature were unnerving.

Finally, after the half-dozen attacks, we lost sight of the shark in midwater. I circled several times in search of it, and as we failed to catch sight of the beast, I felt a confusing mixture of disappointment and relief. We were getting low on air, so we headed back across the channel in the direction of Jedrol Island.

There seems little question that the gray reef shark is quite a different animal from the other sharks that live around the reef. Though not great in size, the gray has by far the most aggressive spirit that I've encountered in a fish. Aggressive, that is, toward meddling humans. It is uniquely dangerous to even well-meaning skin divers and swimmers who do not suspect its hostile, mercurial behavior. It does not appear that many of the attacks of this species are motivated by hunger, but this may make it even more dangerous. An unaware diver might interpret the shark's reluctance to flee as the result of a calm disposition. Pressing on, the diver would find it easy to approach the seemingly relaxed shark, getting a close-up view of the display as it began. The display may be so intense as to immobilize the shark, perhaps encouraging the diver to move in even closer for a good look. Then, if the shark were in an attacking mood, as this one today had been, it would suddenly whirl into action with such speed and agility that the diver would be helpless. There is no time for self-defense.

Areas of the Pacific are quickly opening to tourism and skin diving (the remote atolls of Palau and Truk, for example, have suddenly become accessible to divers via Air Micronesia and offer underwater sights that are among the best in the world). More tourists will find themselves face to face with sharks underwater, and it is important that they know something of the habits of the gray reef shark. I would say that this shark does not normally constitute a hazard to divers—as long as it is not molested. If people learn to recognize the shark (not difficult) and its behavior (unmistakable), there should be few or no attacks on humans. But when divers are spearing fish or otherwise creating a disturbance that might draw it in, it is necessary to treat this animal with a special respect. It is an unsuitable target for gestures of bravura on the part of divers who pride themselves on fearlessness.

As we headed back across the channel, I sighted another *Cheilinus* and chased it briefly, only to lose the trail once again in a deep hole in a patch reef. I then realized that I was just about out of air and that Jerry had already run out and had been breathing from the submarine's supply. There was still enough for both of us, but I quickly started up the sub. I used the very last possible breath I could get from the regulator just as we approached the top. I spit out the mouthpiece and held my breath till we broke the surface, then gulped in some sweet air straight from the atmosphere.

OUR violent encounter with the gray reef shark set me to thinking about bang sticks again, so the next day I drilled a one-inch hole in the bow of the submarine so that I could fire an explosive device from inside the cockpit. My hope was that if we ran into another shark as aggressive as the previous day's, we could collect it after observing its display behavior. We still have almost no information on the feeding preferences of these sharks. We want to know what they eat in hopes of finding what, in addition to submarines, they will attack.

The reason for drilling the hole is that it is very difficult to hit a shark

with a bang stick held out a window. The sub has to be maneuvered precisely so that the shark passes just to one side; it is easier to aim the sub
straight ahead. Also, steering is clumsy with a window open. At the same
time I rigged one of the extreme wide-angle lenses to a camera, hoping to
get some pictures of an attack from inside the plexiglass canopy.

Jo's sinuses were plaguing her still, so Jerry and I again went out in
the sub, heading back toward the tall mounds of coral on the other side of
the channel where we had seen the sharks the day before. We chased another *Cheilinus* into a hole guarded by a moray eel that was large enough
to discourage me from following. I had rigged a long bang stick, which
protruded from the front of the sub about four feet. But alas, the whole
scheme came to naught when I noticed after chasing the wrasse that the
bang stick was no longer visible in front of the sub. I felt the handle beside
me in the sub and realized that the tube had been bent right around
backward. The tubular handle was collapsed from the bending, so I had to
break it off, leaving us with only a short bang stick and the experimental
device Rhett McNair, another biologist, had brought over from Hawaii.
We soon spotted two wrasses, and I opted to chase the larger across the
sandy bottom. It passed up a couple of small coral clumps, apparently
judging them unsuitable as hiding places, and then found an appropriate
hole in a third clump, disappearing from sight. I stopped, set the sub
down, and hopped out with the new powerhead device. I could barely get
my head and shoulders in the hole, and it was quite dark inside. A small
cloud of cardinalfish were also resting there, cutting visibility still further.
I put the bang stick in and waved it around to move the cardinalfish out of
the way, and then I could see the tail of the *Cheilinus* sticking out from a
right-angle bend in the cave.

As I extended my arm as far as it would go toward the fish and prepared to cock back on the powerhead device, I had some second thoughts.
I had never fired this particular powerhead, and a small, enclosed space
like this one was a poor place to experiment. The concussion could be potent enough to take me along with the wrasse. Some dozen years ago I was
experimenting with different powerhead devices, building guns with very
heavy steel barrels, special brass cartridge cases, and a large charge of
bull's-eye pistol powder. Such a load—30 or 40 grains instead of the normal 4 or so—would have blown even a magnum pistol apart, but our barrels were heavy enough to take it. One bang stick in particular used
strictly blanks, killing by concussion alone. We were using it to collect
small fish, simply pointing the stick at them and detonating the charge

about a foot away. This would knock the fish out so that we could collect specimens that were undamaged.

Unfortunately, the device was capricious and hypersensitive. It seemed that below a certain critical mass of powder the charge would simply fizzle without developing enough pressure to ignite explosively. On the other hand, an amount of powder above the critical mass would reach a peak pressure extremely rapidly, producing an explosion so violent it would damage the bearer almost as much as the targets and force the diver to reexamine the whole premise of bang-sticking. There seemed to be no way to predict whether the charge was too small or too large. The first too-large explosion with that particular device came after several mild detonations, knocking half a dozen members of a school of grunts unconscious and shaking me up rather severely. The next time it occurred was in much deeper water—about 100 feet down—when I was diving with another undergraduate at Miami. My friend was doing the handloading right behind me when I spotted a fish called a fat sleeper (*Dormitator maculatus*) hovering above its hole in the silty bottom. I pointed the gun at it and triggered the charge. A violent explosion followed, momentarily stunning me and causing a good deal of pain in the sinuses, throat, and chest. Even my friend, who was about 10 feet away, was violently shaken, and a great cloud of silt billowed up from the bottom. When the cloud finally cleared, there was no sign of the sleeper; we had either blown it away or pulverized it. After that we were pretty cautious about using that particular gun. Eventually we discovered that depth has a great deal to do with the violence of a bang stick explosion. A water-filled barrel, whether it holds a bullet or just a blank, explodes with greater shock the greater the pressure. A gun that is only moderately powerful in shallow water can become quite violent in deep water. A bang stick with an air-filled barrel, however, does not exhibit this behavior. It is capped at the surface, so that the pressure of the gas inside the barrel is low enough to allow a less forceful explosion.

At any rate, the memory of previous bang stick experiences went through my head as I paused in the wrasse's cave. I also thought over what I knew of this particular gun, which bore a good charge of pistol powder plus a large charge of rifle powder. But Rhett, who had shot with the gun for several days, had not described its action as exceptional, and since I was in only 25 or 30 feet of water, I decided to go ahead and fire. I turned my head away from the gun, shielding myself partly by a rock, and pushed my arm out all the way. As I let it go, there was a substantial explosion which shook me but did not hurt. The mud billowed around me so that I couldn't see. I backed out a bit and felt around up in the cave for the *Cheilinus*. Eventually I located its tail and then a pectoral fin and began to haul it out. The fish wasn't quivering or moving, so I guessed I had hit something vital. I slid it around and finally got it out where I could see that I'd blown a large chunk out of the middle of the back, killing it instantly. I hauled it over to the sub, where I tied it onto a wing much as a deer hunter throws his kill over the fender of an automobile (or used to, when they had fenders).

We surfaced only 100 feet away from the *El Territo*, and Jerry swam the *Cheilinus* around to the stern (pulling backward, as one might do in a lifesaving course). We hauled it onto the platform, and I cut it open and found in its stomach a few bits of shell. The bits looked like the remains of cowries, so it seems that these large fish eat mollusks as well as crown-of-thorns starfish. We filleted a large chunk off one side, and Jo fried it for dinner. The meat was white and quite tasty; I am not a big fish eater, but I tried some. I trusted this meal would not prove to be toxic, and by ten o'clock at night our stomachs had not yet begun to convulse, nor had any other symptoms of fish poisoning appeared. (One peculiar symptom of such poisoning is a tricky taste reversal, by which hot seems to be cold and cold hot.)

We hung the carcass beneath the stern of the boat in hopes of attracting some sharks. Rather than keep watch on deck, we fetched the closed-circuit television camera and set it up over the stern and connected it to the TV set belowdecks so we could keep an eye on it. We had seen several blacktips and a couple of butterflyfish come up and begin picking shreds of flesh from the carcass, but no larger sharks. I also rigged up the underwater speaker and played some pulsed, low-frequency tones into the sea in hopes of calling sharks. The fact that these tones often attract sharks has been established by several biologists, including Arthur Myrberg at the University of Miami and Donald Nelson of California State College at Long Beach, who began their research from a common point of experience. Skin divers and fishermen have noticed for years that sharks gather very rapidly whenever a good-sized fish is speared or hooked on a line—much too fast to have smelled blood and often from a distance well beyond the limit of visibility. When these studies began, there were various attempts to record the actual struggling fish in order to lure sharks with authentic, "real life" sounds. The task of recording real sounds proved far more complex than supposed, however, for various technical reasons, so Nelson, for one, simply tried to simulate the sounds of a struggle by artificial low-frequency tones derived randomly from a signal generator. The result, to the surprise of some people, was that the sharks were not at all fussy about the authenticity of the sounds, rushing in from considerable distances as if on cue. Nelson tried his sound machine here at Enewetak last winter, a short distance from where we are just now, and in a few minutes was able to attract about thirty gray reef sharks to his hydrophone.

I tried some of these sounds this afternoon, but there seemed to be little response. It may be that the particular pulsed frequencies I am using are for some reason unappealing, so I'll try some different ones, as well as using natural sounds of speared fish and the sight and smell of actual dead fish (which I hope to spear). I would dearly like to attract some gray sharks to the bait in order to observe them during feeding.

Just before I went below for the night, I took a look at the dead *Cheilinus* and saw three or four small blacktips milling around. I went to the sound machine and began playing some oohs and burps and barks, and the sharks seemed immediately to move closer to the carcass. These blacktips are instinctively shy creatures, hesitating a few feet away from the bait without daring to take a bite. I went to fetch one of Rhett McNair's bang sticks, since one of the blacktips was large enough to make a suitable test target. I turned off the sound while I put the powerhead together; when it was set, I turned it on again and stood on the stern platform. As soon as I got set, a shark about five feet long came in to within a foot or so of the carcass; I wasn't sure if it was a gray. Rather than wait, the shark being only about 18 inches below the surface, I went ahead and hit it. There was a considerable explosion which threw salt water all over me; Jo and Jerry were below cleaning the supper dishes and thought that a battery or something had exploded. They came rushing up topside just in time to see me standing there with a cascade of water dripping from me and an assortment of shark parts on the stern. We shone a light to the bottom and saw the shark lying there. It was just beyond the reach of the boat hook, so we decided to wait till the following day to retrieve it.

18

PURSUING SHARKS

A S it turned out, we never found the shark the next day, and because a stiff breeze had built up during the night, we had to move the *El Territo* slightly to the lee side of the island.

I have been frustrated by our poor luck in finding gray sharks when I want to, and today we began a more active campaign to draw them in so we could study their behavior. This increased the danger somewhat but seemed the only course to follow if we were to learn much during our few remaining weeks.

We set out in bright sunlight to chum up some sharks. First, of course, we had to secure some chum. I decided to head for Pole Pinnacle, about a mile away, and when we arrived, we saw that a shark line had been set and tied to the pole. A large shark was lying on the bottom right next to the pole, and I guessed (correctly, as it turned out) that Rhett McNair and Paul Allen from the lab had set the line yesterday so that they could try Rhett's new powerhead on a shark carcass. There are usually large numbers of *Caesio* just up-current of the pole, and I tossed a half-pound block of TNT overboard there. I had my camera equipment all ready to film any sharks that might come in to feed on the *Caesio* killed by the blast. We moved a small distance away and waited for the explosion. As soon as I heard the familiar sharp crack, we quickly circled back and anchored. Jerry Condit began to pick up the few fish that were drifting slowly to the surface, and Jo and I put on our gear and jumped in. Immediately I saw below me a gray shark circling among the stunned fish. I began to film it, and it responded by rising toward me. It had been at a depth of 50 or 60 feet when I jumped in, and it rose quickly to meet me about 20 feet below the surface. For a bad moment I thought it was going to come at me, who may have looked like the largest *Caesio* in the school, but then I saw that my fins had been blocking my view of a small fish drifting just beneath me. I saw the fish as I twisted to keep the shark in the viewfinder of the camera.

Just as the shark approached the small fish, it made a short dart at a high rate of speed. This was puzzling. Normally when sharks are feeding on dead fish—particularly small fish—they simply swim along at a leisurely pace, open their mouths just as they reach the prey, and scuff it down in a motion as gentle as yawning. There is no frenzied rush or, indeed, any movement to indicate anything but routine swimming. The gray shark seems to follow this general pattern, and momentarily I couldn't understand why this one had suddenly charged. Then I noticed that a number of large snappers were also feeding on stunned fish, and while there were several hundred *Caesio* floating in the area, the two sharks (a second had arrived) preferred to chase the snappers with great speed and high excitement. The snappers easily eluded the sharks, so that I'm really not sure why the sharks bothered to chase them; perhaps they were trying to take advantage of the snappers' reduced wariness while feeding, or perhaps the shark simply is stimulated by the presence of another animal feeding to chase the food that the other animal is chasing. It is known that if a few members of a group of sharks begin feeding, the rest of them will be stimulated into not only feeding but also chasing and attacking anything that moves.

Within a couple of minutes the two grays had eaten their fill and left; I didn't see them again. Jo came down behind me just as they were cleaning up the last of the prey they wanted, and she began to collect fish. Jerry came down as well, and I spent some time filming them picking up *Caesio* and swimming near the vast crowd of live *Caesio* that still filled the area. One of the sharks, just before leaving, rose and made a sudden rush into the school of *Caesio*, which magically parted to let it pass harmlessly through like an airplane through a cloud. One of the great mysteries in marine biology is the nature of the mind force that controls with such speed and precision the movements of hundreds of schooling fish.

I flippered my way up to the top of the pinnacle, where the shark was hooked on the long line. It proved to be a female tiger shark about 10 feet in length and probably 400 pounds in weight. She was still alive, breathing slowly, despite a chewed area and several gashes on one side near a pectoral fin. It looked as though another large shark had tried to eat her as she struggled against the hook, but we didn't see one around. During the struggles she had wrapped about 50 feet of line around the pole, so that it was now snubbed up short and she could barely move.

By that time Jo and Jerry had collected enough chum in their nets, so we went on back to the *El Territo*. The *Cheilinus* carcass we had hung in the water the day before had been devoured except for the head, and the shark I had killed the night before was also gone—presumably eaten. We dumped the chum beneath the boat, and I turned on the underwater speaker to broadcast some pulsed, low-frequency sounds. Although I tried several different series of sounds, no sharks seemed interested in either listening or eating. The underwater TV camera we had set out yesterday turned out to be leaking, so that's another piece of equipment that's going to need some work.

Shortly after we got back to the boat, Rhett and Paul showed up, carrying a portable aluminum shark cage. They wanted to hang it in the water in the baited area. We told them there was a large tiger shark on their line, and they set out to retrieve it. Rhett and I had already discussed an experiment we wanted to try with the bang sticks. While they were gone, I rigged up a handload in a special barrel that we use for large sharks. It is slightly longer than standard and has a brass cartridge case inside the barrel. We fill the barrel about three-quarters full of fine-grain black powder, set the slug on top of the powder, and then cap it. We use black powder instead of smokeless powder for a simple reason: the purpose of this particular load is to carry as much of the explosion as possible into the shark's body. If we used a large charge of smokeless powder, one of two things could happen. If the powder is fast-burning, the outward pressure during the explosion will build almost instantly to intolerable levels and blow up the barrel; it may even knock out the user. A slower-burning smokeless powder blows out of the barrel too early—before it ignites. Once out of the barrel, it can't ignite because smokeless powder relies upon great pressure to explode. Black powder, however, continues to burn even when blown out of the barrel; with a large charge, the portion of powder to ignite first propels the slug as well as a large mass of igniting powder into the target. The result is that the shark is ripped not only by a bullet but by a bullet surrounded by exploding powder.

When Rhett and Paul got back, we went down to compare his experimental powerhead with a traditional type. We laid the now-dead shark on the bottom in about 10 feet of water. We found, however, that the carcass refused to lie flat, giving us trouble even after death. No matter how we set it down, the carcass turned belly up. We wanted a "natural-looking" situation because Jo was trying to film the tests and an upside-down shark just doesn't look right. I thought there might have been air in the stomach, so Paul got his knife and slit open the belly. No air. Then I realized that we were dealing with the natural buoyancy of the shark's large liver. This organ in sharks weighs something like 70 to 100 pounds, almost a quarter of the body weight. The shark stores huge amounts of oil in the liver, which apparently functions as a hydrostatic "float," maintaining neutral buoyancy so that the shark neither floats nor sinks. I don't know if this is the sole function of the huge liver, but I did realize that we were going to have to shoot the shark belly up or not at all.

We got set to go, and then a great cloud of blood suddenly spewed out of one of the wounds. The cloud obscured the area and made it impossible to film, so we had to drag the carcass 20 or 30 feet away and start again. I went down the first time with a magnum load, hit it against the shark, and braced myself while nothing happened. It turned out the powder was wet. Then I got one of the regular bang sticks with an inertial firing pin and put the magnum barrel on it. This gun is only four feet long, however, and is used primarily as a defensive weapon, so I swam up to the shark and then lay down with my head as far from the shark as I could get it. Jo was ready with the camera, and I cocked the powerhead and hit the shark. There was a tremendous explosion; I felt as though I had been punched in the throat. My mask half filled with water. When I pulled the bang stick back, I saw that the whole end of it had blown off, directing a good deal of the explosion back toward me. It had also blown a substantial hole in the shark; the bullet had gone completely through the body and landed in the sand, where we found it. I took down another load, smaller this time, and shot again, and the bullet again went all the way through. It did not make as large a hole, however. Then Rhett went down with two different loads and fired them both, and we put a rope around the shark and hauled it out of the water with the crane. We slit the beast open, immediately saw the huge liver, but found nothing in the stomach. We explored the wounds where we had tested the guns and found there didn't seem much to choose from; they all made a devastating wound.

Rhett proceeded to cut the jaws out of the tiger shark for a souvenir, and Jo and I went out in the submarine. We ran through beautiful clouds of *Caesio* and unicorn surgeonfish and large snappers, but no sharks. When we got back to the *El Territo*, we found that nothing had touched any of the bait or the carcass of the tiger shark, which we had dropped in the water. In the past I've found that when you use sharks for bait, other sharks will either come in immediately or not at all. Sharks seem to avoid an area where a shark is decomposing, although they will feed on a freshly killed individual.

The next day was calm and generally sunny, so we cruised along the rim of the atoll for about two miles and landed on a small islet where a large colony of noddy terns was roosting. We wanted some more chum, since none of the bait beneath the boat had attracted any sharks, but we didn't find anything that would help us. On the way back we stopped at a site where a group of researchers several months earlier had stretched a rope from the breaker zone across the coral into the ledge of the lagoon. They were studying reef metabolism—the way the organisms of the reef use phosphates and nitrates, oxygen and carbon dioxide, and so on. On the lagoon side was a lot of coral growth—primarily stinging coral—until the water became shallower. Where the lagoon was only about two feet deep I could see only relatively barren rock and sand and large numbers of sea cucumbers. To seaward there is more of the common stony coral until you get into the breaker region, where there are some sparse algae and largely barren rock. We went to the edge of the surf zone, but the constant breakers made it difficult to go any farther. This, of course, is what has stopped most ecologists from working to seaward. The only way to do it is to go around to the outside in a boat and swim in.

After struggling to get out as far as we did, it was a delight to drift back in with the surf current. At one point Jo looked like Neptune's shepherd, moving along slowly behind a considerable flock of parrotfish and surgeonfish that were grazing as they went, keeping just ahead of her. The farther she went, the larger the flock grew until shortly she had hundreds of fishes drifting in a huge group ahead of her. As I was carried along, I thought of how well we had already grown to know some of the habits of our fellow reef creatures. A small blacktip shark came cruising toward us without paying any attention and then broke off and disappeared. This was a large one, about the size of a small gray shark, and very streamlined. In theory, the blacktip is capable of inflicting as much harm on a human as is a gray reef shark. But they are very timid animals, and when I recognize one, I never give a thought to danger. Had the animal been a gray shark, I would have been immediately on guard.

Just as we neared the boat, I came across a giant clam about 3 feet in length and probably weighing 200 or 300 pounds. I stopped and called to

Jo, who was a little distance away, and she came over. She swam right above it in water about 4 feet deep, but she was expecting me to point out a fish, so she didn't pay much attention to the bottom. Finally, I pointed down, and she looked down and let out an exclamation of surprise; it was the largest giant clam we had seen there, although they do grow even larger. I shot some footage of it and then took off my swim fin and stuck it between the valves. It closed, but it couldn't close far enough to pin the fin. This is commonly the case, because their mantle and fleshy parts are so thick that the two valves fail to touch. In the folklore of the sea these clams are frequently depicted as deadly dangers, snapping shut on a human limb. Indeed, if a person were determined enough to shove a whole leg or arm between the valves, he might be held prisoner. But this would have to be done deliberately. The mantle of the creature is brilliantly colored and easily noticeable, and the valves close quite slowly when they do shut. More to the point, perhaps, is that a diver does not often stuff arms or legs into strange holes in a reef. The stories of people being trapped and drowned by giant clams must be regarded as fiction.

T HAT same day we managed to provoke a shark attack, and again the pattern varied from what we were used to. Jo's sinuses were bothering her again, so Jerry Condit and I went out in the afternoon, around the shore of Japtan Island farther to seaward than we had been before. The bottom coral was fairly lush, with large formations of plate coral. As we came about and started back toward the lagoon, we noticed a large leopard ray whose tail was bobbed. Normally a leopard ray such as this one, with a wingspan of four or five feet, has a tail six or seven feet long— a whiplike affair with a series of barbs at the end. I followed the ray for a few moments, and then, as it turned and I turned, we came across another one. While that one moved away from us, flapping in ponderous slow motion, Jerry tapped me on the shoulder and pointed to a gray shark coming down the slope toward us. I saw it when it was about 50 feet away and moving in fast. It swam in as we have seen a dog-toothed tuna do, aiming toward the tail end, apparently attracted by the whirling propeller. As we turned toward it, it turned toward us so that we were making a circle chasing each other. We made almost one complete circle and were climbing slightly when we began to lose our momentum and hence our planing ability; the sub began to sink on the inward side of a tight turn—

just enough so that we were going to hit the coral. I pulled out of the circle and tried to head straightaway to get up some speed, but we touched bottom and then came to a halt against a large clump of coral. The only way I could get started again was to blow the ballast tanks slightly. We had lost the shark momentarily, but we found it farther up the slope. It was about four or five feet long. As I headed toward it, the display began, but mildly. I have noticed since we've been chasing after sharks here that none of the sharks that have actually attacked the submarine has displayed violently; it seems that an exaggerated display reflects a powerful inhibition against attacking. Instead, the sharks performing a mild display have been the ones to attack, so I kept my eye on this one. I headed toward it, and it moved slowly away, continuing a moderate arching of the back and lateral swimming. I finally got it lined up, in about 20 feet of water where the coral was dense, so it was more or less trapped just under the sub's nose, and then I dived down on it. As I did so, the shark suddenly darted upward at us, disappearing under the nose and hitting the sub, not at the propeller or the clear plexiglass, but along the fiberglass hull. The three shark attacks, then, manifest no consistent pattern; each has chosen a different target. The shark may simply be choosing the part of the sub that for some reason attracts attention, and this time it may have been the red cap on the bang stick barrel, which was sticking out the hole I made in the front of the sub. Or the shark may have responded to the fact that the nose portion of the sub was nearest to it, bearing down threateningly.

The shark broke off the attack, and by the time we had turned around, it had vanished in the blue haze. We cruised for a while longer and then went back in. At sunset we were greeted with a freshening fall of rain, which came just in time to wash the salt off all our diving equipment. After the rain everything grew calm. With the lights off, a half-moon lit the lagoon and just enough of the deck to walk and work, and then we listened to the steady fall of the breakers coming in against the reef and watched the pale glimmer of lights to the south on the island of Enewetak. To the west the water was silken smooth, undulating gently, and the silhouettes of Jedrol Island and the concrete ship rose against the fading sunset. We decided to charcoal-broil some steaks on deck for dinner.

THE next day was clear and beautiful, and Jo and I made another excursion in the sub before leaving Japtan, starting from the pier and moving along the shore of the island to the deep eastern channel for half a mile or so. For the first twenty minutes we saw no rays or sharks or *Cheilinus*. Then, cruising down the slope of the channel at a depth of about 70 feet, I spotted a large gray reef shark near the top of the slope. I turned toward it while Jo was looking in the other direction, and she never saw it coming. It had begun to display mildly when we approached, and I guessed that this one would probably attack. Sure enough, I bore in straight at the shark, which was about six feet long, and when we were within five or six feet of it, the creature swirled into action, hitting the plexiglass canopy just in front of Jo. She was startled, to say the least, since she hadn't yet seen the shark. It hit the canopy with a good loud whop—the top of the canopy even sprang up slightly. But it is held down by elastic cord, so it immediately closed again.

I lost sight of the shark momentarily, as I usually do after an attack, and then spotted it again and charged. It counterattacked, this time from the front, and hit the plexiglass, bearing in rather fast. I managed to get some footage of the attack, from the charge to the collision, but afterward we couldn't find it. We ran along the channel for a few minutes and then decided to retrace our course. We came across a beautiful leopard ray that wouldn't let us get very close, then a whitetip that we filmed swimming away from us to show its typical nonaggressive behavior. As we followed it, we moved right through the middle of a large school of peculiar reddish-brown snappers with concave foreheads; the school gracefully parted to allow our small procession to pass and then closed in formation again. Farther on we passed a large eagle ray, then a large school of small barracudas, 18 to 24 inches in length, and Jo opened the window to film them. As I was circling the school for her, I suddenly noticed out of the corner of my eye that Jo was quickly pulling the window closed. I guessed that something was heading for us, and as I turned the sub, I saw first one and then two gray sharks. The second was emaciated and must have been injured in some way so that it could not catch enough to eat. We started after the sleeker of the two and caught it at a depth of about 125 feet. It was quite a distance away at first, about 75 feet, but the water was so clear we could follow easily. It began to display in typical fashion, but since we couldn't provoke an attack and it was too dark at that depth to do any filming, I decided after ten minutes not to waste any more time. Moving back up the slope, we came upon the emaciated shark again and chased it for several passes, but it seemed too weak to attack, contenting itself with a halfhearted display.

On the way back we spied the largest shark we have seen here, seven
or eight feet long, but it vanished immediately in the murk of shallow
water. Our air was getting short, so we motored on back to the *El Territo*
and then steamed down to Enewetak to ship our film on next morning's
plane.

T HAT day brought a flat calm, so we took the boat into the pier to take
on our weekly supply of water and to change the oil in the generator. While we were there, I noticed several small inshore squid near the
foot of the pier. It seemed to be the same group from which Jo had
speared one for Mikka a few weeks ago. I got the camera and went in the
water to film them; with the light on them, they offered brilliant patterns
flashing translucent green and other colors. They are also able to glide
through the air, a fact most people are unaware of. More familiar is the
open-ocean flying squid, which can sail hundreds of feet through the air,
sometimes landing on the decks of ships. Similarly, this little inshore species can glide easily for 20 or 30 feet. It does this by a sudden contraction
of its muscular body, which forces a jet of water out of its siphon. The reaction to this action is to force the squid clear of the water as it holds its
tentacles together for streamlining.

I remember the time in British Honduras a year ago when one of
these squid propelled itself into the air and at the same moment shot ink
all over Jo. Years before that, I took part in an inking operation that was
not so accidental. A friend of mine and I were both graduate students at
the University of Miami, and we were out in a boat off the Keys at night
using a light to attract squid, larvae, juvenile sailfish, and anything else we
could find. We dipped up several squid and dumped them into a bucket.
As we shone the light on them, they pulsed with color, changing patterns
so fast that I counted a dozen or so in just a few seconds. I reached into
the bucket and held one of them in my hand. I could feel the body expand and contract as it pulsed water out of its jet; it couldn't move because I was holding it firmly. Then, when I felt it expand, I picked it up
and tilted the animal's siphon. When the contraction came, it shot a jet of
water several feet across the boat. My friend Clyde was busy with the net
and didn't see what was going on, and I called, "Hey, Clyde, come over
here and take a look at this." Clyde, who wears glasses, came for a look,
and as he got there, I felt the squid expand. I tilted the siphon again, this
time toward Clyde; but the squid decided at that moment not only to

squirt water but to discharge its ink sac as well, shooting a mixture of water and black ink right into Clyde's face and glasses. Fortunately he is good-natured and loves squid (he is a squid specialist today at the Smithsonian Institution), so he was not angry.

After we had finished taking on water, I took Rhett out in the sub; he was interested in seeing the attack behavior of the gray reef shark. We towed the sub around the end of the island for a mile or so to save the battery, and stopped at the edge of the drop-off. It was calm, and we passed a large school of porpoises or dolphins on the way. (The terms "porpoise" and "dolphin" are often used interchangeably, although taxonomists recognize certain differences. The mammalian dolphin is not to be confused with the edible game fish of the same name.) They came up beneath the bow, where Jo was sitting, and played beneath her feet. They left us as we rounded the end of the island. No sooner had we stopped than a gray shark came up from the depths and circled the ship and the sub. Jo dropped a jig overboard with a spinning rod to see if she could catch a fish, and the shark made a dive at the jig. It only nosed the bait, however, and when Rhett and I got down in the sub, we couldn't see the shark. I circled a few times and then headed for the drop-off, where, just beyond a school of about 150 paddle-tailed snappers, we saw a silvertip shark. They are smoothly streamlined and look as though they would be very aggressive, being larger than the gray sharks, but this one, like others we have met, made no overt display of any kind and steadily moved out of range. We went on along the edge of the drop-off at 75 feet or so, saw only one whitetip, and came back the same way. As we approached the school of snappers again, I heard a high-pitched squeaking at irregular intervals. At first I thought that either it was Rhett's regulator or I was imagining it, but soon a movement caught my eye, and we were greeted by yet another fantastic Enewetak performance. About halfway between us and the surface, outlined against the setting sun, was a school of six or seven porpoises moving in time with the sub. The water was crystal clear and blue, and the sleek porpoises moved with a grace that can be appreciated but not imitated by humans. Soon a second group, including a mother with a very small baby, came toward us from the front. They appeared to be spinner dolphins, an offshore species about 6 feet long and 150 to 200 pounds in weight. The baby was only about 2½ feet long, and it swam very close to its mother. As the dolphins swirled around and peered at us, I turned with them and followed them about in a game they seemed to enjoy. They carried on a rapid conversation of high-pitched squeaks, with

two adults in particular doing most of the "talking." They put on a glori-
ous display for us, racing together in tight formation, making great circles
and arcs, up to the surface and down. They would leap clear of the water,
breaking through as though through a mirror and throwing up a cloud of
spray as they reentered the water. They stayed with us for perhaps ten
minutes, intelligent spirits sharing their fun. As I began to change course
and head up the reef, they soon broke away.

Just as we got back to the area where the school of snappers had
been, I saw a gray shark and headed toward it. The behavioral display
began immediately and grew more violent as I closed in. I kept pushing
closer, and eventually the shark whirled and charged the sub, striking the
canopy beside Rhett's head. Rhett spent the last split second before the
collision staring down the shark's throat past scores of needle-sharp teeth.
The shark glanced off the plexiglass and headed into deeper water. I followed to about 150 feet and then broke off the chase. Coming back up the
slope, we met another gray shark, started to follow it, and then saw another, larger one and went after it. This shark displayed in exaggerated
fashion whenever we could get close to it, but as usual, the exaggerated
display was not followed by an attack. We lost it finally in an area of large
coral heads.

On the way back to the *El Territo*, Rhett and I talked about the
shark attacks. I was describing to him how the sharks making the most
violent displays seldom attack and how those presenting a mild display
more often do. Rhett had spent five or six years bullfighting in Mexico,
and he told me that the bulls that stop and paw the ground and put on a
dramatic show of aggression are generally the cowardly ones. It struck me
that the behavior phenomena here are similar, both being forms of displacement behavior. That is, when an animal experiences two conflicting
drives, it frequently responds to neither, but does something entirely different to release tension. In the case of the shark and the bull, for example, both are responding to two simultaneous drives, one that says
"attack" and another that says "flee." Instead of either attacking or fleeing, the animal does neither. When such conflicting drives afflict a human
being, he may pound a wall or desk or get high blood pressure. The shark
carries out in midwater what I believe is a mock attack directed at no particular object. We hope to demonstrate this more positively later by observing the "real" behavior when a shark attacks a large bait; I believe that
the mock-attack behavior is derived directly from the real one. Further, I
think we shall be able to say that when a shark has an overpowering drive

to attack, the display is kept to a minimum and is finally overridden by the attack reflex itself.

One question that still baffles me is why this particular species of shark is so markedly more aggressive than the other sharks of this area. Neither the whitetip nor the silvertip exhibits this behavior. The gray is about the same size as the whitetip and smaller than the silvertip, and all three species must compete for food, but the gray is far more aggressive than either of its cousins.

An interesting detail about today's observation was that we encountered all three gray sharks just a few minutes and a few hundred feet from where a large group of porpoises had been cavorting and making a considerable amount of noise. The sharks did not appear in any way to behave differently from the way they usually do. It appeared that the porpoises presented no threat to them and that they did not threaten the porpoises. These two forms of life—one a primitive fish and the other a high-order mammal—appear remarkably similar in their gross features: general body form, color, a line of light gray down the side, size. Of course, the snouts are different and the tails oriented 90 degrees differently, but the similarities as seen underwater are far more striking. Yet, while both compete for prey in the same environment, evolution has produced in the porpoise one of the most complex brains of any creature, and in the shark one of the feeblest.

It is generally concluded by researchers today that the porpoise is extraordinarily intelligent, with brain activity that approaches that of humans. Why should a porpoise be so smart? In man, the high development of the brain allows for the ability to manipulate objects with the hands, to make tools, and ultimately to control the operation of rivers, forests, cities, and other gross features on the surface of the earth. In the porpoise, however—a diving predator whose living depends upon the ability to do without oxygen for long periods underwater—a large and complex brain which demands a large and constant supply of oxygen would seem, at first thought, to be a disadvantage. A smaller brain would use less oxygen and therefore allow dives of longer duration.

Some people have dismissed the problem by suggesting that it simply represents an evolutionary accident—a freak of nature. But if we are not content with this explanation, the only reasonable hypothesis for the development of smart porpoises (and whales) is that these creatures need superior intelligence to survive in their stressful lifestyle and hostile environment. Although we are not yet sure how much "higher" intelligence porpoises need or have—the ability to think in abstract terms, for example—we know of several abilities that far exceed those of sharks. In hunting, porpoises depend to a large extent upon a powerful and accurate echo-ranging, or sonar, system, and a large brain certainly seems to be a necessary natural "computer" for transmitting and receiving sound signals. Porpoises have also developed a complex social system that involves considerable dependence upon one another. Again, their large brains control the transmission and reception of interporpoise communication, or speech if you will. It seems that teamwork while hunting, care for one another, and cooperation in general are essential to the porpoise's evolutionary success.

The comprehension of intelligence in the order Cetacea, which contains whales, dolphins, and porpoises, could be extremely revealing. Cetacean intelligence seems to be very high, and yet it is obviously different from the high intelligence of humans. Our own kind of intelligence is approached by some of the primates—the chimpanzee, the gorilla, the orangutan—but it seems that studying these creatures is much like studying a rather dull human being. The apes may be too much like us to expand our understanding of the nature of intelligence. Porpoises, on the other hand, have developed and learned to use their "minds" in a different environment, in response to different challenges. Understanding this process could be invaluable in "getting to know" creatures of other kinds of environment, such as those thought to exist on other planets.

19

A CASE OF THE BENDS

THE next day we had a bad scare during our dive in the submarine. Jo and I waited until afternoon to go out because we hoped to find the porpoises again. We towed the sub out just after four and went down along the edge of the drop-off for a distance of several hundred yards, saw one or two silvertips and no grays, and then turned to head back down the reef. We cruised through a large school of paddle-tailed snappers and spotted a large *Cheilinus*. We decided to pursue it—in the absence of sharks and porpoises we didn't seem to have anything better to do. The *Cheilinus* wove its way parallel to the beach, swinging up and down along the drop-off face from a depth of 125 feet up to 50 or 60. The bottom configuration is by now very familiar. From the shore of Enewetak Island it gradually drops to the edge of the reef, a distance of about 50 yards or so. The reef edge is still near the surface, but then it drops straight down 10 or 15 feet in a series of surge channels. From these channels outward the slope is again very slight, so that over a distance of 100 yards the bottom declines gradually to a depth of 30 or 40 feet; by a quarter of a mile out the bottom is still only 50 feet deep. Then it suddenly breaks and plunges in a steep slope, angling downward at about 45 degrees, to 175 feet, where it again falls vertically, this time into the oceanic abyss.

We'd been running along the gentle bottom just at the edge of the break-off when suddenly the *Cheilinus* broke downward, apparently to hole up in a clump of bottom coral. I went down after it, saw it duck into a crevice, and parked the sub on the sand. I was putting on my scuba tank to go look for the fish when Jo tapped me on the shoulder. Coming at us from the blue yonder was what looked like a Phantom jet fighter—a creature with a robust body and two short wings sticking out at the sides. The body turned out to belong to a very husky silvertip shark, and the "wings" were its pectoral fins. It was about 8 feet long and 18 inches or 2 feet in diameter through the body, so it probably weighed 300 pounds. It came straight at us, and I hastily amended my itinerary to stay right where I was. I decided to get the sub started again to see if we could provoke any attack or threat behavior. So far we had been unable to do this with any silvertip. We followed it closely, and Jo took a lot of footage, but there was no success in provoking an attack. That didn't mean it wasn't a dangerous shark; it may have been more dangerous than a gray shark, giving less warning of a threat. It could be that because of its size, this shark would view a diver not as a competitor but as a meal. It was an extremely streamlined and beautiful shark, and made us feel slow and clumsy in our expensive submarine.

As we circled, another silvertip showed up, and then another and another until there were four of them cruising in circles at depths between 125 and 175 feet, where the bottom fell vertically. Also present were several large schools of big snappers, a couple of leopard rays, and then some gray reef sharks, so we did not lack for sizable company. But we did run into a problem with the sub. We were deeper than we had ever been before, and the foam flotation in one of the rear compartments apparently collapsed under the water pressure. As a result, the tail dipped slightly, and I could no longer make the sub dive. The thrust of the motor would drive us in the direction we were pointed, which was up, so to remain among the sharks, I had to stop the engine and sink, then start it again and climb. We spent what seemed like a long time doing this—probably five to seven minutes, in reality—and milling about with the sharks, rays, and snappers, while Jo filmed them in various positions. We did get a fairly aggressive display out of one shark, which sped off, whirled, and appeared to plan an attack; but because of our lack of maneuverability we weren't able to pursue it, and when it had widened the distance between us somewhat, it seemed to feel there was no longer a need for attack.

Finally, a little too late, I began to realize we had been down a long time. Conscious of the need for decompression, I started heading gradually back up the slope. We topped the rise where the coral grows thickly and then bore straight inshore about 40 feet down. When we broke the surface, I blew ballast and Jerry came over in the skiff to tow us toward the

El Territo. We'd gone along for fifteen or twenty minutes, discussing the sharks we had seen and taking some pictures of the children, when suddenly Jo said both her legs were beginning to feel like pins and needles. That was followed by sharp pains in her lower back, and we knew immediately that she was being hit by the bends. Fortunately Rhett McNair and Jerry Allen, who had both been visiting the lab, were coming in another skiff behind us, and we just cast off the sub, yelled to them to bring it along, and took off at full speed for the *El Territo* and its decompression chamber.

After what seemed like an eternity, but was probably no more than four or five minutes, we reached the ship. By that time the pain had become virtually unbearable and both of Jo's legs were paralyzed. It was a very rapid and violent hit. Fortunately I had been keeping the decompression chamber pumped up, so it would be ready to go at a moment's notice. We depressurized the outer lock, and Jo got in, or rather we picked her up and just slid her in, as quickly as possible. She helped as well as she could without the use of her legs, and we immediately closed the door and then opened the pressure valve to the outside chamber. As soon as the pressure equalized, the pain ceased, so we knew we had caught the bubble before it had grown too large. We started treatment on pure oxygen for a depth equivalent of 30 feet, but there was still some residual pain. So we went by the standard oxygen treatment table for 60 feet, which calls for a total of two hours' decompression. In the meantime, I got the compressor going and started topping off our air banks and refilling oxygen bottles, et cetera, to have refills for everything if needed. Then I got in the outer lock of the chamber and repressurized and went in with Jo and helped her set up a new oxygen bottle; the one in the chamber was getting low. Next I went out and adjusted the pressure lines and fixed her some tea, brought her a pillow, and got fresh carbon dioxide absorbent for the breathing system. Then I locked myself back in with her. We had painted the inside of the chamber with epoxy paint a year ago, but the inside had been sealed for some time, and the fumes were still strong. They aren't dangerous, fortunately, but unpleasant to smell, so we vented the chamber as best we could by letting air in and out simultaneously, maintaining a constant pressure.

After the two hours were up, we gradually bled the last few pounds of pressure out and opened the door. Jo seemed to be in fine shape, with no more pain.

The children had been with us in the afternoon when the bends hit, and of course they were upset to see their mother in pain. Varrina, the younger one, had missed her nap and then, when Jo was in the chamber, had insisted on staying up until she was out; she fell asleep in her high-chair while trying to eat dinner. Marissa had insisted on staying up, too, so Mommy went to reassure them that she was feeling fine now.

What turned out to be a relatively minor incident could, of course, have left some permanent disability if we had not had a decompression chamber right on board. It is interesting to note that sports divers have a high incidence of permanent damage from the bends, whereas military divers, who suffer considerably more attacks, have a much lower incidence of disability. The reason is that military divers almost always have ready access to a decompression chamber, and sports divers do not. If a sports diver is hit, he is usually taken by boat or car, or both, on an hours-long journey to a hospital, where people ask slow questions about insurance and financial situations before they will even admit him. So it can be considerable time before the victim gets into a chamber; by then permanent nerve damage may have been done. The key to success in decompression treatment is to get the person under pressure immediately, to squeeze the bubble of nitrogen back to a size where it can no longer block a blood vessel. Decompression in the water, where the problem started, is possible as a last-ditch measure, but it frequently makes a bad situation worse. Another dive adds to the bottom time and usually cannot last long enough to do any good. Also, the most effective treatment involves breathing pure oxygen. I just can't say too much in favor of having a chamber right on hand. The decompression meters and tables that divers use are helpful, but even when they are properly followed, it is still possible to get the bends. The tables are based only on mathematical abstractions and do not represent what is actually happening within the individual human body.

The basic idea behind conventional decompression tables, which are used by the world's navies and by commercial diving organizations, is that nitrogen comes out of solution at known rates under various pressures. Thus the decompression tables tell you how fast you can come up from various depths and how long you must wait at intermediate points along the way. As pressure decreases, the blood becomes supersaturated with nitrogen—that is, the blood as a solution can no longer hold the amount of nitrogen it could hold at greater depth. Conventional theory described the release of nitrogen without the formation of bubbles; the supersaturated solution was thought simply to drive the nitrogen out molecule by molecule. However, this idea has been seriously undermined by recent discoveries in physical chemistry and is no longer tenable.

Much more attractive is the routine developed by an English physiologist, Dr. Brian Hills, who began his work in Australia and later came to the United States. Dr. Hills has come up with a different approach to decompression which appears to be more realistic than the old supersaturation theory. He contends that when a diver makes that long ascent to the first decompression stop, the nitrogen does not leave the blood molecule by molecule, but instead forms tiny bubbles of gas in the body. These bubbles are microscopic, emerging as films of gas between different types of tissues and between cells, small enough in size and quantity at this stage that they cause no pain. In reality, however, what we have is a sub-symptomatic case of the bends—bubbles without pain. Only if these bubbles concentrate and coalesce can enough pressure be brought to squeeze a nerve. And, when conventional tables are followed, this can happen. The goal, according to Hills, should be to rise slowly enough so that there is no chance of these tiny bubbles growing into larger ones. Thus he advocates starting the first decompression stop much lower and ascending more gradually to a depth of 20 feet or so for the last stop. From there, he says, it is safe to rise the remaining distance with impunity, because when you reach the surface, there will be no further lessening of pressure and, therefore, no further chance for bubbles to enlarge and coalesce. The last stop by the traditional system is made at 10 or 5 feet, and from there to the surface, following that system, there is still a danger of the bends.

Empirically, Hills's theory seems to hold up well; indeed, he was first led to it by empirical observations. In the vicinity of Thursday Island and the Torres Strait, off the coast of Australia, there is a tremendous amount of conventional hard-hat diving for pearls. For many years native divers have been going down as deep as 300 feet, sometimes making two dives a day and staying below for as much as an hour at a time. Hills observed that these divers were decompressing much faster than the conventional tables called for, and he found further that most of their decompressing was done at greater depths and that they skipped the shallower stops. This routine had been derived completely by trial and error over a period of fifty years. The system is not written down but kept in the minds of the Australian diving tenders.

Dr. Hills himself is not a diver, but he studied the system of these pearl divers and concluded that some erroneous assumptions lay behind the conventional decompression tables. This is not surprising, really, since the tables were devised fifty years ago. We took some of his ideas and tested them last year in the Bahamas with some interesting results. In our

Electro-lung we made thirty exposures to 300 feet, each lasting about fifteen minutes; after each we decompressed in about fifteen minutes also. Conventional schedules require about two hours of decompression for the same dive, but we completed the thirty tests without a single incident of the bends.

Some further work of Hills's has also indicated that rapid descent below the surface may be dangerous for reasons other than those associated with the bends. When a diver sinks swiftly, he creates a strong osmotic gradient by suddenly saturating the blood with dissolved gases. The tissues that can absorb these gases only slowly, such as bone, can become dehydrated as water flows out of them more quickly than gases can move in, just as your hands can become dehydrated when submerged in salt water. This is probably the cause of the mysterious diver's disease known as aseptic bone necrosis, in which bone tissue dies, the bone weakens, and in severe cases the whole structure can gradually crumble. There is no known cure, and it can lead to permanent disability. It was incipient bone necrosis that forced the former astronaut Scott Carpenter to withdraw from the Sealab program.

It is also quite possible to pass out underwater—and then drown—from any number of physiological problems that diving human flesh is heir to. One familiar problem is the rapid loss of carbon dioxide from the blood. This might seem to be a good thing since the body constantly rids itself of this gas, but a certain amount of carbon dioxide is important for regulating the acid-base balance of the blood, and its sudden removal can cause loss of consciousness. This can happen as well if a diver is breathing a helium-oxygen mixture for deep diving and becomes excited in shallow water, either on the way down or up; rapid breathing can flush most of the CO_2 from the system. It is possible to do this even on land; just breathe deeply and fast for thirty seconds or so, and you will flush much of the carbon dioxide from your system. By contrast, in deep water, when the breathing mixture is under pressure and becomes so dense that it doesn't circulate adequately around the lungs, carbon dioxide, which is not removed as fast as it is produced, may build up to levels that can cause a diver to pass out. Likewise, breathing too much oxygen in deep water can cause loss of consciousness.

What all this adds up to, of course, is a demonstration of just how poorly suited to underwater living we are, and how sophisticated is the metabolic adaptation of the dolphins. All we can hope for is limited visiting rights, all the while exercising extreme caution and watching for physiological danger signs. It is not a realm for the daring; underwater problems cannot be solved by extra bravado. In this respect I have noticed that women divers often do better than men because they are more realistic about their human, air-breathing limitations than men are.

I'll admit it: I am terribly envious of the dolphins of Enewetak that speed along at 15 or 20 knots on the surface or dive to 1,000 feet or more with equal facility, free of the multiple physical problems we encounter even at lesser depths. I think sometimes the dolphins are even aware of our insecurity underwater. The other day, as they raced to and fro before the sub, they seemed to be showing off, slight smiles on their faces, as we blundered through the water in our wundercraft of technology.

The next day Jo was still feeling the aftereffects of the bends, so she rested. Jerry and I took the sub out to inspect the damage done to the foam flotation during the deep dive yesterday. It had been crushed. The foam was designed to withstand pressure at a depth greater than that of the dive, but designs are one thing and the ocean another.

20

ATTRACTING SHARKS

THE next day we had a little more luck in enticing sharks to approach bait within range of the movie camera. Observations like this are needed if we are to learn the sharks' body language of aggression.

We had anchored the *El Territo* at the seaward end of one of the surge channels (these are quite clean of coral on the bottom, where the ocean surge scours back and forth), and had gone down in scuba gear. Dense schools of surgeonfish and parrotfish grazed on the flat reef areas between channels, and some of them were resting in the channels themselves. After doing a good bit of photography, I was reloading at the surface when Jo came up to tell me that there were a couple of gray sharks circling below and that Jerry was standing watch with the bang stick just under her feet on the ladder. It seemed like a good chance to film some feeding behavior, so I immediately went down with the sling spear and shot a surgeonfish. Even though this took only thirty seconds or so, the sharks had retreated, so I stuck the spear and its impaled fish on top of a clump of coral. The fish was wriggling and splashing a good deal and making noises. Soon I heard *tink, tink, tink, tink* and turned to see Jo tapping on her oxygen tank with her ring to attract my attention. As I looked over, I saw her swimming quickly in my direction; just behind her was a large gray shark. As she reached the surge channel, the shark veered off to circle in the distance. Meanwhile, a small blacktip about four feet long had sensed the surgeonfish and moved quickly toward it. It circled several times and then went right up to the fish; I was waiting with the camera about eight feet away. The blacktip came in and nudged the bait with its snout, shied off, then repeated this routine. Just as the shark would reach the spear, the surgeonfish would begin to flutter about, apparently in response to the presence of the shark, but the blacktip was just a little too timid to grab it. The exhaust bubbles from my regulator and my own presence were probably frightening it.

The gray shark then returned, apparently attracted by the excitement of both the blacktip and the surgeonfish. It circled once, then came right toward me as I filmed it. It kept on coming until it was three feet away, then swerved to the side. At that point it appeared to pick up the sound or scent of the speared fish and lost interest in me. The shark worked its jaws a couple of times, as though to prepare itself, then went suddenly toward the spear and grabbed the fish, spear and all. It swam off (I was still filming), shook its head, and tossed the spear shaft out from between its teeth. The shark then settled on the bottom.

I really didn't get the behavior I was after—the technique of chewing a chunk out of a large prey—but the place and time seemed right to try again. I retrieved the spear and shot another, larger surgeonfish, left it lying on the bottom of the channel, and again stationed myself about eight feet away, this time behind a little clump of coral that I could hang onto. The blacktip was still circling and coming in, and still too shy to take the bait. Several very large jacks came through, but they seemed to be more curious than hungry. Then a whitetip showed up and headed directly toward me, just as the gray had done. At three or four feet it veered off, then seemed to pick up the scent of the bait. Although the shark was larger than the gray—about five or six feet long—whitetips are more slender, and when this one grabbed the bait and spear, it had more difficulty swallowing than the gray had. Again the spear slid free as the shark swam off, and again I picked up the spear and shot another surgeonfish. The gray reef shark came back, along with a larger companion, five or six feet long. The smaller one, about five feet, had a wound near the gill slit on the right side. It was also carrying a remora; these specialized beasts, also called shark suckers, attach themselves to sharks, sailfishes, and other large fish (or to skin divers) by a suction disk on the top of the head. They feed off "dinner scraps" left by the host. This remora was simply riding most of the time, but at one point I saw it take a bite at the wounded area. The shark responded by speeding up slightly, and the remora returned to its post beneath the stomach.

The grays never picked up the scent again, probably because there was very little current; they continued to circle at the limit of visibility, about 100 feet away.

I looked at my watch and realized we'd stayed longer than planned, so we went back to the *El Territo.* Later I hoisted the skiff with the crane and set it down on the dock. It had been in the water continuously for a month, and the growth of algae on the bottom was beginning to have its effect. With the 100-horsepower outboard the skiff usually does 27 or 28 knots, but I doubted that it would do 18 now. The thin film of algae doesn't look like much, but it adds tremendously to the wet surface area and cuts speed by an inordinate amount. This film can be scrubbed off while the boat is in the water, but it is much easier to let it dry first.

After dark I took a look at the rising full moon and noticed that the tide was at its lowest. The bow of the boat was only 30 feet or so away from the beach at Japtan Island, and the small waves were gently rolling onto the beach, bubbling and foaming in the bright moonlight like puddles of molten metal. Unable to resist the appeal of this scene, I stepped up on the dock, walked shoreward, and jumped down onto the beach/cauldron for a moonlight walk. It was bright enough to read by, and I could see dozens of large hermit crabs moving about. Some were so large they inhabited shells five and six inches in diameter. These land hermit crabs are closely related to the marine hermit crab; there are hundreds of species, but only a few genera have learned to live in a terrestrial environment. These land genera still return to the sea to breed, but most of the time they can be found wandering through the islands hundreds of yards from water, even crawling up trees in search of food. "Shellwise" the hermit crabs have catholic tastes, so that the variety of mobile housing I could see on the beach gave a fair indication of the variety of local mollusks.

As I approached each hermit, it pulled back into its shell and rolled down the slope a short way. Land hermits actually make good pets; they eat almost anything, and quickly adapt to the presence of humans.

The ghost crabs were out as well. These are the most common crabs on the beach. They live in burrows they dig in the sand and come out at night, looking just like the sand they live in. They have large eyes mounted on long stalks. Standing tiptoe on the ends of their feelers, they can run about as fast as a human along the beach. As I approached, they either darted into their burrows or headed for the water. Sometimes carnivorous fishes learn to take advantage of this. I remember reading a paper out of the Tortugas Laboratory at the Dry Tortugas Islands off Florida that described the ingenuity of the gray snappers along the beach. These fish learned to spot a human walking close to the water and to follow him; as the ghost crabs darted into the water, the snappers would snap them up.

I walked back to the ship, the beach glowing with the slanting moonlight, pure and unmarked except for my single, shadowed set of footprints and the tiny trails of the ghost crabs.

T HE following day we were lucky enough to film a gray shark in the midst of its feeding routine. The day had got off to a mediocre start, thanks to Mikka. He has taken to following Jo everywhere, day and night, seldom leaving a three-foot circle of which Jo is the center. We've taken to forcing him to stay outside during the night, because if he has a fish to chew on, he makes a mess of it. The first thing in the morning, Marissa goes up and opens the door for him. He bolts downstairs into our bedroom, where he screams and squeaks for a few minutes, romping over, around, and under Jo. Then he snuggles up against her and goes to sleep for as long as she will stay there. Last night he grabbed our only remaining functional underwater light meter and dragged it all the way down the stairs. Jo was below when she heard *thump, thump, thump,* and looked up to see Mikka leaping down the steps, pulling the light meter by its carrying cord. Upon arriving at the bottom, he dragged it across the room and threw it into his bowl of water. That last was an idle gesture, since it is an underwater meter. But it is hard to tell whether the stairs damaged it, because it was not working perfectly even before its down-steps trauma. In any case, it doesn't work now. Mikka also tried to run away with one of the still cameras as I laid it on the deck, but I caught him just in time.

Short on underwater equipment, I was just starting to put on my gear when I looked down at the 10-pound snapper I had tethered at the end of a wire. That is, I looked at where the bait had been; now a gray shark was there with the bait in its mouth, tail end first. Apparently the shark had already bitten off what it could chew and had then come back for the rest. The shark's body was tilted at a 45-degree angle, with its pectoral fins down, and it was shaking its head. The position, I was interested to see, was much the same as that of the midwater threat display we have seen so many times. As I watched, the shark chewed on the snapper for a moment, then broke free with another chunk and circled around, swallowing it. Again it came back and seized what was left of the head and began munching on that part. It didn't seem to be able to cut through the larger bones, so I went back up to the skiff and quickly grabbed a camera with a long lens to get some movies of the jaw action. The shark broke off several times to circle, passing close to Jo and me, returning each time to the head. Finally, it came very close—about three feet away from me and directly over Jo's head. It worked its jaws a couple of times and then blinked, or rather flicked the nictitating membrane over its eyes (fish don't have true eyelids). It began to shake its head in a manner that suggested the first stage of the threat display, probably because we were so close to the bait. Without the submarine for protection we chose to back off a bit; the shark continued to circle but at a greater distance. I believe it was very close to beginning the full threat display or even attacking at that point, but as we moved back, the urge seemed to pass. It circled and passed close to the bait but didn't bite; eventually it lost interest altogether and moved off.

Jo and I went up to troll for more bait fish, landing two mackerels by rod and reel. We rigged them on the line as we had done in the morning, and a whitetip and a blacktip soon appeared. Both were shy and somewhat bothered by our presence, but when a second whitetip came in, one of them decided—perhaps because of the added competition—that the time had come to feed. Both were five or six feet long, and suddenly one swam up to the mackerel, grabbed it in the middle and shook its head violently enough to tear it loose. I was filming, and the shark turned and swam directly toward me after it had wrenched the bait off the line, chomping on the mackerel and releasing great puffs of blood from its gill slits with each bite. At a distance of two feet it finally turned away, circled, chewed the mackerel in half, and then picked up the second piece and swam off, eating. Despite the large cloud of blood this created and the small bits of floating mackerel, the other two sharks lost interest when the first one left. We went away, too, and when we discovered that some large snappers were attacking the rest of our bait, we pulled the line in.

What we had seen was exciting, for it was the first link we had discovered between the threat display and feeding activity. I was now willing to conjecture that the threat display we had seen so many times in midwater was really displaced feeding behavior executed in mock form. Another experiment that suggests itself is to suspend the baits as we did today, lure a shark in to feed, and then charge toward it in the submarine, acting like a large predator competing for the bait.

The more we found out about the display of the gray reef shark, the less we seemed to know. Why should the gray shark do something that is totally absent from the behavioral repertoire of the whitetip and blacktip and silvertip sharks? The display could be simply a displacement behavior triggered by conflicting drives to attack or to flee when confronted by a strange stimulus like the yellow submarine or a scuba diver. However, if this were the case, we might expect to find at least some trace of a similar display in other species of sharks under similar conditions. We might also expect the shark, if the strange new stimulus continued, to become dominated by the instinct to flee, leaving the scene as do the other species when approached too closely.

If this is an aggressive threat display, on the other hand, what is it meant for? It surely was not developed just for skin divers and yellow submarines. It is hard to believe that such behavior would be used against larger sharks, since larger sharks would simply eat *them* if attacked. In the feeding situations we have seen, there have been no displays against other species of sharks present, so it does not seem to be a behavior meant for smaller sharks. The best guess I have at the moment is that the display is for use against other members of its own species, which are its most threatening competitors. At least this is true in other species; many reef fishes, including damselfishes and butterflyfishes, behave aggressively against members of their own species, with the result of limiting the numbers of their species in any one place and assuring that they will not deplete available food supplies.

Still, the question remains: why only this shark? To answer that, we need a good deal more information not only about the gray but also about the blacktip and whitetip. This includes going through a good many stomachs to see what they all eat. If there are basic differences in the kinds of fish these sharks eat, they will not be competing with each other as directly. This is a problem in the case of sharks, since most stomachs turn out to be empty. If you catch sharks on a set line, they almost invariably regurgitate what they have in their stomachs during the struggle against the hook. So I expect a long program of accumulating tiny bits of information—one that will take years.

I might as well set down the possibility that has suggested itself to me as an answer. The whitetips, to judge by their general behavior and morphology, likely feed in and about the reef caves and crevices where they sleep—probably at dawn or dusk, when the day and night "shifts" of prey fishes are changing, or on sleeping parrotfish and surgeonfish at night. The blacktip, by contrast, is often seen during daylight hours, active in shallow water, taking advantage of its highly streamlined little body to run down healthy, active prey in schools of surgeonfish, parrotfish, and the like. With both the whitetip and the blacktip, the feeding situations are not very competitive, since food supplies are abundant and the only trick to eating is to exert enough individual effort to catch a speedy fish.

In the case of the gray shark, however, individuals may have learned to rely upon a diet of sick or wounded or otherwise slowed-down prey, therefore making it dependent on a source of food which is much less reliable. This behavior is suggested by the aggressiveness of the grays in arriving quickly to take a bait fish; such wounded prey is not naturally abundant, so the shark has to take rapid advantage of every individual it encounters. If its energy requirements are rather low—something we don't know yet—the species could conceivably live in this fashion, provided each individual has a fairly large forage area that it patrols regularly. If this is true, the gray sharks would find themselves in a far more competitive intraspecific feeding situation than the whitetip or the blacktip. It would be easy to understand the need for some aggressive mechanisms to keep their populations spread out. They will, however, gather in groups under some conditions, and we don't understand their biology well enough to account for this. But the willingness of the grays to attack the submarine seems to indicate an aggressiveness that surpasses the business of eating; it is highly unlikely they are trying to eat the submarine. Such nonfeeding aggression must have a natural target, and the only one I can imagine at the moment is other gray reef sharks.

I T occurs to me that I have been rather casual in describing how we caught our shark bait. In fact, it would not be an exaggeration to say that any sport fisherman I know would be willing to give a good deal to do some of this "bait catching." The following day included some fishing for bait, although we attracted no sharks, and the richness of fish life ("bait") throughout our journey along the seaward side of Japtan Island was nothing short of astonishing for one accustomed to the modest fish life that surrounds shorelines inhabited by humans. The tide was coming in, and the water was very clear, with visibility as much as 150 feet. The bottom consisted of flat-topped areas of coral interspersed with patches of sand. The height of the coral, of course, was dictated by the level of maximum low tide. It was a convenient bottom for dropping down with a camera to photograph fish. The sandy patches were calm, and from them I could shoot the fish swimming around the adjacent corals. There were good-sized groupers and snappers, big schools of parrotfish and surgeonfish, a dazzling variety of wrasses, butterflyfish, cardinalfish, squirrelfish, gobies, blennies, jacks—I could name twenty more families like this, and each of them would contain as many as twenty or more species. I'm sure that a real census would contain several hundred different species of fish, all in this rather constricted region of one island channel of one atoll. The colors stood out with abnormal clarity because of the shallow water; the strong sunlight from above was reflected by the white sand bottom. Because of the cleansing effect of wave action, there was little sediment to cloud the water—just white sand and clean, living coral. What we really had in this place was a sport fisherman's dream—a spin-casting paradise. There is a strike on every third or fourth cast; the skiff would be full of fish in an hour if we kept casting. By any "normal" standards, our bait fishing alone was worth a trip halfway around the world.

I went ashore on a whim, hoping to photograph one of the monitor lizards that prowl Japtan Island. These fierce-looking creatures were introduced apparently by the Japanese, when they ruled Enewetak, to control the rat population. Without any controls these rats, which also were introduced by man and which have no natural enemies on this atoll, would overrun the island and ravage both the plant and the animal population; they are known to feed on young and even adult birds. Where albatrosses nest, the rats have learned the trick of climbing upon the backs of nesting adults and gnawing through the skin, leaving large wounds that eventually can kill the birds.

The monitor lizards have been effective in limiting the rat population and have adapted successfully to island life. They are charcoal gray, with small yellow flecks sprinkled over the skin, and very large. Some of them are as much as four feet long, although a good bit of this length is tail. The head is long, and the snout pointed, like that of a baby alligator, and the long, pointed tongue flicks in and out, snakelike. They are also fast-moving and, with their large, hooked claws, can easily climb the trunks of coconut trees.

I suddenly heard a rustling behind some brush and stepped around a bush to see a monitor standing at the base of a coconut tree. Its hind feet were on the ground, and its forefeet on the trunk of the tree. I had never seen one climb, so I moved forward in hopes that this one would; I also wanted a photo, and the only good light was higher up the trunk. I moved around so the sun would be at my back, and up the tree it went, emerging into the rich light of the afternoon sun. I shot a lot of film and then moved in closer. I threw a few stones and pieces of coconut husk to see if the lizard would run all the way into the crown, but it stopped about 50 or

60 feet above the ground, 4 or 5 feet below the crown. Later, in one of the abandoned tin buildings, I opened the door of an old cabinet and a half-grown rat fell out, so the lizards have not eaten them all.

W E tried again the next day to obtain some good footage of sharks feeding, especially the gray reef shark. For bait we trolled around the side of Japtan, and Jo caught a large snapper. We then raced at full speed to the place where we have been baiting sharks, and because the snapper was only out of the water for four or five minutes, it was still very much alive when we threw it over the side with a weight and a buoy. Visibility was only 60 feet or so; it seemed that some of the cloudy water from the lagoon was sweeping along the reef front. But it was still clear enough for photography. I took down my sling spear to try for several more fishes; it is only by the sounds of fish struggling and the scent of their blood that we can hope to attract sharks. A small blacktip was in the neighborhood, but shy as usual, it didn't show much interest in the bait. I managed to spear a surgeonfish and placed it next to the snapper. The blacktip nosed up against it a few times but always shied away at the last minute. I think we humans were too close for his liking. A large snapper weighing about 20 pounds came in and took several nibbles on the slightly smaller snapper that was our bait but was able to dislodge only a few scales.

Soon a whitetip came in, circled a few times, and then dived to the bottom to grab the surgeonfish. The shark ran off with its prey and the spear—my good collecting spear—dangling from its mouth. The spear shook free, however, and Jo went off and brought back a large emperor angelfish (*Pomacanthus imperator*), one of the most strikingly beautiful of all Indo-Pacific reef fishes. It was about a foot-and-a-half long and almost that deep through the body. It had been speared only through the fleshy part of the body and was very much alive, making a loud grunting sound which I could hear clearly 20 feet away. To make this sound, it apparently grinds its teeth, and the swim bladder acts as a reverberation chamber. *Onk, onk, onk,* it went.

Jo placed the spear and fish in the same place, and soon a whitetip shark was there, and then two whitetips and then two blacktips. The whitetips seemed to be more excited now that there were two of them, and one went quickly to the snapper on the line as though to make off with it, but it veered away at the last minute. Then one of them came in and grabbed the angelfish. I was surprised by this, because the emperor's deep, rigid body seemed to be too big for the shark to swallow. The shark was about five feet long, but its mouth was smaller than the prey. Nonetheless, the shark seized the fish whole and swam off with the four-foot shaft of the spear sticking forward from its mouth like the bowsprit of a ship. I shivered in sympathy as the inevitable happened: the shark swam too close to the bottom and rammed the butt of the spear into the coral and the point down its throat. It then fled off into the distance, the spear still protruding, with me in hot pursuit. The spear shaft was made from tempered stainless steel, spring steel, actually, and I was loath to lose it. There would be no way to replace it here. It is a free type of spear that we shoot with a rubber sling called a Hawaiian sling, and it is highly useful for collecting small fishes.

Finally, as I chased the shark, it again ran into the bottom, this time bending the spear almost double. Being spring steel, it straightened right out again, and the shark went into a convulsion on the bottom. I thought for a moment that the spear had penetrated a vital organ, but it was probably shaking to rid itself of the spear and the angelfish, whose dorsal and anal spines and rigid body structure had jammed crossways in the shark's mouth so it could neither swallow nor spit it out. As the shark shook and arched its back and rolled on the bottom the way a dog rolls on the ground, the spear finally came free and fell to the sand. I immediately went to reclaim it, and the shark disappeared into the haze, shaking its head vigorously.

21

LEARNING MARINE BIOLOGY

ON the way back to the *El Territo* I heard another scuba rig going, and I turned to see Bill Eschmeyer and Jerry Allen nearby. They were photographing the lionfish I had found earlier in a drum. By now it had moved to another drum that was open at both ends, so that both Jerry and I could get a look at it. The lionfish, seeing humans at both ends of the drum, turned upside down and "sat" on the ceiling; perhaps Jerry and I looked less threatening from an upside-down perspective.

Later that evening Jerry and Bill came over to talk awhile, and we caught up on everyone's movements. Jerry had just received his doctorate and is taking a job as research director of a small lab on the island of Palau, where we are going in a few weeks. Bill and I were graduate students together at Miami; he's now director of ichthyology at the California State Museum in San Francisco.

We talked over old times and old classmates and agreed that although some of them had gone on to good jobs, they were the exception. Jobs seemed to be growing scarce. In the late 1950s and 1960s, after the launching of the Russian satellite Sputnik, the U.S. government poured money into research to "catch up" with the Soviet Union, and suddenly there was a great deal of research money in fields that were accustomed to poverty. When I was first a graduate student, there were only about half a dozen others in marine biology; by the time I graduated there were seventy-five. Students flocked into the field with great enthusiasm, but little guidance or sense of where they were going. Traditionally a professor is considered to have done well if in his lifetime he trains two or three students. It takes only one to replace him as a researcher; the one or two others may teach or eventually move from the field. If there are *ten* graduate students for each professor, nine of them are going to have to find new jobs—or none. If they all got jobs, and if their students in turn got jobs, the whole gross national product would be quickly usurped by marine biologists. That might be a lot of fun, especially from my standpoint, but it isn't going to happen, and the general aura of euphoria that accompanied this new money has already faded, as has much of the enthusiasm for science in general. A sad symbol of this turnabout is the case of a fellow doctoral graduate of Miami who is now picking up papers with a pointed stick for the parks department in Miami. Others manage to find jobs in their general field but not really what they want. Usually the jobs that are available are those at small universities; those at the major oceanographic institutions and universities and museums tend to be already filled; there are not many more positions at such places than there were before Sputnik.

Jerry had decided to take the "little" job at Palau because a tentative job at one of the Ivy League universities—I think it was Harvard—had not yet been funded. I for one think he made the right choice whether or not the job at Harvard was funded. I don't really buy the argument of many career-oriented scientists that the stimulation of a major university environment is necessary to produce good work. The best stimulation, the best thoughts, are those that are capable of reasoned expression and worthy of being written down—in short, books and articles. One can tap these sources of ideas anywhere, even on a desert island. There is more information in writing than anyone can read in one lifetime, but there is far more time to try on a desert island than there is at a major institution, where 80 or 90 percent of the working day is spent sitting in meetings, writing memos, and running back and forth, attending to the politics of science.

This is not to say that a major research institution or center of learning is not a stimulating place. I am saying simply that there are other ways and places to achieve intellectual stimulation and enlightenment. Personal contact with other scientists is important, but personal contact with the subjects you are studying is also important, and if I had to drop one, it would be the former. In terms of results, one can find just as many highly productive people tucked away in odd corners of the world as in the major institutions. Taken as wholes, the universities are extremely productive,

but not all their researches are so; they become submerged in the la-
byrinth of bureaucracy. Perhaps the greatest danger at these places is success. If any individual shows real ability and rises above the general level
to produce original work, that person is recognized as a coming star and
saddled with a load of inappropriate administrative duties, or chosen to
head large grant programs, or appointed to time-consuming committees.
Soon the person is no longer producing scientific work himself—only directing it. It is foolish to pull the best people out of productive work situations in order to supervise the work of less productive people. It is
probably not a coincidence that much of the best work at major institutions is done by graduate students who do not yet have any administrative
duties. I would guess that from the standpoint of productivity the ideal
situation would be a remote outpost for a single researcher who is aided by
a couple of assistants and a secretary and the cash to subscribe to a good
range of scientific journals. Someplace not unlike Enewetak, perhaps.

THE next day a group of fifteen people from the Scripps Institution of
Oceanography came in on the plane to do some work at one of the
islands farther up the atoll, where the bomb craters are. Rumor has it that
they are going to drill a deep hole in the crater, penetrating the face of the
atoll for several thousand feet. The idea would be to tap the deep, nutrient-rich water at those depths and let it flow to the surface. Nutrients at
surface levels are relatively depleted by plankton and the rest of the food
pyramid, but the deep water is "used" by relatively few organisms. The
deep water is also denser than surface water because it is colder. So if you
put a pipe down into this water and start it moving, it will continue to
flow to the surface—the region of less dense water—indefinitely, without
adding any external energy. The idea, of course, is to "fertilize" the shallow sunlit water of a lagoon or pond with this deep, nutrient-rich water
and grow plants or animals in it. The cold water would gradually warm at
the surface and produce lush blooms of plankton (perhaps of a desired
species which could be injected in small "seed" populations). These
stands of plankton could in turn serve as food for zooplankton and eventually for some creature prized by humans as food, such as shrimps, oysters, or fish. Similar projects are being considered for the Caribbean as
well as for the atolls of the Pacific and other tropical parts of the world.
     For this project, however worthy, the Scripps people had insisted on
taking all the small boats, outboards, and scuba gear up to the island
where they want to work, thus leaving the people at the laboratory with-

out boats or diving gear. The lab here at Enewetak has the usual problem of incompetent handling of small boats. Most scientists have little experience in using small boats, especially in such rough conditions as those encountered around oceanic atolls. In fact, there is no reason why they should be expected to be competent, since there is nothing in their academic training that would make them so. It is one thing to study for a few hectic years and earn a doctorate; it is quite another to become a good boat handler or fisherman. Either of these usually takes years of experience, for which laboratory work cannot substitute. This probably seems unlikely to land-based folks, and the scientists themselves do nothing to change this impression. There is a general attitude that once a person becomes a marine biologist or oceanographer and grows a beard and takes a few voyages somewhere he is then a master mariner, or at least an old salt. And there is no telling these people that they don't know what they are doing without delivering a deadly insult. But here at the laboratory the small boats are frequently tied improperly so that they break loose and beat on the reef. Outboards are left turned down in the water so electrolysis eats away at them. Or they are left with the outboard down on the beach, where the surf beats the boat up and down and may knock the motor off so that it is soaked by salt water and has to be completely torn apart and cleaned or else is ruined. Anyone can learn to operate an outboard in a couple of hours; it is not physically difficult to start, stop, and reverse. The trick is judgment—where to go, when, what to do with the boat when you get there, and a thousand other things that must be learned through experience.

Rhett McNair, who is now responsible for the equipment at the lab, particularly the expensive new skiff that we brought down from Hawaii, had the audacity to ask the group of scientists if anyone was experienced in handling small boats, and one of the scientists replied that *all* the people in his group were competent boat handlers. Well, it is a safe guess that there is no single group of fifteen people anywhere in the world all of whom are competent boatmen; in any such group you would be lucky to find one. The truth is that the requisite practical tools for marine biology—boat handling, diving, maintenance, building of equipment, judgment in general—are not available at most teaching institutions, and most students neglect these skills under the assumption that they must be easier than academic work. They may or may not be easier, but they are different. Before you can build equipment, for example, you have to learn to use lathes and milling machines and drill presses and grinders—tools that are not commonly part of the oceanography curriculum. And much of this building skill is common sense of the kind that cannot be taught other than by experience. Fortunately most of the major institutions have at least diving training programs, but even these are deficient in maintenance instruction, such as in rebuilding regulators. This is partly the result of the mystique perpetrated by diving instructors, who give the false impression that regulators can be torn apart and rebuilt only by master divers. Actually they are extremely simple devices which every diver should be able to repair, just as every rifleman in the military is expected to know how to disassemble and reassemble a rifle—a tool considerably more complex than a regulator.

Learning to capture marine animals—most commonly by fishing—is another area in which most biologists are inexperienced. It is not fair to expect a biologist to become an expert fisherman, but he does need some basics. Any marine biologist should be able to master the basic routines of collecting juvenile fishes around drifting seaweed or catching schooling fishes in the open ocean, and so forth. They should also be instructed in the use of various spears, poles, spear guns, multi-barreled spears, power-heads, and nooses. Most biologists simply go to a store and buy a spear gun, but this is only one kind of tool, useful only for large fish. They should also learn the use of anesthetics, poisons, hand nets, and various traps. If a biologist is at least aware of such tools and techniques, he can seek them out as the need arises. Let me illustrate how the lack of such knowledge can waste our tax money and other funds. I watched the administrator of a research grant amounting to hundreds of thousands of dollars a year, involving the efforts of half a dozen people, waste six months trying to capture sharks that any sixteen-year-old kid in the Florida Keys would be able to get every day. And that's eventually how they solved their problem—by paying kids to go out and get small sharks for them. The biologists were trying out tricks like encirclement of a section of beach with a 200-foot beach seine. This is like trying to collect butterflies with a hunting rifle. The easiest way to catch a small shark is with a small throw net. It is also easy enough to catch them with rod and reel, but this requires the skill of poling a boat in the shallow grass flats so as not to frighten the fishes, in addition to skill with the rod and reel. You have to use Polaroid glasses, to cut the glare from the surface, and learn to spot the sharks from a great enough distance so as not to scare them off. You then stalk them by poling silently to within 50 feet or so and casting the throw net just to the other side and slightly ahead of the shark so as not to frighten it; then you pull it right back in front of their path of motion. The business of poling is an acquired skill, like riding a pogo stick or a bicycle, and although it is not needed by every marine biologist, it is good to know that such a skill is available for certain needs.

Speaking of needs, the surge built up this afternoon, and we were in need of a bit of calm. Any place you tie a boat in a surge will cause trouble. The tide was high, and the *El Territo* was riding against the pier and at one point bumped a porthole against the pilings. Fortunately it didn't break, but it was a warning, so I decided to move back up to Japtan Island. There was a slight delay; Jo was taking a ride on a bike borrowed from one of the loran Coast Guard crew, and Marissa, who was riding on the back, got her foot into the rear wheel, so we had to bandage up what she began proudly to call her "bump" and get her back aboard. We came into Japtan after dark—a tricky maneuver with the reefs around. I had the radar on, so it was fairly easy to judge the distances, and I could even see the breakers at various points. I had also heard a rumor, third-hand, that a typhoon was somewhere in the area, so I wanted to be sure we were near a heavy mooring and had a thick line ready in case it came close.

W E still wanted more footage of the gray reef shark feeding, so the next day we set out to catch some larger fish for bait. I particularly wanted to try a new lure I had developed several years ago. We had with us some of the first production models and had had good luck with them. The lure combines a number of features that attract hungry predators. Most fishing lures are simply made to suit someone's fancy and take little account of the needs and desires of the fish themselves. However, the color, pattern, and action of lures are all-important if predator fish are to recognize them as something desirable, so a good lure design must somehow make "sense" as a prospective meal. In the sea the most widely recognized food is a member of the herring family, most of which have a deep body, a knife-edged belly, and flat sides. This type of fish is popular prey all over the world, even in some fresh-water areas. Yet to my knowledge that body form, which my lure imitates, has never been used realistically: flat sides; deep body; sharp belly line.

The next feature I mimicked was color. The belly and sides are silver, like those of a real herring, and the back is blue-green, also like that of a herring. The next point about herring predation is that an injured herring will swim eccentrically, unable to maintain its normal upright position. Then the silver sides catch the light from above and reflect brightly. The fish immediately becomes a beacon for predators in the area, flashing on and off as it turns rapidly and erratically. Normally this flashing serves a school of herring well, for as they wheel in a group, they all flash at once, distracting the predator by offering hundreds of flashes moving very quickly, making it very difficult to get a visual fix on any one of them. We guaranteed an easy-to-catch silver target by giving the lure a slightly asymmetrical shape that makes it rock back and forth as it moves through the water, flashing silver.

Another appealing feature is the eye. Under normal conditions a predator makes its final fix on the eye of the prey, because it is a distinctive point in most fishes and a ready target. Many fishes, as I mentioned earlier, have ways of hiding or disguising the eye, such as a black line through the pupil or a false eye in the tail. I decided to give this lure an exaggerated eye made out of molded plastic, with a yellow iris and a large black pupil.

As a final touch we used a bit of fluorescent pigment. This grew out of an experiment where we marked fish with pigment to find out if they returned to the same school in the day after foraging at night and also to learn what school an individual forager had come from. That particular experiment was a failure because the fish we marked bore a conspicuous green or red blotch on the side, and they stood out in the school like beacons for predators. Blood fluoresces green at any depth in the water, so the predators quickly eliminated the fish we had so carefully tagged. But while that experiment told us nothing about the travels of schooling fishes, it did tell us that predators like green blotches, so we've put a patch of fluorescent green on the side of our lure. It looks underwater like a bloody wound and serves as a visual fix for an attacker. So our lure resembles in most important ways a wounded or ill member of a common prey group and invites a predator to zero in on its "eye" and "wound." These prototypes we are using, made by Beckwin Instruments in California, have caught half-a-dozen kinds of fish and seem to be working very well. We got the large snapper we wanted for shark bait and were pleased with our new product.

WE went around to the outside of the island and decided to try the edge of the deep channel with our bait, in about 20 feet of water. We'd no sooner got down than a small gray shark came in, but it seemed to be more interested in us than in the large snapper flapping on the line. It left, and I took the spear and speared a surgeonfish and a parrotfish, and then a large paddle-tailed snapper which I put on the coral, the spear still in it, just below the snapper that was moored in midwater. I started to swim toward deep water and a few seconds later looked back to see the snapper on the line being jerked about. I moved closer and found it was just a moray eel that had taken a bite too big for its mouth or its stomach.

We continued to hang around the area. Jo discovered a giant clam about a foot and a half in length, and I was interested to find that its mantle and fleshy parts were so thick that it could not close tight. I could insert my whole finger between the valves, so that the clam seemed at least partially defenseless. A whitetip shark appeared and paid a good deal of attention to the snapper on the line, but the shark was only a little more than twice as big as that snapper, and it didn't seem to see the smaller one impaled on the spear below. As the shark swam straight toward me, I could see the tips of the dermal denticles standing out in the light. Under the right illumination they glare like a dry surface. For five minutes the shark circled from the snapper to me to Jo to the snapper again, coming very close but showing no aggression. Suddenly it spotted the snapper on the spear and went to it immediately. It tried to swallow the bait, spear and all, but I had made sure the spear was stuck completely through the snapper. The shark went into a really vicious spasm of head shaking and violent rolling against the bottom. Still the spear stayed in; the shark went away a bit, and I went swimming after. In another 20 feet came another spasm, and the spear finally slid out. The shark swam off, swallowing the snapper. I had hoped all the activity would attract more sharks, but it didn't, and I ran out of air. I hung the other snapper alongside the *El Territo* to keep it alive, figuring to use it after lunch, and as I came up on deck, I saw a big landing craft and Harry, the boatman, waving his empty coffee cup at us. He tossed it over but aimed too high, and it smashed against the bulkhead behind me. Jo went below to get a plastic cup of coffee for Harry, and I found then that only the head of the snapper was left; a shark had come up and bitten the bait right beside the boat. Harry, in his mid- or late forties, is a former career Navy man who is now working here as a diver, boatman, and radio man. While in the Navy he served on a Seal Team, and was involved in some rather exotic activities in Vietnam, both North and South. I got into the skiff and ran the coffee over to him.

We went down again after lunch without much luck, and Jo brought back a crown-of-thorns starfish from a crevice about 100 feet deep, and I found one at 30 feet. When you pick up an *Acanthaster*, it immediately closes its arms, forming a spiny ball like a European hedgehog. We laid one on the coral, and soon it straightened out and began to crawl methodically ahead. Its tube feet (powered hydraulically) were so tenacious that when Jo stuck her net handle in front of the starfish, it started to crawl on it, and when she lifted the net, the whole animal was able to cling to the handle by just a few feet. When she pulled the handle away, the feet came with it. We brought the starfish back because I wanted to look at the skeletal elements as an aid to identifying starfish remains in fish stomachs.

After supper we went for a night dive off Japtan Island. We fired up the little single-cylinder portable gas engine as a generator and took down the 650-watt movie light. Soon we began to spot sleeping parrotfish tucked in crevices everywhere on the reef, as well as surgeonfish, also sleeping, and a number of shells crawling around. Suddenly I looked up and saw a pair of eyes I knew belonged to a shark. Sharks have a reflective layer in the eye like that of a deer or cat or other nocturnal animals. This reflective layer bounces the light that passes through the retina back again, acting as a kind of image intensifier, so that it makes more efficient use of the light coming into the eye. Sharks have only rods in their retinas, rather than the cones we have, and presumably only black-and-white vision. But an all-rod retina is much more sensitive to low light than our own rod-and-cone type. The shark's pupil is also like a cat's, being an elliptical slit designed for a light-sensitive eye. A round pupil like ours can close only a certain minimal amount; if we had a round pupil large enough to allow us to see in the dark, it would not close sufficiently to protect the retina during the daytime. While an elliptical pupil is not as precise optically, giving only a rough image, it can close down to zero in sunlight if necessary or open very wide at night. The optical nerve structure of the shark is also designed to enhance contrast, so it can probably see us at night at distances where we cannot see it. One often catches a glimpse of a shark in the distance, dimly visible in the haze; it is probably approaching and circling at a distance where it can see the human, but the human can see it barely or not at all.

This one was a blacktip, and it came right toward the light. I held the light to one side and prepared to fend off the shark, but at a distance of five or six feet it suddenly whirled and disappeared. Later Jo yelled at me to warn of the approach of another shark, which turned out to be a gray, but as soon as I turned around and put the light on it, it vanished into the darkness.

T HE next night, after a dive, we came back to a sight we had never seen before. I had left the deck lights burning on the *El Territo*, and throughout the lighted area around the boat were hundreds of brown jellyfish. Apparently they are phototropic, strongly attracted by a light source, so that even as the current pressed them toward the end of the island, they swam steadily to remain in place beneath the lighted ship. When we had tied up the skiff, I hung the movie light above them so as to point a very strong beam straight down, and within five minutes or so the water lit by the beam was a thick soup of jellyfishes. Before I turned on the movie light, each animal had been a foot or so from its neighbors, so that they cast an interesting pattern of distinct black shadows on the bottom. As they pulled together, however, they closed in so tightly that they actually were touching, back to back and jelly to jelly. I went into the water with the movie camera and a full wet suit, so that I didn't have to worry about being stung except on the face and hands. I dived to the bottom, about 15 feet down, and filmed upward into what was then a solid but translucent mass, shifting and seething. Then I went up and shot at close range, mixing among these tight-packed creatures, oozing and squirming my way like a fly in a bowl of Jello.

22

WINDING DOWN

MY strategy continued to revolve around catching snappers or other large fishes to use for shark bait, in an effort to observe more shark feeding behavior. This, I hoped, would teach us more about the aggressive display of the gray reef shark. If we got to know it well enough, we might be able to devise a set of rules of human behavior that would reduce the danger to skin divers.

The next morning we set out to catch some fish, and, after little success, set off a depth charge near an isolated mound of coral. There were *Caesio* nearby, and Jerry picked up those that were killed while I swam around with the camera. On the down-current side of one mound I found a large stingray resting on the bottom. I held my breath and eased as slowly toward him as I could, hoping to film some feeding activity. In feeding, these large rays use a process like hydraulic mining, pressing the flat ventral surface against the bottom and squirting water against the sand to expose prey. They take in clean water through the spiracles atop the head and blow it out the mouth with such energy that a single ray may excavate a hole 3 or 4 feet in diameter and 18 inches deep. The goal is to uncover any of a variety of tasty mollusks and crustaceans.

This ray, however, declined my invitation to dine, so I went back beneath the boat to pick up tools and other items that Varrina had decided to toss from the skiff. When we're diving in shallow water, we frequently take the children; wearing life jackets, they can't sink if they fall in, and we can safely leave them in the boat if we glance above the surface every few minutes. However, the atrocities perpetrated inside the skiff cannot be seen, and Varrina takes advantage of this protection to get into the tackle box or the tool box and do a little depth-charging.

I still needed a fish large enough for bait, and we trolled for fifteen minutes or so without success, even though I was using two lures. It is fascinating that fish can catch on so quickly to the true nature of any fishing lure. The first two or three days we trolled around this side of the island, we would get three or four strikes in just one short pass, but yesterday and today I got none. I have seen this phenomenon many times in Florida. Along the Keys, for example, large numbers of fish—big snappers, snooks, tarpons, groupers—gather beneath the bridges of U.S. Route 1 that connect the islands. Fishermen stand on these bridges by the hour, their lines hanging untouched among the schools of fish. After a short period of interest, fish learn to avoid even the cleverest of lures in any given spot, and this goes for the entire populations—not just the "smart" ones. I remember when bucktail lures first became popular in the Keys. They came in with the introduction of spinning tackle, and they were so effective we could catch one fish after another. Now they are just another lure. In the same way the Mirror Lure, when it first came out, was miraculously effective, and everyone bought it. Within a few years, however, it, too, was just another lure. This happens even with natural baits. My father was the first person to use live mullet for catching sailfish, and for a number of years it never failed: he would catch four or five times as many sailfish as any of the other boats. Then a few of the competitors started using mullet, and its effectiveness dropped.

Sure enough, I went around to the other side of the channel by Medren Island, where we had not yet fished, and in five minutes I caught a five-pound snapper. I fastened it onto a line and turned away; when I looked back, I saw a large puffer nibbling at it. The puffer was even larger than the one that had sheared off the end of my snorkel, and when I pulled the snapper up to check it, I found that the puffer had removed the skull and part of the brain with a casual bite of its powerful jaws. It made me wonder whether some of the snappers supposedly eaten by sharks had actually been taken by these dull-looking fish.

When I was photographing gobies later, I happened upon a small pipefish along the side of Pole Pinnacle. These creatures are related to sea horses and bear them some resemblance externally in the leathery appearance of their skin. Both live near shore and feed on minute organisms, and neither looks particularly fishlike. A peculiar habit of both pipefishes and sea horses is that the female deposits the eggs in a pouch on the underside of the male's body, where they remain until they emerge as miniature versions of the parents. Most of both kinds of fish live in grass beds, but this pipefish was a member of one of the few species that have adapted to life on coral reefs. It swims with a stiff body, weakly driven by the high-speed fluttering of the dorsal and anal fins, both of which are virtually invisible. Pipefishes are able to kick with their long, sinewy tails if necessary, but in most cases they swim only short distances before settling down in the coral. They have prehensile tails that can fasten to the coral in the face of a surge, and their tiny, tubelike mouths seem to be well suited to securing the microscopic creatures they feed on around the reef.

On the way back to the *El Territo* I witnessed the unusual sight of a halfbeak soaring out of the water for 50 feet or so, then splashing back in. The halfbeaks, like their cousins the needlefishes, are predatory surface creatures that feed upon smaller fishes, which they seize with a sharp, oversized bill. In the needlefish both upper and lower jaws are extended and heavily toothed; in the halfbeak only the lower jaw is long. Both are related to flying fishes, and when they are young some flying fishes have an enlarged lower jaw which may be a holdover from halfbeak ancestors. The halfbeak I saw has enlarged pectoral fins—not actual wings, like the flying fishes—that allow it to glide for long distances, although not as long as their cousins. Nor do they hold their body straight as they glide, curving instead into a J shape. First one jumped and glided away from the skiff; then it was followed by five more. Just near the stern of the ship I passed a very large group of true flying fishes, which broke water from right under my bow and skittered away in all directions like a covey of quail. These fishes do not actually flap-fly, like birds, but by spreading their pectoral fins and sculling rapidly with the lower lobe of the tail fin, they can skim-glide above the surface for hundreds of feet.

WE had been having rough weather, with clouds and a lot of swell, but the next day it finally broke. The wind settled to a light breeze, and the sun was bright. For humans and fish alike it turned out to be an active and somewhat dangerous day, and in some respects an omen of things soon to come. It was September 13 and, as I look back on it, the last really productive day at Enewetak.

We got a late start because I first rigged up an aluminum pole that allowed us to troll a live or dead bait from the submarine at the same time we were searching for sharks. I brought along the sling spear (which I had to retrieve from the bottom of the sea where Varrina had managed to throw it) to shoot a bait, snapper or grouper, but all I saw for some time were triggerfishes. I finally spotted a grouper of the right size and speared it, whereupon two large *Cheilinus* appeared from the up-current side of a pinnacle. I wanted to look at some more stomach contents, and when the smaller of the two sped away, I swam after the larger. It disappeared behind a coral mound, but when I swam around after it, I saw the tip of its tail sticking out of a cave. When I approached, it wriggled farther back by six or eight feet to where it was dark. I went around to another point where there was a larger opening. Most of these coral mounds are hollow to some extent; the heart of the coral, after the growing organisms are superseded by new generations, erodes slowly, leaving large caves for fish, morays, and other creatures to hide in. After a few stings from hydroids that were growing on rocks inside, I managed to work my way up through crevices to the top, but I saw no trace of the fish. I gave up and went back to the sub, and we towed the grouper along as bait. Toward deeper water we saw one whitetip that paid us no attention and one small *Cheilinus* in an area of very heavy plate coral, so that we couldn't set down.

At the edge of the deep channel we turned left and ran along the bank. I was cruising at 50 feet when Jo tapped my shoulder and pointed to her ears; her sinuses were giving her trouble. I pulled up and waited awhile and descended again, but she still couldn't clear them. We climbed again, and then I spotted a large *Cheilinus* and a second one right with it, and I chased the larger one until it went into a cave right on the edge of the channel about 65 feet down. I descended, and Jo's ears cleared at last, so we put down on a patch of sand. Just as I got out of the sub, I saw the *Cheilinus* come out of the rock and look at me, so I swam directly at it so as to scare it back into the cave. Then I turned quickly and went back for the bang stick. I reached the cave, which turned out to be just a ledge, and jabbed the bang stick at the *Cheilinus* just as it started out, but it was a glancing blow with no explosion. Then it wedged itself in where I could get a clear shot, and I did. After some struggle I managed to pull it out and tug it toward the sub, where I noticed Jo standing up with the movie camera, filming my return. I was trying to fasten the fish onto the aluminum pole when Jo got my attention and pointed to a gray shark coming in. It was over five feet long and very peculiar. Its head was large, but the body was very skinny, bearing a strange bump on the ventral surface just back of the pectoral fin. I suspected that it had swallowed something too tough even for a shark's stomach and that the meal had become wedged in its gut, preventing normal feeding. Just above its head swam a school of small jacks only two or three inches long. Since it looked so gaunt, I feared it might attack, but it came in only to mouth the large wrasse, which, being about 100 pounds, was too large for it to eat. Jo filmed as it went off and circled and returned, swimming completely around us an arm's length away, then returning to mouth the wrasse again. I kept the bang stick loaded and cocked, but it was more interested in the wrasse. Finally, a second, healthy gray showed up and circled, and then I noticed that there were eight large *Cheilinus* in the area—the most I've ever seen gathered in one place. Some were more than 100 pounds, and the smallest was about 50 pounds. They hovered in midwater, and then two whitetips appeared and circled as well. One of the big wrasses went down behind the same rock where I'd collected the other one, so I followed to take a look. First I thought I'd better get rid of the long, sick-looking gray shark because it worried me the most. I didn't want to dangle my bare legs from underneath the rock while I was trying to capture a *Cheilinus*. I loaded the long bang stick, and the next time the shark came in I killed it. I wanted to take it back to look at the peculiar lump, but it was still kicking a bit, and I decided to leave it on the bottom. I reloaded the bang stick and found that the big wrasse was in the same cave as the first, but much farther up. I went around to the other side of the rock, where I could see its head peeking out. I put the bang stick underneath the rock to line it up for a shot when suddenly a six-foot moray eel struck the end of it. The end of the bar was stoppered with a fluorescent orange cap, which appears even brighter than normal underwater, and apparently the thing had sufficiently outraged the moray to draw a really vicious strike. I tried again and managed to shoot the wrasse. With the explosion the moray took off and, unbeknownst to me, settled right beneath the submarine.

I went to the other side of the rock and pushed at the wrasse with the stick, trying to force it back out so I could reach it from the other side. I did so, checking every few seconds to make sure the second gray shark was not becoming too interested in what I was doing. The *Cheilinus* was slippery, and I had to dig my fingers into its tail, inching it backward until I could finally get my arm into the rock and reach the eye sockets. I was just getting there when suddenly I felt my regulator beginning to signal the end of my air supply, and almost out of oxygen, I made one last quick effort and managed to yank the fish all the way free and pull it rapidly over to the sub. I grabbed the regulator from the sub's air supply, and then Jo signaled me that her tank too was running out, so I quickly gripped the other *Cheilinus* and pointed to Jo to go on up. She didn't much like that idea, however, with the sharks milling about, so she held out for a little longer while I stuffed the second *Cheilinus*, aluminum pole and all, into the sub and blew the ballast tanks.

We bobbed to the surface, and as soon as we did, I closed off the ballast tanks and blew them completely so that we were floating high and dry. But with a couple of hundred pounds of dead wrasse in the sub I couldn't even get to the front cockpit, and we were out in the middle of the channel about three-quarters of a mile from the *El Territo*. When the sub is on the surface with all that weight in front of the propeller, the prop simply fans air, so Jo had to take off her fins and crawl back to add her weight to the stern while I crouched behind the regular seats as low in the water as I could so that my weight did not push the bow down any more than necessary. We barely managed to get the prop in the water, and once we got moving I put out the diving planes, and they helped bring the nose up. After a fifteen-minute run we pulled up to the ship, a strange-looking craft and cargo by any standards, with me squatting in water up to my neck, Jo perched on the rear, and a huge load of dead green wrasses filling the cockpit. Later I found that both stomachs were virtually empty, save for a small piece of gastropod shell in one and in the other a piece of a bivalve shell, the tails of some shrimps, and the bones of some very small fish. That made four *Cheilinus* stomachs examined; the first, taken in the morning, had an *Acanthaster* in it, and the rest, taken in the afternoon, were essentially empty. It made me suspect that this animal feeds either just at dawn or at night. That would be unusual, because all other wrasses I know of are diurnal, feeding by day and resting at night. We cut a couple of huge fillets from the larger *Cheilinus*, and Jo baked one for dinner, but the meat had a jellylike consistency that we didn't much care for. We had cut one of the previous wrasses into finger-sized pieces which were not bad at all, fried.

THAT night Jerry and I made a dive, using the big floodlight powered by the alternator, while Jo wrote up a list of provisions to order on the next plane. The plankton were atrocious that night, aggregating in a huge pink cloud wherever I turned on the light. Most of them were tiny shrimps. When I turned the light off, I could see thousands of little lights mixed in with the shrimp—apparently the luminescent larva of some creature. A number of large groupers, snappers, mackerels, and a whitetip shark also came to the light, and at one point a large gray shark cruised in, its eye glowing fiercely. Two large morays and a couple of beautiful lionfish foraged around a coral mound. It would have been a beautiful dive without the plankton. I had to keep swimming constantly; each time I stopped they enveloped me in their single-minded pursuit of the movie light. If I turned the light off, they would blunder around in the dark, getting in my hair and ears. After half an hour of swimming in circles we gave it up and retreated to the more orderly world aboard ship.

23

SHARK ATTACK

THERE followed three days for which I can't say much good, when the wind blew and the rain fell and the dim light allowed for little or no photography. It dampened our spirits as well as the boat and the atoll, and we felt gripped once again by the whim of the monstrous weather machine, helpless and tiny. On the fourth day, when it was still blowing and raining, we decided against my better judgment to make an excursion no matter what the elements attempted. That decision turned into disaster and near tragedy for both Jo and me as well as for the submarine.

In the morning I went out in the skiff for a couple of hundred yards in just 8 or 10 feet of water to try to collect some cardinalfish of the genus *Siphamia*, which I had heard were living in interesting proximity to some sea urchins, but none was around. Late in the afternoon Jo and I set out in the submarine to go—we thought—only a short way out into the channel. It was blowing quite hard from the east, and the tide was just beginning to go out, but we decided to go anyway.

The mail plane had brought the two light meters that we had sent for repairs. We tried the older of the two, and it seemed to be working perfectly, so we took it along for a trial. We had no more than started when we discovered it leaked like a sieve, so we came back and opened it to get the water out and took the other meter. It was around five-thirty when we finally left. Most of the way it rained, and the water was lagoonal and muddy, so that the visibility was only about 30 feet. When we pulled around to the south side of Japtan Island, however, the water suddenly cleared to the normal 100-foot-plus visibility of the ocean water. We went on out to the same little spur of reef where Jo and I had got the two *Cheilinus* the other day, and we had no more than arrived when we saw several more big *Cheilinus* and a very large school of jacks; there must have been 150 or so, all about 18 inches to 2 feet long. As usual, they swept in as one large cloud and then began to follow the submarine. We pulled up at a little sand patch in about 80 feet of water, stopped the sub, and got out the cameras. I filmed in the direction of the sub as the huge school of jacks swam around Jo.

At about that time Jo shouted to me and signaled with her hand that she had seen a shark. I turned quickly and saw a gray milling around the area; I was a little uneasy when I saw that it was in the initial stages of display. So I swam back and got into the sub and decided to go after it for some attack footage. Since we were sitting on the sand with some coral around, I had to blow a little air into the ballast tanks to pick us up. As soon as we were clear of the coral, I planned to start the motor and let the air back out of the tanks, leaving us "airborne," so to speak, and flying on the power of the motor. So I blew the tanks, and we rose about five feet off the bottom. I turned the engine switch to start, and a hideous grinding sound came from the bowels of the sub. There was no propulsion—not forward, not reverse, not anything. We continued to drift upward without propulsion; I had no choice but to let it rise all the way to the surface. At that point I went ahead and blew the ballast tanks completely, and there we were, afloat perhaps 100 yards off the shore of Japtan Island, right on the edge of the deep channel. Without power, that 100 yards seemed oh, so far. I sat there for a minute, fiddling with the switch and trying to decide what to do: wait for Jerry to miss us and come out in the skiff, or leave the sub and swim in, walk over to the skiff, and then come back out to find the sub in the dark.

Because the wind was blowing from the east, which would push us in, and the usual flow of water was also shoreward, I decided just to drift for a while. We didn't seem to be moving very much, however, as I could see by keeping an eye on the bottom. Gradually we began to drift more to the south, toward Jedrol Island, so I resolved to see if we could "swim" the sub. Jo and I both got out, each hanging onto a wing of the sub, and kicked with our flippers. We pushed hard for several minutes and seemed to be making a slight bit of progress when I glanced down and noticed that while we had been flipping as hard as we could, a gray shark had moved in beneath us and was keeping track of our activities. By this time we'd drifted out over the edge of the deep channel so that I couldn't see bottom anymore. I kept a close watch on the shark below, but it didn't seem to be paying much attention. I finally realized that we weren't going to make it to shore in this fashion, so we got back inside and sat there awhile. After some time spent unproductively thinking about our plight, we made up our minds that since we were still only about 200 yards off Japtan Island, we would go ahead and swim it. It wasn't a long swim, and we could leave our weight belts in the sub, relax, and just kick ourselves in. I picked up a bang stick, and we got out of the sub and started toward shore.

We'd only gone a distance of 75 feet or so when we got the scare of the year. Suddenly, up from the blue, came a gray shark on the attack. With no provocation, with no blood in the water or speared fish or unusual activity, it charged at full speed—the attack charge. I was slightly ahead of Jo, and it came first at me, the lead duck, and as it sped by, I shot at it with the bang stick. The shark veered off and swirled around behind me, undoubtedly pulling the trick the other sharks had performed in attacking the submarine, circling faster than I could move, and biting from the rear. It might have worked except that Jo was there. The shark came in without seeing her, and she kicked at it and apparently confused it, with the result that it darted off and came at me from the front instead of the rear. By then I was ready and again jabbed at it with the bang stick, fending off the charge while Jo started moving carefully back toward the sub. I kept watch for the shark until she made it safely, and then I turned around and got back to safety also, happier than ever before to feel the security of that plexiglass.

We both settled down in the sub to wait; with an aggressive shark around, it was too dangerous to swim. As we waited, we drifted more and more to the south. To compound that difficulty, the outgoing tide from the main pass began to pick up and carry us out to sea. By then it was getting late and the light was fading rapidly. We kept hoping to see the skiff, and we kept standing up to get a better look. We must have made a picture of helplessness, adrift in the wrong direction, bobbing to our feet every half-minute to get a look at where we wanted to be. I decided to lighten the sub as much as I could so it would ride higher and be more easily visible. I took the lead ballast from the back and threw it overboard; that made us float quite high and also made the sub unsinkable, even with the wing ballast tanks flooded.

The farther we drifted in the main channel, the rougher it became.

By now a big sea was coming in, and squalls were blowing at 20 and 30 knots, throwing up waves that were 8 and 10 feet high and breaking.

We bobbed around like a cork in the big seas, and it was pretty miserable, but the sub was sound, and we were in little danger of sinking. I began to figure our fate. If nobody saw us—and it was by now unlikely that anyone would—I calculated that one of two things would happen. Either the tide would change and carry us back toward shore in the main channel, or since we were fading southward with the winds and sliding diagonally across the channel current, we'd move out of the current altogether so that the winds would push us in.

The wind won out. By the time it grew completely dark we were half or three-quarters of a mile off Medren Island. Although I couldn't see the land well, I could see the breakers rushing white against the beach, and gradually it became apparent that we were drawing slowly closer to land. We sat and waited, and waited, and by around nine o'clock we were right at the edge of the reef. Much as we wanted to get back to shore, it now appeared that the shore was our enemy. With such a big sea running, there were very large breakers pounding the reef. Along a gently sloping sandy beach this would have been a small worry, promising a wet and confusing landing but little danger. On this shore, however, the reef rises steeply from the ocean depths, and the waves were leaping up and crashing down abruptly on rock. The reason for this abrupt breaking was partly the uncompromising nature of the shoreline itself. On a "mature" shore that has been eroded and reduced to sand, wave action evenly distributes and smooths the sand into a gentle shelf extending hundreds of yards seaward, depending upon the nature of the near-shore currents. On an atoll, however, it is rare to find a shelf that slopes gently. By definition an atoll is a steep-sided affair, rising from the abyssal depths atop a volcanic cone and in some places topped with a barricade of live and growing coral that resists erosion. Here was such a place, and the waves were breaking so sharply on the jagged coral formations that we dared not swim in. As waves like this break, they do not drive you forward as much as downward, and the zone where downward movement is greatest may hold water only a foot or so deep. If we were seized by such a wave, we would probably be slammed into the bottom and knocked unconscious—at best.

I ruminated on that one for a while and decided that the course of least danger was to stay put in the submarine, letting it be our guide. Close in, we would try to ride the outside of the sub, like pilotfish on a shark, ready to jump free if it started to roll out of control on a big breaker.

We got our fins on and stepped outside as we came into the breaker zone. Jo perched on the wing on one side of the sub while I swung my body across the back of it, trying to keep the nose up. The rest was up to the whim of the night sea.

The wait was not long. In less than a minute we bumped the bottom a couple of times between waves; that was how shallow the water was. I tried to keep the sub from rolling over, pitting my meager weight against the heaving of the waves. We got to a place where a few more small waves would have us in close and then a big one—as long as it broke before it reached us—could carry us the rest of the way. If it came in over the top of the undertow, however, we would get the full breaking force, which was exactly what I did not want. Almost the instant these thoughts went through my mind I looked back over my shoulder and realized we had been ambushed. A huge wave 8 or 10 feet high hissed straight down upon us, hurtling nonstop across the backs of its smaller cousins to hit us squarely on the downbreak. It plucked me cleanly off my unsteady perch and bowled me topsy-turvy through the foam for more than 50 feet, where I discovered to my amazement that I was allowed to get to my feet without further punishment. I was standing in only a foot or two of water, inside the reef. Immediately I realized Jo was nowhere in sight, and I yelled to her. At first I heard nothing, nor did I see the submarine. I shivered with fear and adrenaline reaction, and then I heard her call to me that she was trapped.

As it happened, I, in answering her call, stumbled into almost the same trap. The sub had rolled over and come down on her leg, pinning her to the rough coral. I quickly clambered over toward her voice, and just as I got there, the sub bounced upward and then, as I was trying to push it off, dropped down on her again. I began to push again, and at that moment the next wave came along, plucking the sub from Jo's leg and dropping it on me. I remember thinking that the sub weighs about 1,200 pounds and wondering whether the human body could withstand that much weight. My answer came quickly as it crushed me into the coral, coming down across my hips and pinning me just as it had Jo. Then the sea mercifully grew bored with us; the next wave carried the sub away shoreward and washed both of us along after it. We both tumbled into the shallows and came to rest on a pavementlike reef flat covered by only a veneer of six or eight inches of water.

The submarine didn't make it that far in, catching on some coral just inside the breakers, but our first concern at that point was with ourselves.

Jo thought her leg was broken, but because it was so numb, she couldn't be sure. I examined it as best I could, and at least it didn't seem to be a compound fracture; when that happens, the leg just sort of dangles like that of a rag doll. As some feeling began to come back, she tried to move it, discovered that she could, and then tried to put some weight on it. Little by little she found she could stand and even walk, so my worry subsided a bit. We hobbled into shore, which was about 100 feet across the flat, smooth reef. There we stopped, and I took a better look at Jo's leg and found a nasty gash at the knee. We made our way up to the beach rubble and then onto the island itself, heading for the road on the other side. All this seemed to take hours but was probably only a few minutes.

After just a few steps I could see a light flashing around on the near side of Medren Island, so we knew that people were searching for us. That was good to know, even though we had no obvious way to attract their attention from so far away. We stumbled across the weeds and rocks, Jo's knee aching badly and my hips very sore but still functional. Finally, we reached the other side (again, probably only ten minutes that seemed like an hour), and I walked out to the end of the large pier that juts into the channel. We could plainly see the boat from the base sweeping the shore with a searchlight; apparently they had already checked Medren, where we were, and found nothing. I looked around for some means to signal them and, failing that, began to yell. That turned out to be a frail gesture, so I walked over to some of the abandoned buildings in hopes of discovering an old match or light (well, there was little else I could do), and, of course, it was black inside the buildings and I could see nothing. In addition, it had been raining and everything was wet. I gave up on that and went back to the dock to wave and jump and shout whenever the light seemed to flash our way.

Finally, the search boat cruised over toward the *El Territo* at Japtan Island and tied up alongside. I thought about this for a while, and decided they would eventually search back this way, going on toward Enewetak Island. When that happened, I wanted to have something better than my own small human form to wave at them. I remembered there was some aluminum siding falling off one of the abandoned buildings, so I hiked the few hundred yards to the center of the island, picked up one of the sheets, and hauled it back down to the pier. We waited awhile, and then, sure enough, they started the search again and moved back our way. They came closer and closer until it seemed they couldn't fail to see us; the light would shine directly at us and I would hold up my signal slab, which was about four by eight feet, and still they missed us. At one point they stopped and circled, shining their light down on something in the water. That worried me because I thought that the sub might have rolled on around to where the search boat now was. If they saw the sub empty, they might think we were lost, and in that case, might not even think of looking on the pier where we stood. I was worried not so much for our safety, as that seemed to be assured now, but because neither of us wanted to spend the night on the dock in the uncomfortable state we were in.

They started up again. It turned out that they had found the skiff, which had broken loose, and circled to pick it up. Soon the light was flashing, and in seconds they had picked up the sheet of siding and then us. They came in and took us aboard and told us how they had spent *their* evening. Just about dusk Jerry, who had been with the children, had decided to look for us, so he put the children to bed in their room and locked the door. He came on around the corner of Japtan with the skiff and got worried when he failed to spot us. He looked on the concrete ship, a perennial diving favorite, and on Medren and Japtan and even on Enewetak, where he notified the men at the base. They got in the larger boat with the searchlight and came back up, searching. I recalled that just before we went onto the reef, we saw a light flash on the lee side of the island. They had checked the docks at Medren first, but of course we weren't there yet, so they hadn't looked again until an hour or so later.

The Coast Guardsmen took us directly to Enewetak to the dispensary, where their medical corpsman washed the sand out of our various cuts, particularly the deep one on Jo's knee, which he had to sew up. Then they returned us to the *El Territo*, where we cleaned up and went to bed. It was a miserable night. We both felt as though we had been in a car wreck.

The outstanding feature of this whole episode, if there is one, is that there was no reason for it. Stupidity—the most common reason for accidents, and in this case my own—had got us into it. I should have laid out a plan, including exactly where we were going and for how long, and asked Jerry to come look for us if we didn't come back. The deceptive feature of the excursion, of course, was that we told ourselves we were just going a few hundred yards from shore—easy swimming distance. The ocean is no place to get careless or to take anything for granted. The difference between an enjoyable situation that is danger-free and a situation where you are fighting for your life is a thin line. Often this line consists only in the design of a proper plan—which someone besides you knows about.

24

HEALING

THE accident had a strong effect on us, and on the expedition as a
whole. It was now September 18, and we had been on Enewetak
Atoll nearly two months. We had about two weeks more here before setting sail for Truk and Palau, far to the southwest. Yet those two weeks, as
I look back on them, produced almost nothing in terms of new observations or insights. It was as though we had been injured in an athletic con-
test and had to sit out the rest of the game on the sidelines. We tried to
work, we went through the motions, but we were limited by both the
technical problems caused by the accident and the psychic healing that
seemed to be needed. The gray reef shark and the submarine had combined to deliver a rude demonstration of our human frailty.

The next morning we woke up sore, and Jerry went to Enewetak Island at dawn to get some more painkilling pills for Jo; her knee was hurt-
ing badly. After a very late breakfast Jerry and Marissa and I went down to
Medren to look for our battered submarine. We tied up on the lee side of
the island and could easily see the sub high and dry on the beach, where it
had been deposited by the sea. It seemed to be intact, and all the gear was
in it except for the two cameras and light meters. Luckily we found one
camera about 50 yards down the beach—one of the Beaulieus—which
had bounced around in the surf a good deal. But although it was scraped
and a few knobs were broken off, it hadn't leaked and seemed to be in
working order. Even the lens cover had stayed in place, protecting the lens
glass from scratches. The Rebikoff camera, however, was nowhere to be
seen. I waded onto the reef flat, trying to judge where we had come in, hit

upon a scraped spot on a rock where the sub had bumped, and then found bits of the sub's yellow fiberglass. So I knew I was in the right area. But the camera had had a float on it and was undoubtedly on the bottom somewhere, probably in one of the surge channels. The water was just too rough and muddy to see the bottom. Once I spotted something in a channel and felt around with my foot before a wave knocked me down, but it turned out to be just a white piece of dead coral.

We returned that afternoon at high tide to try to retrieve the sub. The plan was to bring the skiff around the south end of Medren Island between the reef and the shore, move along the reef flat there, and tow the sub back around to the lagoon side. But when we got there, it turned out to be too rough. The tide was full, and breaking waves were reaching all the way to shore. There wasn't enough water for the skiff; rocks were visible throughout the entire route we would have to travel. So we went back around to the lagoon side and crossed to the sub on foot. It was bouncing around on the rubble zone of the beach, so we took the bow line and made it fast to a tree limb, pulling the sub as far from the water as we could; with each supporting wave we inched it a little farther until the waves were no longer bouncing it. It was clear that this was a retrieval job for a terrestrial vehicle and not a boat. We didn't have many worries about the shape it was in, with the exception of the canopy, which had been shattered by the rough coral. I was eager to get at the sub and find out what had caused the motor failure. But whether that would help us in the future or not would not matter: I intended after this always to attach a small surface boat to the sub by a floating polyethylene line. The floating line would not get tangled in coral when the sub was near the bottom, and a bright marker on the boat would tell observers at the surface where the sub was at all times, in case of emergency.

R ETRIEVAL day: we got the sub back. Both Jo and I slept a little better, and some of the soreness was going away. Shortly after we got up, the landing barge from the base came by. They were headed up to Runit to pick up some of the Scripps people, and they told us that they had already deposited a small bulldozer on Medren. With it was a geologist who was searching for one of the deep borings that had been made on the island. After it stopped raining, we got in the skiff and headed over to Medren ourselves. But it began to rain again, heavily this time, just after we left. We couldn't even see Medren, which was only about half a mile away. We knew the way, of course, and were quickly there and heading toward the beach where the sub was. It rained all the way. The sub was right where we had tied it the day before, and we fastened a line to the towing bar in the front. We threw some planks down on the rubble and tied the other end of the line to the front of the bulldozer. The driver backed up slowly until the rope tightened, then pulled the sub slowly along the skids up the beach. When we got it to firmer ground, we took a couple of short cranes and hooked them to the lifting sites in the sub. Then it was a simple matter of hoisting the craft by the bulldozer's front loader (this one was equipped with a bucket loader rather than a blade). Then back across the island with the sub dangling below the loader like a stricken gazelle from the jaws of a lion. There was some maneuvering done around trees and bushes, and finally we were at the pier, where the driver set the sub down gently within reach of the *El Territo*'s crane. Home at last.

Back at Japtan I pulled off the cover of the battery compartment and found that only a small amount of acid had spilled when the sub rolled over. There was virtually no damage there. But there was repair work elsewhere: electrolysis had again eaten up the main motor connection, which had been unplugged during the accident; the shroud around the power housing had to be repaired, and the shattered canopy replaced. All in all the machine had shown itself to be amazingly tough. But I was still impatient to discover why it had failed in the first place; I guess I was driven partly because I wanted a pretty good reason for almost being killed and partly because I wanted to know what little piece of technology to blame it on.

The next morning I went to Medren again, this time at dead low tide. I hoped to find that the missing camera had been washed up during the night, and if not, I thought there was a good chance of spying it on the bottom. The tide was indeed lower than I had ever seen it there before, and I was able to walk right to the edge of the reef, tracing the path of the bouncing sub all the way by bits of broken rock and smears of yellow paint. I went to where the sharp edge of the reef comes up, and right there was a short surge channel that ended just where we had hit the reef. Unfortunately, while the surf was calmer than before, it was still substantial and constant. The water in the channel was a mass of cloudy foam; I peered into it for fifteen minutes without catching a glimpse of anything but water. Dizzy, I finally gave it up and retreated to Japtan.

There I started tearing into the submarine in earnest. It turned out that the reason the sub had stopped dead was complex on one level and simple on another. Complexity is involved in explaining where (a rotary switch that activates a series of solenoids that pass power to the motor —two speeds forward, two speeds reverse, and neutral) and simplicity in explaining how (the switch housing had leaked, shorting it and activating two or more sets of solenoids at once, so that one set of solenoids was telling the motor to go ahead while the other was telling it to reverse, shorting the whole and blowing a 100-amp fuse in the motor housing). But at least I ascertained that the motor still functions correctly, the batteries are good, and the switch, dry now, works as before. The shroud around the propeller is bent a bit, as are the diving planes, but these can both be repaired without new parts.

Around three-thirty Jerry and I went back over to try for the missing camera at full high tide. The wind had died slightly, but the surf was still heavy, and we anchored the skiff just outside the first breakers. I had taken a careful bearing in the morning, lining up a tree and a pole, so we'd be able to find the surge channel at high tide. I got the bearing again, and while Jerry checked the bottom to be sure the anchor was secure, I swam in scuba gear toward the channel. After 30 or 40 feet, *voilà!* the camera. I looked back, saw Jerry coming, and signaled that I'd found it. The camera looked as if it had been sandblasted, having been swept up and down the surge channel for three days, but the works appeared to be intact. The lens, which is recessed slightly, had not been scratched at all. I passed it to Jerry and searched further. I found a couple of bang stick barrels and a bang stick, and then a weight belt, all within 10 feet of where the camera had been. That pretty well accounted for everything, except the lead ballast weights I'd thrown overboard in deep water, so we swam on back to the skiff and secured our recovered treasures. Just as I was feeling pretty lucky about the whole thing, I glanced at the camera again and noticed some moisture on the inside. I unlatched the back, and about a quarter of a cup of seawater ran out. That may not sound like much, but further investigation revealed that the quarter of a cup had been evenly and constantly distributed throughout the works for three days, achieving what is known colloquially as a total loss. Or so I thought. I took it back to the *El Territo* and dumped the whole thing in fresh water and sprayed it thoroughly. I wiped off as much rust as I could, then blasted the mechanism with compressed air to get the fresh water out. Next I put it in a plastic garbage can with Jo's hairdryer blowing hot air on it. After all the components were fairly dry, I took the mechanism out and sprayed it with a petroleum distillate that displaces water and lubricates at the same time. It still seemed to be pretty stiff, but I'd done what I could to halt the corrosion where it was.

N EEDLESS to say, the events of the accident stayed in my mind for some time, replaying in the form of dreams by day and by night. Exercising hindsight, I could pick out a number of conscious measures we could have taken, or fortuitous events fortune might have supplied, that would have prevented our modest excursion from becoming an accident at all. Overall, however, going over the details the following day, I decided that the single most important element I had neglected was the most obvious of all: the behavior of the gray reef shark. And it was most surprising that this should be the thing to overlook, since we had spent more time studying that behavior than any other subject at Enewetak.

Our normal custom has been to take the skiff along on any trip in the submarine outside the reef or any place where it might break down, leaving the skiff standing close by the area we planned to explore. But because we were using the sub right in our own watery backyard, in the channel, and within swimming distance of the ship, we had indulged in the luxury of carelessness. It hardly seemed necessary since even in the event of total breakdown we could take a short swim to the island, a short walk over to the skiff, and then easy retrieval of the stricken sub. But here was the trick: we had tried to swim home on the surface. I now believe that any sort of diving operation around Pacific reefs like Enewetak should be planned to exclude swimming on the surface if there is any possibility of meeting gray reef sharks. I think that if we had left the submarine on the bottom when it malfunctioned and simply swum to shore across the bottom in our scuba gear, we'd have had no gashed knees, no sore hips, no wounded submarine. We have seen dozens of gray sharks at close range while swimming around in midwater or near the bottom. Unless we have been spearing fish or somehow antagonizing the sharks, there have been no problems. Swimming on the surface, however, is different. On the surface, a diver is executing much the same motions, in roughly the same place, as a dying or injured fish, or even a dead fish that floats to the surface. Looking back on it, I am now able to construe our behavior as a provocation of the gray shark almost as direct as our aggressive pursuit with the submarine.

In our particular case, one might call the attack a totally unprovoked one; we were minding our own business and were not releasing blood in the water or making peculiar noises. In contrast are many other so-called unprovoked attacks, where a fisherman has just speared a fish and a shark rushes in at the fisherman, not the fish. The shark may mistake the diver for a large fish, or the fish itself may have escaped, or the shark may consider the diver—correctly, in this case—a competitor. We had not caused any of these conditions, yet I'm virtually certain that if I had not shot at the shark with the bang stick, and if Jo had not kicked at him with her flippers, the gray would definitely have grabbed me on the first rush or Jo on the second, after circling behind her. It might even have rushed around behind me as I've seen gray sharks do to the submarine.

I N the eight days that remained for us on Enewetak Atoll, we accomplished little beyond a stepwise gathering of ourselves together, our bodies and minds and tools, for the journey to Truk and Palau. There were really only four items of note. First, we made an exploratory journey to the northern islands of the atoll in a fruitless search for one of the largest bomb craters; the trip was uneventful except for the sighting of a pair of rare hawkbill turtles and an equally rare, gigantic triton that was 14 to 16 inches long and feeds upon the crown-of-thorns starfish. Also, a dog named Pimba, who was traveling with us, leaped clear of the skiff as we were speeding at flank speed across the lagoon in a gesture that lacked any obvious purpose, unless dogs can be said to do something for the hell of it.

Secondly, I explored a final relic of historic jetsam we had discovered upon the island of our small shipwreck. What appeared at first to be a large pile of scrap iron on the beach turned out to be the remains of a small Japanese tank which had been quietly decomposing since World War II. Its gun was still mounted in front, and its hatches were still in place. The hatches were very small, so much so that I doubt the average American could have passed through them. Nearby, around the surge channel where the sub came to grief, were a number of slender copper-jacketed bullets around 6.5 millimeters in caliber and one gigantic 5-inch projectile half buried in the sand. I realized that these remains came from the very ship whose bow was still intact nearby, off Japtan. The vessel had been torpedoed by an American submarine, and the captain had decided to run his ship ashore to keep her from sinking with her much-needed cargo of ammunition.

The third event was an unexpectedly rough trip next door to Enewe-

tak Island to take on fuel. As soon as we got out of the lee of Japtan Island, we encountered a very heavy swell rolling in through the deep
channel. The wind had pulled around to the northeast and was screaming
in at around 30 knots, so that within five minutes of leaving the dock we
were rocking and rolling vigorously. I was in the wheelhouse, and suddenly there came a steep roll in one direction, sending all the drawers in
the steel chest flying out; as I grabbed at them, we rolled in the other direction, and a heavy steel file cabinet came crashing over, along with some
underwater housing and a couple of underwater lights, onto my feet. I
managed to hold everything in place for a second, get the cabinet back upright and then the drawers closed and locked, and keep cameras and
charts still for a few minutes until we were just as quickly out of the waves
and into the lee of Medren Island. For the rest of the trip to Enewetak
I didn't pay much attention to my feet, other than to note that the ankle
of one and the instep of the other had been badly slammed. As we
took on fuel and Jo found some fresh vegetables for our coming journey,
my feet started to hurt more and I began to notice that I no longer
trusted them entirely. As a result, my agility dwindled until I couldn't
count on being able to get from one side of the deck to the other. Later
I slipped on some diesel fuel and fell on the steel deck; I managed to
catch myself and partly break my fall by grabbing the bulwarks. Then
I stepped off the dock onto the boat, and my feet flew out from under
me; that time I grasped a cable on the rail to keep from bouncing my
head on the deck. On the way back to Japtan late in the afternoon the
port throttle lever began to malfunction, and I removed it after reaching the pier; I took off the heavy brass casting where the throttle is
mounted, put it carefully next to the steering wheel, and then knocked it
off onto my foot. Both feet were so sore by the end of the day I could
hardly walk.

The fourth item was the gradual repair of the submarine. The job
was done between short dives and side trips and other chores, and it was
as important symbolically as the healing of knees, feet, and hips were
medically (my own low-grade pain around the waist mysteriously moved
first into my back and finally up to my diaphragm before fading at last
from consciousness). I may have understated the extent of the submarine's wounds, for there were plenty, but we were so relieved to find the
basic hull and motor components sound that the external wounds seemed
small. Nonetheless, healing, as with all wounds around salt water, took
some time. I got out the acetylene torch we carry, heated the metal parts

of the propeller housing, and used a hammer to get it roughly back into shape. Then, at the points where it was broken, I applied small splints of aluminum and screwed them across the broken areas and cracks. After that the housing looked almost like new.

That was one day. The next, I got a new fuse for the motor, this one with a replaceable bus bar in it so it would be easy to replace in the event of another burnout. I rebuilt the rotary switch that controls the speed and resealed it and then put the whole motor assembly and propeller shaft back together. Then I straightened one of the slightly bent diving planes and took out the other; that was a job because the heavy one-inch stainless steel shaft was bent and didn't want to come out. I had to beat it out; then I heated it with the torch, took a hammer to it, and bent it back straight. Finally, I put it in the lathe, cleaned it all up, and then reassembled the diving mechanism.

By the next day the stitches were ready to come out of Jo's knee, which was a bit infected, and my soreness was up to the area of my diaphragm. I took some movies of gobies and sea whips, had the still camera jam up on me, and cursed at the strong wind that roiled the water and spoiled the visibility.

The following day was our last, and it was an active one. In the morning we made a final dive (I spent a good deal of time aiming my camera at an emperor angelfish that made loud, burping noises at me whenever I turned the light on). The rest of the day was devoted to finishing the repair job on the sub, this time fixing the rudder. The T-shaped arm on top of the rudder that holds the control cables was bent, and the lower pivot point was broken. So I had to make a new pivot on the lathe, disassemble the control assembly, and straighten the T. That took most of the afternoon, but I finally got it back in, made a new shear pin for the propeller, and put that back on. Finally, one of the two wooden skids on the bottom of the sub was broken, and all four of its bolts were rusted completely solid, so I had to break them off and find some stainless bolts to replace them. After a few more touches —polishing of the scratches on the windows and sealing of a couple of small cracks on the edge of the rear windows—the sub would be operational again. Jo and I were fairly well healed by then also, and ready to face the 750-mile journey to Truk, where we planned roughly the same kind of exploration we had conducted on Enewetak. For a number of reasons, however, our work there, or later at Palau, never measured up, and the experience was not as rich. It seemed to me that night, as I lay listening to the rain drumming on the deck, that our accident had been a turning point, for that year at least. It also seemed to contain a message, a message I was unwilling to accept, about man's place in the sea.

We left the next day, and on that day arrived about twenty men to begin a new test project up north involving conventional explosives.

INDEX

Acanthaster (crown-of-thorns starfish),
107–8, 113, 114, 118–19, 139, 174–5,
229–30
agriculture, 66–9, 126, 128
alcinarians (sea whips), 44
Alembel Island, 111–12, 162
algae, 214; radioactivity of, 153, 159; reef
ecology and, 95–100; *see also* coralline
algae; zooxanthellae
Allen, Jerry, 207, 222, 223
Allen, Paul, 192, 194, 195, 207
Alligator Reef, 123–4, 147
Amazon Basin, 68
anchovies, 15–16
anemone fish (clownfish), 102, 104
angelfish, 39; emperor, 220–1
animals, nuclear testing and, 151
Anthias, 42, 88
Aomon Island, 56, 58, 127, 162
artificial reefs, 94–5
Aspidontus taeniatus, 40–1
Atomic Energy Commission (AEC), 57,
58, 153, 156–7, 161

bait, 233; *see also* chum; lures
Baldridge, D. H., 79
baleen whales, 97
bang sticks, 86–7, 89, 91, 179, 187–9,
194, 195; *see also* powerhead
barracudas, 45, 88, 90
barrier reefs, 25
bends, the, 50, 83, 206–11
Bijile Island, 58, 112, 157
Biken Island, 161, 162
Bikini Atoll, 23, 25, 57; nuclear testing
on, 150–60
Bikini-Eniwetok Resurveys (1948 and
1949), 153–4, 158–9
Bikini Island, 151
Bikini Lagoon, 155, 159, 160
biologists, marine, 175–6, 222–6
biomass, 96–7
birds, 161–3, 219; *see also specific species*
blacktip reef sharks, 50–1, 61–2, 175,
190, 191, 196, 212–13, 217–18, 220,
230

black jacks, 19, 20
blennies, 102, 163; *see also Aspidontus
taeniatus; Meiacanthus atrodorsalus*
blowfish, *see* pufferfish
boats, small, 224–6
Bogorov, V. G., 96
Bokoluo Island, 58, 161, 162
Bokombako Island, 161, 162
Bolger, Gary, 180–1
bonefish, 169–70
bone necrosis, aseptic, 210
Bora Bora (island), 27
bull shark, 134
butterflyfish, 9, 39, 104, 217

Caesio, 44, 88, 90, 107, 113–14, 116,
145, 182, 185, 192, 193
cameras, retrieval of, after accident,
246–7, 249–50
camouflage (among fish), 37–40
carbon dioxide, loss of (from blood), 210
Carcharhinus menisorrah, see gray reef
shark
cardinalfish, 95, 102, 114
Caroline Islands, 54, 55
cetacea, 204; *see also* dolphins; whales
Cheilinus, see wrasses
Cheilinus undulatus (giant wrasse), 33,
169, 172–5
clams, 153, 196–7, 229
cleaning wrasse (*Labroides dimidiatus*),
40–1, 95
clownfish (anemone), 102, 104
conchs, 99
Condit, Jerry, 35, 45–6, 61, 65, 90–1,
104, 110, 114, 130, 184–5, 190, 192–4,
197, 206–7, 237, 245, 246, 249
cone shell, 113
consciousness, 141–2; loss of, due to loss
of carbon dioxide, 210
coralline algae, 24, 26
coral reefs (coral atolls), 4–5, 14–15,
18–19, 140; ecology of, 95–100; features common to, 24; fishes of, *see*
fishes, coral reef; fore, 97–8; origin and
formation of, 23–8

corals, 98, 104; plate, 172; radioactivity of, 155, 156; stinging (fire), 178–9, 182, 183
Coriolis force, 15
cornetfish, 109–10
corrosion, 32
courting behavior (unicorn surgeonfish), 91
crabs, 99, 100, 183, 214
craters, A-bomb, 110–12
crown-of-thorns starfish (*Acanthaster*), 107–8, 113, 114, 118–19, 139, 174–5, 229–30
crustaceans, 98, 107; *see also specific species*
cyclones (hurricanes or typhoons), 121–4

damselfish, 102, 217
Darwin, Charles, 23, 25
Davis, Bill, 71
decompression, 50, 83, 106, 206–11
decompression chamber, 207–9
decompression tables, 208–10
Defense, U.S. Department of, 57
derris plant, *see* rotenone
dog-toothed tuna, 44
dolphins (porpoises), 129, 201–2, 205, 210–11; intelligence of, 203–4
Donaldson, Lauren, 157, 158
Donna (hurricane), 122–4

East Channel, 12, 14, 17
ecology, 66–70, 78; of reefs, 95–100
ecosystem, 67–9
eels, 98, 100; *see also* garden eels; moray eels
Elugelab (Eluklab) Island, 58, 161
emperor angelfish, 220–1
Enewetak Atoll, 3–5; absence of humans from, 66; fauna species found in, 16–18; history of, 55–9; names of islands of, 11–12; origin and formation of, 25–8; resettlement of human population of, 4, 5; *see also specific islands*
Enewetakese people, 10–12, 55, 56, 125–9; culture and language of, 125–6; diet of, 128–9; sociopolitical structure of, 126–8
Enewetak Island, 4, 57–8, 64, 126–8
Eniwetok Marine Biological Laboratory, 18–19, 163; *see also* Mid-Pacific Marine Laboratory
Enjebi Island, 56, 58, 126, 127, 157, 159, 164
equator, cyclonic storms and, 121–2
equatorial ocean currents, 15, 16, 19
Eschmeyer, Bill, 222
evolution, 140, 141

explosives, collecting fish by means of, 146–8; *see also* bang sticks

fairy terns, 72–3, 184
fat sleeper, 189
fishes, coral reef: camouflage in, 37–40; collecting, 143–8, 155, 157–8; coloration of, 35–9; mimicry by, 40–2; nocturnal, diurnal, and crepuscular, 102–3; philosophical motivation for studying, 139–41; radioactivity and, 153–5, 162–3; *see also specific species*
Florida Keys, 122–4, 233
food chain, 96–9
food gathering, 126, 128
forests, rain, 68–9
French grunt, 37

garden eels, 51–2, 99, 106
Germany, 55
ghost crabs, 214
giant wrasse, 33, 169, 172–5
goatfish, 102, 116
gobies, 21, 71, 95, 99, 100, 178, 183
God, nature of, 140, 142
gray reef shark (*Carcharhinus menisorrah*), 5–8, 45, 79–91, 169, 185–6, 198–200, 212, 228, 235–6, 240; aggressiveness of, 8, 186, 203, 217, 218; agonistic behavior (warning display) of, 6, 79–82, 84–5, 132–4, 187, 198, 202–3, 216–17; attacks on humans by, 79, 84–5, 179–80, 198, 199, 202–3, 241, 250–1; bang sticks used on, 187–8, 191; chum (bait) used for, 192–4, 215, 216; feeding attacks by, 84, 85; feeding behavior of, 215–18, 220; iridescence of, 134; submarine attacked by, 82–5, 185–6, 198–9, 218
gray snapper, 147
groupers, 48–9
Guam, 54, 56
Gulf Stream, 15
Gushman, Dick, 7, 35, 45–6, 71, 86–9, 94, 102, 104, 110, 114, 130, 172–4, 178
gyres (in ocean currents), 15

halfbeak, 234
hammerhead sharks, 85, 180–1
Heine, Carl, 54–5
hermit crabs, 214
herring, 227–8
Hills, Brian, 209–10
Hines, Neal, 152, 156, 165
Holocentrus, 116, 171–2
hurricanes (or typhoons), 121–4
hydrogen bomb, 160–5

Ikuren Island, 162

jacks, 38–9, 48, 88, 240
Japan, 55–6, 163–4
Japtan Island, 60, 73, 166
Jedrol Island, 168, 169
jellyfish, 230–1
jewfishes, 48, 49
Johnson, Richard H., 80–1

kelp bass, 48–9
krill, 97
Krutch, Joseph Wood, 140

lagoon, 24; Bikini, 155, 159, 160; Enewe-
    tak, 27–8, 43, 73, 98, 100
lanternfishes, 117–18
lemon sharks, 120
leopard rays, 47–8, 112, 197, 199
lights for underwater photography, 101–2,
    104, 107, 112, 113, 115–16, 119
lionfishes (scorpionfishes), 38, 167–8
lizards, monitor, 219–20
Lojwa Island, 112
longline vessels, 62–3
Lorenz, Konrad, 36
lures, 227–8, 233

Mack Tower, 143–5
Magellan, Ferdinand, 54
manta ray, 47
mantis shrimp, 183
Marianas Islands, 54
marine biologists, 175–6, 222–6
marine laboratories, see Eniwetok Marine
    Biological Laboratory; Mid-Pacific Ma-
    rine Laboratory
Marshall Islands, 54, 55, 125
McNair, Rhett, 188, 189, 192, 194, 195,
    201, 202, 207, 225
mechanical problems, 43, 86, 104,
    112–13, 130–2, 169–70; of submarine,
    32–3, 42, 45–6, 83, 84, 133–4, 240–2
Medren Island, 58, 106–7; bore hole in,
    26–8
Meiacanthus atrodorsalus, 41
Micronesia, history of, 53–60; see also
    Enewetakese people
Mid-Pacific Marine Laboratory (MPML),
    4, 19, 78
Mikka (pet otter), 32, 70, 92–3, 113–14,
    144, 177, 215
Millepora (stinging coral), 178–9, 182,
    183
mimicry (among fishes), 40–2
monitor lizards, 219–20

Moorish idols, 36, 37, 39, 109
moray eels, 105, 236
mullet (as bait), 233
myctophids, 117–18
Myrberg, Arthur, 190
Myripristis species, 116–17

Naso, see unicorn surgeonfish
Navy, U.S., 153–6
needlefish, 234
Nelson, Donald R., 80–1, 190, 191
night diving, 101–20, 230, 237–8
nuclear power plants, 64–5, 78
nuclear testing, 4, 57–9, 64–5, 69–70, 78,
    150–60; collecting fish after, 155,
    157–8; target ships used in, 151–2,
    154; see also radiation

ocean currents, 14–16
O'Connor, Edward C., 59
octopus, 114–15
Operation Castle, 163
Operation Crossroads, 151
Operation Ivy, 161
Operation Sandstone, 157

Pacific jewfish, 49
Pacific Ocean, equatorial, 14–15
parrotfish, 102, 104–5
patch reefs, 20, 94–7, 100, 118
pearlfish, 167
Perry Sharkhunter submarine, 9–10, 47,
    237; blowing air into ballast tanks of
    (for emergency ascent), 83; mechanical
    problems of, 32–3, 42, 45–6, 83, 84,
    133–4, 240–2; plexiglass panels of, 86;
    repaired after accident, 252–3; retrieved
    after accident, 246–9
philosophy, rational, 76–8
photography, underwater, 115, 182; lights
    for, 101–2, 104, 107, 112, 113, 115–16,
    119
Photo Tower Mack, 143–5
phytoplankton, 13, 96
pipefish, 95, 233–4
plankton, 13–19, 28, 43, 97, 224, 237–8;
    lagoon, 98, 100; nonplanktonic, 18; ra-
    dioactivity of, 155, 158–9, 162
plankton-feeding fish, 17–19, 44; diurnal
    and nocturnal, 103; see also specific
    species
plants: effect of nuclear tests on, 160–2;
    reef ecology and, 96–100
plate coral, 172
poisons, collecting fish by means of,
    146–7; see also rotenone
Pole Pinnacle, 41, 71, 72, 87–90, 105–6,
    192–4

porpoises, *see* dolphins
powerhead, 86, 87, 179, 180, 188,
    194–5
pufferfishes, 49–50, 170–1, 233

rabbitfishes (siganids), 145
radiation (radioactivity), 64, 65, 69, 70,
    111, 150–65
rain forests, agriculture in, 68–9
Randall, John, 137
rational philosophy, 76–8
rays, 47; *see also specific species*
reefs, *see* artificial reefs; coral reefs
Reese, Ernie, 8–9
rotenone, 42, 146–7, 183
Runit Island, 58, 60–1, 64, 110–11, 149,
    157, 161–2

science (scientific research), 74–6; motiva-
    tion for doing, 139–42
scientists (career-oriented vs. curiosity-
    oriented), 138–9; *see also* marine
    biologists
scorpionfishes (lionfishes), 38, 167–8
Scripps Institution of Oceanography,
    26–8, 224–5
sea basses, 48; see also *Anthias*
sea biscuits, 99
sea cucumbers, 43, 99, 166–7
sea fans, 44
sea horses, 233–4
sea urchins, 99, 146, 156
seawater, 29–31
sea whips, 44, 71
shark guns, 86–7; *see also* bang sticks
sharks, 38–9, 48, 139, 143–5, 148, 182;
    attacks on humans by, 179–81; bang
    sticks used to kill, *see* bang sticks;
    catching small, 226–7; chum (bait) for,
    218–20, 228–9; eyes of, 230; propellers
    attacked by, 180; sounds used to at-
    tract, 190–1, 194; *see also* blacktip
    reef sharks; gray reef sharks; silvertip
    reef sharks; tiger sharks; whitetip reef
    sharks
shark sucker, 213
shrimp, 95, 100, 104, 109, 170–1; mantis,
    183; snapping, 21, 178
shrimp-goby relationship, 21–2
siganids, 145
silvertip reef sharks, 47, 48, 201, 203, 206
snappers, 38–9, 89, 104, 193, 199, 228–9,
    233; gray, 147, 214
snapping shrimp, 21, 178
soldierfish, 102, 107
sounds, use of, to attract sharks, 190–1,
    194
space program, 74–5

Spain, 54–5
sponges, 98, 108
squid, 92, 200–1
squirrelfish, 95, 102, 114, 116, 118–20,
    171–2
Starck, Jo, 7, 32, 50, 64, 70, 71, 87, 88,
    92–4, 102, 104–6, 110, 112–14, 118,
    130–3, 136, 144, 174, 183, 188, 192–9,
    206–8, 212, 215, 216, 220, 227–30,
    235–7, 239–47, 252, 253
Starck, Marissa, 70–1, 92, 106, 144, 174,
    207–8, 215
Starck, Varrina, 70–1, 92, 106, 144, 174,
    207–8, 232
starfish, 117; brittle, 108; crown-of-thorns,
    107–8, 113, 114, 118–19, 174–5,
    229–30
stinging coral, 178–9, 182, 183
stingray, 232
stomach eversion, 120
submarine, *see* Perry Sharkhunter
    submarine
sunken ships, *see* wrecks
surgeonfish, 20–1, 51, 71, 90, 102, 104,
    162–3, 185, 212–13; unicorn, 44, 88,
    91–2

Tahiti, 27
Tektite undersea habitat, 137–8
Ten Commandments, 77
terns, fairy, 72–3, 184
Test Able, 151–2
Test Baker, 152
Test Bravo, 163–4
Test Mike, 161
tiger sharks, 85, 193–6
trees, cyclonic storms and, 123, 124
triggerfish, 168
Truk Island, 27, 129, 253
Truman, Harry S, 57, 59, 157
Trust Territory of the Pacific Islands, 54,
    57; *see also* Micronesia
tunas, 62, 63; dog-toothed, 44
turtles, 99
typhoons, 121–4

Ujelang Atoll, 57, 127
underwater photography, *see* photogra-
    phy, underwater
undisturbed environments, 66–8
unicorn surgeonfish, 44, 88, 91–2
United Nations, 56
United States, 56–7, 126, 127; *see also*
    Atomic Energy Commission; Defense,
    U.S. Department of; Navy, U.S.; Tru-
    man, Harry S
universities, 223–4
upwellings, 15–16

volcanoes, 25–6

water, chemical characteristics of,
    29–31
westward rotation of the earth, 15
whales, 97, 129, 203–4
whitetip reef sharks, 33–4, 45, 88–9,
    168, 172, 173, 185, 199, 203, 213,
    216–18
Williams, J., 79

World War II, 56, 127
wrasses (*Cheilinus*), 88, 184–5, 189–91,
    194, 205–6, 235–7, 240; cleaning,
    40–1, 95; giant (*C. undulatus*), 33,
    169, 172–5
wrecks (sunken ships), 12–13, 19–20, 29,
    32, 61–3, 73, 130, 151–2, 156, 251

zooplankton, 13, 96, 98
zooxanthellae (algae), 24, 25

A NOTE ON THE TYPE

This book was set in the film version of Electra, a type face designed by W. A. Dwiggins. The Electra face is a simple and readable type suitable for printing books by present-day processes. It is not based on any historical model, and hence does not echo any particular time or fashion.

Composed, printed and bound by American Book-Stratford Press, Saddlebrook, New Jersey. Color lithography by Longacre Press, New York.

Typography and binding design by Virginia Tan.

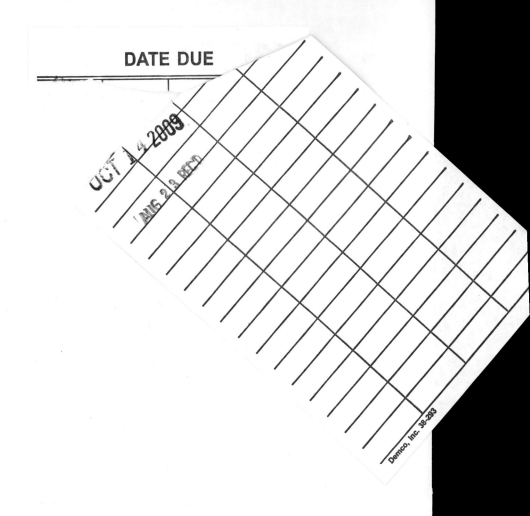

DATE DUE

OCT 14 2009

AUG 23 REC'D